SIR WILLIAM HINGSTON
Montreal mayor, surgeon and banker

By Alan Hustak

Library and Archives Canada Cataloguing in Publication

Hustak, Alan, 1944-
Sir William Hingston: Montreal mayor, surgeon and banker / Alan Hustak.

Includes bibliographical references and index.
ISBN 1-896881-37-8 (bound). – ISBN 1-896881-48-3 (pbk.)

1. Hingston, William H. (William Hales), 1829-1907. 2. Mayors – Québec (Province)
– Montréal – Biography. 3. Surgeons – Québec (Province) – Montréal – Biography.
4. Montréal (Québec) – Biography. I. Title.

FC2947.26.H55H88 2004   971.4'28'03092   C2004-905223-3

Cover by Susan Ferguson. Cameo portraits were painted in Dresden, 1892

Printed in Canada

Price-Patterson Ltd.
Canadian Publishers, Montreal, Quebec, Canada
www.pricepatterson.com

Hard cover version: ISBN 1-896881-37-8
Soft cover version: ISBN 1-896881-48-3

For Brian and Nancy
and
especially for their grandchidlren

DEUM POSUI ADIUTORE

CONTENTS

INTRODUCTION 7

FOREWORD 9

PROLOGUE. 15

CHAPTER ONE   Major Sam's Boy 21

CHAPTER TWO   Edinburgh, Paris, Berlin and Medicine 41

CHAPTER THREE   Private Practice, Public Service 55

CHAPTER FOUR   Making Better Men and Men Better 63

CHAPTER FIVE   The Bishop's Gamble 73

CHAPTER SIX   Friends in High Places 81

CHAPTER SEVEN   "A Funeral as Canada Has Never Seen" 97

CHAPTER EIGHT   "Smallpox is as Common as Dirt" 109

CHAPTER NINE   A School of One's Own. 125

CHAPTER TEN   The Climate of Canada. 139

CHAPTER ELEVEN   A Second Plague 149

CHAPTER TWELVE   Deus ex Machina. 161

CHAPTER THIRTEEN   Well Earned Honours. 171

CHAPTER FOURTEEN   Vigorous Old Age 193

CHAPTER FIFTEEN   "He Loved a Good Horse" 201

CHAPTER SIXTEEN   Mother and Sons. 211

AFTERWORD 225

BIBLIOGRAPHY. 227

INDEX. 230

WILLIAM HALES HINGSTON (1829 – 1907)

INTRODUCTION

Sir William Hingston was my maternal great-grandfather. I was two years old when his widow, Lady Hingston, died.

As a youngster, I vaguely understood who they were. The family rarely discussed their accomplishments or just how influential a role Sir William played in Montreal's history.

It was only when I grew older and I was given some of Sir William's private papers that I began to comprehend the full extent of his contributions to medicine, politics, religion and finance. It was then, with the encouragement of my mother, Katherine Hingston Gallery, that I began to appreciate how Sir William's sons, including my grandfather, Donald, and my great-uncle, a Jesuit priest, William Hales Hingston, continued his legacy.

My purpose in asking Alan Hustak to write this book is two-fold. First, as the current Chair of the Canadian Irish Studies Foundation I obviously wanted to know more about my Irish ancestors and the role they played in the development of Montreal and Canada. The Foundation has repeatedly expressed the belief that "You cannot be proud of your heritage unless you know it."

Second, I wanted to raise money for the Foundation. Therefore, all profits from the sales of this book will help fund the *Sir William Hingston Scholarship in Canadian Irish Studies* at Concordia University.

In telling our family's story author Alan Hustak has written a vivid account of a little known chapter in the history of Victorian Montreal, shed new light on the religious and political divisions of the period, and at the same time allowed me to become better acquainted with the great-grandfather I never knew.

Brian O'Neill Gallery
Knowlton, Quebec
August 2004

FOREWORD

I first saw the name of Hingston at Loyola College because it was in Hingston Hall that I taught my first class. Then I heard it as the name of a high school that some of my students had attended. It embarrasses me now to admit that was all I knew of the family. I should have known more, much more, because this was a family whose work still touches the lives of most Montrealers, from children in their playgrounds to scholars in their universities. The Hingston influence begins very early in our lives, with that childhood injection to protect us from smallpox. Children survived, and still survive, thanks to Sir William Hingston, who did more than any other man to end the ravages of smallpox in this city. And who did more than even that.

Sir William Hingston was a man of his time and place. His time was the nineteenth century. His place was the business and professional world of Montreal. That time and that place meant he was politically a conservative; but Hingston's conservatism was more than a political label. It was rooted in his Roman Catholic faith which saw his social status not as a personal privilege but as something which gave him the means and the responsibility to serve others. It was this same conservatism of faith that would be profoundly reflected in the lives of Lady Hingston and their children.

But to understand Sir William and his family, we have to start with their time and place. We have to look at the Montreal of the second half of the nineteenth century.

Montreal was never just a village looking in unto itself. It always looked eastward on its river and the oceans all the way to France and Britain, even to Africa and India and China. And it always looked westward where the waters divided, one stream carrying Montreal into the lands around the Great Lakes, the other to the fur country beyond the Ottawa. Everything that moved in or out of that richest and most populous part of British North America – missionaries, soldiers, settlers, ploughs, timber, potash, wheat, boots and books and clothes – everything passed by river and canal through the traders and stevedores and warehouses of Montreal.

By the 1850s, trade also moved on a railway that ran even in the months the river was frozen. But Montreal remained so much the centre of trade that the railway built a bridge to reach the city. The Victoria Bridge also put Montreal in the news around the world. It was such a triumph of engineering that headlines declared it the eighth wonder of the world.

All of this was done with a population that barely reached 50,000.

Nor did accomplishment end in the 1850s. Within a decade, Montrealers were considering the unprecedented challenge of a railway right across North America through land that was still mostly wilderness and mostly unsurveyed. They would have to build a new country to do it, too. But they did it, and did it within a generation. At the same time, they added to their human muscle a new energy drawn from water power and coal to build the factories that would supply the new Canada. Then Montrealers reached out to build some of the great railways of Africa and South America and even of China.

By the last quarter of the 1800s, Montreal was the giant that straddled Canada. Its businessmen, though few in number, controlled most of the wealth of its millions of people. One man was so wealthy he could raise, train and equip a whole regiment of a thousand soldiers and provide them with thousands of horses all on a single donation. He and his friends could confidently say they owned the Conservative governments of John A. Macdonald that dominated the federal scene. They could even claim, with truth, that the very constitution of Canada had been designed for them.

But prosperity built on coal and factories made their homes in the old part of the city noisy and choking with soot. So the rich moved up the hill to Dorchester, to St. Catherine, and then to Sherbrooke Street. At each level, they built increasingly palatial homes, the homes then giving way to shops and hotels as commerce moved up with them from about 1900. Even the greatest symbol of their triumph, St. James Methodist Church on St. Catherine Street, fell to advancing commerce as it had to rent out shops around its Gothic exterior to make up for congregants lost to the slopes of Westmount.

Social centres for the rich were the Windsor Hotel on Peel Street and, just behind it on Stanley, the great, indoor Victoria Rink. Such was the standing of the wealthy of Montreal that aristocratic governors-general like Dufferin and Lorne and Stanley were regular guests at the lavish social events of the rink.

The Victoria Rink is gone; but it had something that survives over a century and more. That something was the size of its ice surface. It was the same size as the regulation size of a modern ice hockey rink. Well, of course it was. The Victoria Rink is where two older games, shinty and rugby, were combined to create the modern game of ice hockey in 1885. Nor is that the whole story of Montreal and sport.

The Montreal wealthy of the 1800s were not an intellectual lot, so they weren't much interested in music or painting or theatre. It's true that in the 1820s they had built the library and lecture hall they named The Mechanics' Institute. But that wasn't for any love of literature. Rather, it was intended to train the lower classes to be productive and obedient workers. No, the ruling passion for most of Montreal's wealthy was not books or the art gallery or the theatre. It was sport, a passion they adopted in imitation of the officers of the British army who were stationed in Montreal until 1871. The result was remarkable.

In just over forty years, a small group of people in what was still a small city invented four modern sports. They were competitive snowshoeing (whose awkward gait was called jogging), lacrosse, North American football, and modern ice hockey. No other city in the world, of whatever age or size, can match that. Nineteenth century Montreal, with its Montreal Amateur Athletic Association, was the foundation of all organized sport in Canada.

This amassing of wealth, the display of glamour, and the leisure for sport came at a price. Like the wealth and glamour and leisure of other places and other times, that price was paid by the poor with long hours, low pay and hellish living conditions. Lord Strathcona could donate millions for the military and for charities because he could hire men at a dollar a day for a ten-hour day, six days a week. There were no holidays, no benefits, no health care, and no pensions. Nor was there unemployment insurance, though unemployment was common at any time, and almost a certainty in the slow, winter months.

Pay was so low that women and children, as well as men, had to work just for the family to survive. Women could expect fifty cents for a day of ten hours or more. Children as young as seven would be paid half that. Work places were nightmares of presses and saws and drills powered by flywheels and belts. Safety equipment was rare. In the same period that the sons of the rich were inventing hockey, a young boy in a Montreal factory lost his arm to a machine. The employer immediately stopped the boy's pay and sent him home. Nothing more was required under the law. Nothing more was done.

Low pay created great stretches of slums east and south and west of the city. Indoor plumbing was often a luxury, with many depending on water drawn from taps on the street, next to privies that numbered in thousands.

Not until late in the century would there be drinking fountains for people. But there were drinking troughs for horses; so people shared those.

Slum streets were filthy with garbage and with animal droppings from horses and from the many cows, pigs, goats and chickens still kept in the city. Indeed, for the poor, a pig raised in the home might be the family's only chance for some meat in its diet. Add to that an appalling quality of market food that was unregulated but all that was available at affordable prices. Then add to that miles of open sewers running through the streets. It can be no surprise that the Montreal of the latter half of the 1800s was ranked among the unhealthiest cities in the world as smallpox, diphtheria, tuberculosis, cholera and typhoid visited the city almost as often as governors-general skated at the Victoria Rink. In fact, Montreal's infant mortality rate was still the highest in the world well into the twentieth century.

The slums were unrelieved by parks for adults or playgrounds for children. In an age when only property owners could vote for them, city councilors saved their spending for the districts of the rich – who did have the vote.

Poverty, weak labour unions and lack of government help had a defining effect on Montrealers. They were forced to cling together in groups for help, but that clinging in groups also forced the groups apart from each other.

A labourer, unemployed or sick or unable to bear the cost of burying yet another infant, could get help, if he were Irish Catholic, from St. Patrick's parish or from United Irish societies. If he or she were French and Catholic, it would come from the St. Vincent de Paul Society or from a Roman Catholic parish. The small Jewish population could turn to the Spanish and Portuguese synagogues. Scots Protestants had the St. Andrew's Society. And so it was with charities for English and Blacks and Chinese and Baptists and Congregationalists.

To survive, the poor had to stick with their national or religious groups because only through these groups could they get help. And when employment was scarce, as it usually was, these groups of the poor had to fight each other with fists and boots and clubs for jobs. These divisions even carried into sport, as English Protestants played for the Montreal Lacrosse Club, French Catholics for Le Club National, and Irish Catholics for the Shamrocks. Nor were such warring divisions limited to the poor, as mutual distrust also reached upward through the highest offices of business and into the private clubs.

These ugly and sometimes violent divisions were reinforced by theories

of racism which, throughout the western world, were then enjoying a period of scientific respectability. Morality and intelligence were linked to skin
colour and religion and nationality, a linkage accepted at the time even
among the best educated. To be different, then, might mean – usually did
mean – to be discriminated against and shunned.

As well, Montreal is not, and never was, a city of two cultures. It is, and
always has been, a city of dozens of cultures. In the nineteenth century, the
English-speaking were divided into English, Scots, Irish and Welsh; and
those were divided into Anglican, Presbyterian, Methodist, Roman Catholic
and Baptist with many of those subdivided into sects. Some, if few, French
were Protestants; but there was nothing monolithic about the remaining
Catholic majority. It was profoundly divided between the ultramontane
zealots of Bishop Bourget, and those who followed more moderate leaders.

Then there was the deep division between rich and poor. Contrary to
myth, Montreal was not a city of rich English Protestants and poor Irish and
French Catholics, though the Irish Catholics, as a group, probably came
closest to validating the myth. The very rich, it is true, were predominantly
English-speaking and Protestant. But they were only a tiny part of the
English-speaking Protestant population, most of which was at the lower
level of the working class. And there they remained until as late as the 1950s.

Similarly, there was a substantial French-speaking and Catholic group of
wealthy families with their own "golden mile" residential districts. Further
down the social scale, but better paid than the lowest levels, were skilled and
semi-skilled workers. Among these, French-speaking Catholics were well
represented, usually better represented than either English-speaking
Protestants or English-speaking Catholics.

This is the Montreal, a city of deep social divisions and hostilities, of Sir
William and Lady Hingston. He was the son of a common soldier in the
British army who had risen to commissioned rank and then to a colonelcy.
That, in his day, was so extraordinary as to be almost unheard of. No doubt,
the father's position gave the young William a start. But that the son should
be able to take that start to become outstanding in both medicine and business, and to establish himself as a trusted leader among all the religious and
language and economic groups of a bitterly divided city is a feat even more
remarkable than his father's. And, through Lady Hingston and their children, the influence carried into the twentieth century and beyond.

To this day, all Montrealers live better lives because of the Hingstons. It
starts with children who live to be adults thanks to vaccinations and a structure of health regulations, and who can enjoy childhood more thanks to the

parks and swings and see-saws that are the result of the voluntary work of Lady Hingston. It extends to the influence of Loyola College that became a part of Concordia University, of St. Mary's Hospital, and of Université de Montréal on the slopes of Mount Royal, the mountain park that itself is very much a tribute to Hingston's leadership.

These were people of their time and place whose achievements live on into our time and place.

Graeme Decarie
Associate Professor of Canadian History
Concordia University

PROLOGUE

The doctors in their light horse-drawn carriages began arriving at The Windsor, then Montreal's grand hotel, just before seven on the evening of Tuesday, November 5, 1895 for an invitation-only dinner to pay tribute to one of their own, Sir William Hales Hingston. At sixty-five, Hingston was an eminent Irish-Catholic physician, the chief surgeon at the Hôtel-Dieu Hospital, who earlier that year had been knighted by Queen Victoria.

What was unique about the black-tie gathering was not that all present were distinguished medical men, but that the guest list represented a rare cross section of the socially tribal city. English and French in Montreal rarely socialized; for the Protestant ruling class to go out of its way to honour a Roman Catholic was equally uncommon. As testimony to their collective esteem, more than one hundred and fifty doctors were on hand for the pre-dinner cocktails served in the hotel's grand promenade, known as Peacock Alley. Among the early arrivals were Doctor Thomas George Roddick, the first chief surgeon at the Royal Victoria Hospital, who had introduced Joseph Lister's antiseptic surgery to Canada in 1877. Doctor William Osler, who had just published *The Principles and Practice of Medicine*, the seminal textbook that would soon make him one of the best known physicians in the English-speaking world, came up from Baltimore where he was teaching at Johns Hopkins University, and Doctor Lawson Tait, the brilliant surgeon who pioneered appendectomies, made the trip from Birmingham, England to represent the British Medical Association. Doctor James Grant, the personal physician to several governors-general of Canada and Conservative Member of Parliament for Ottawa who was also president of the Canadian Medical Association, was an especially welcome face. Himself a knight, Grant and Hingston had been close friends for years.

With gas lights glowing, the honoured guest took his place on the dais in the Rose Room Banquet Hall where he found himself seated between Senator Michael Sullivan, a Killarney Irish doctor who was professor of surgery and anatomy at Queen's University, and a former mayor of Kingston, Ontario, and Doctor James Guérin, who had just been elected to the Quebec Legislature as the Liberal member for Montreal's Sixth Division. Also present was Doctor Emmanuel-Persillier Lachapelle, dean of medicine at Université Laval.

Greunwald's orchestra played, and as entertainment between the six courses served, Doctor William Henry Drummond delivered some of his light-hearted comic verse in a habitant *patois* dialect and Doctor Patrick Sheridan sang Irish and French airs in a clear tenor voice.

To many of those present, the choice of Doctor Robert Craik as Master of Ceremonies seemed unusual. Craik and Hingston had rarely agreed on anything during the forty years they had known each other. Craik, the Dean of the Medical Faculty at McGill University, acknowledged their differences in his toast: "We have fought together, sometimes against a common adversary, and it must be confessed, sometimes against each other. Someone has said that you can never know a man thoroughly until you have fought with him." But Craik was magnanimous. In spite of their differences, he said he had always respected Hingston's gentlemanly qualities.

"Gentlemen, we are proud of him as a Canadian; we are proud of him as a distinguished member of an honourable profession, we are proud of him as the one who filled the Mayor's chair of our city as few have been able to fill it, and we are proud of him and we drink to him as our courtly Canadian Knight, Sir William Hingston who has honourably won his spurs and who is worthy to have upon his shield the motto, *sans peur et sans reproche*."

Doctor Jean-Philippe Trefflé-Rottot, founder of Hôpital Notre-Dame, now the president of Université Laval, proposed another toast in French.

For Hingston, it was a triumphal, gratifying evening. When the new knight finally rose to speak, he clutched at his black satin lapels and seemed at a loss for words. "The desire of my life has been to keep in close touch with the members of my profession, and in doing so I feel I am keeping in touch with all that is good and true."

A century ago Sir William Hingston was celebrated as a figure of international stature. In a career that spanned more than five decades, Hingston pioneered gynecology and obstetrics before they were recognized as medical specialties, was among the first to attempt the excision of a kidney and the first surgeon in the English-speaking world to remove a tongue and lower jaw. Queen Victoria credited him with preventing ethnic strife in Montreal in the 1870s when he was the city's mayor. Today he is a shadow from a bygone era still admired as a footnote in the history books. Toronto historian Peter B. Waite called him "A courageous and cool man"; French-language medical historian Louis D. Mignault, who was present at the dinner, lauded Hingston for his attachment to his Roman Catholic faith and for his "loyalty and tact beyond all praise" during his public career. "For in his youth, the path an English-speaking Roman Catholic doctor had to follow was not always strewn with roses," Mignault wrote. Quebec historian Robert Rumilly praised Hingston's sagacity, as someone who was "both conservative and Catholic without being a fanatic about either"; Stephen Leacock included him on a select list of McGill graduates reserved for those "whose name forms a roll and scroll of honour unsurpassed."

Today, many of Hingston's accomplishments are largely overlooked, but during the last half of the nineteenth century the pioneering surgeon was at the centre of Montreal's medical, social, business and political life. Honoured with a knighthood as one of the first modern surgeons in Canada, Hingston also served two terms as mayor of Montreal, was president of the Montreal City & District Savings Bank (today the Laurentian Bank of Canada), was a champion horseman and author, and spent eleven years as a senator in Ottawa before his death in 1907.

As chief surgeon for twenty-five years at Montreal's Hôtel-Dieu Hospital, he helped lay the groundwork for the establishment of what is today the Université de Montréal.

His marriage to Margaret Macdonald, the daughter of Ontario's lieutenant governor, John Alexander Macdonald, and the niece of John Sanfield Macdonald, prime minister of the United Province of Canada between 1862 and 1864, increased Hingston's social standing. But because he was a Roman Catholic, he had to prove his worth to Montreal's Protestant ruling class. He had a genius for dispassionate calm, and impressed everyone by refusing to cast judgment even when stones were flying over his head.

He was the patriarch of a remarkable family that left its mark on the city. Doctor Hingston's eldest son, William, was ordained a Jesuit priest and helped build Loyola College, now part of Concordia University, into a major institution before becoming provincial of the Jesuits in English-speaking Canada. A second son, Donald, succeeded his father as both the Hôtel-Dieu's chief surgeon and as a president of the Montreal City & District Savings Bank. A Hingston family member served on the bank's board of directors consecutively for a century. Donald was also the founder of St. Mary's Hospital. A third son, Basil, was killed in action during the First World War, and a fourth, Harold, a stockbroker, was wounded at the Second Battle of Ypres.

The story told in these pages portrays Sir William Hingston as a unique product of his place and time. He was one of those great Montrealers who brought French and English together and forced them to share in the profound mysteries of religion, race and class, and who helped us appreciate how separate, and how distinct, yet how indivisible we really are. He was the quintessential Canadian, whose knowledge, forbearance and decency triumphs over time.

Remember always and under every circumstance,
the practice of medicine is a kind of priesthood.
It too is a vocation. To practise you need to be
schooled in science, just as a priest is schooled in
theology. But no matter how much science you
possess, you will never be an efficient doctor
if you don't have faith in what you practise, if
you don't possess a superior moral quality...

WILLIAM HALES HINGSTON

CHAPTER ONE
Major Sam's Boy

L ate in the summer of 1853, a strapping twenty-four-year-old physician, William Hales Hingston, began his general practice in a house
that he shared with his younger brother, Samuel, at 31 McGill Street
near the Montreal waterfront.

When Doctor Hingston opened his office, medicine was even more of an
imperfect science than it is today. He was one of only fifty doctors in the
city who honed their skills through a series of routine consultations which
required them to be part social worker, part grief counsellor. Those who met
and got to know Hingston swore by his discretion and his effectiveness. "Tall
as a poplar, broad shouldered with a slim waist," the promising young surgeon looked younger than his age as he would all his life. Fashionable side-
whiskers, grown to mask his youthful appearance, framed his square jaw. His
pursed lips and a permanent frown gave him a stern countenance. He rarely
smiled, and according to one contemporary description "he gave some the
impression that he was severe." Hingston was driven, spiritually conflicted
and determined, but hardly severe. He spoke with a low reassuring voice and
had a wry sense of humour. The glint in his startling blue eyes revealed him
to be sympathetic and easily approachable. He exuded quiet charisma. But
he was someone who felt he didn't quite belong.

Much of Montreal in the middle of the nineteenth century was a sickly
place, dank and diseased. Many of the streets and laneways were thick with
muck, contaminated with puddles of slop thrown in the dirt and left to rot.
Horse dung and human waste, garbage and raw sewage were swept under
wooden sidewalks that had been built to conceal the filth. The stench in
summer was overwhelming. Nothing was known of germs or the spread of
infectious disease, sanitation was all but unheard of. In an age before antibiotics and anesthetics, typhus, cholera, scarlet fever, diphtheria and smallpox had each in turn decimated the population. Life expectancy in Montreal
was among the lowest on the continent. The child mortality rate was high:
one in four infants died before reaching their first birthday.

But Montreal had another side. There were about 50,000 residents, and for the first time in its history, those who spoke English were beginning to outnumber those who spoke French. Two out of five residents were Scots or English; two out of five, French, and the rest, about 8,000, had recently arrived from Ireland. The Scots and the English were the most prosperous, the Irish and the French, the least. The Irish were particularly despairing.

Starved out of their homeland by the British, an estimated 60,000 of them found refuge in British North America where they were not especially welcome. Thousands of Irish immigrants perished in a typhus epidemic even as they arrived in Montreal in the summer of 1847. In January 1848, a disastrous flood in the city added to their woes. Four years later one thousand were to die from cholera. That same year, fire destroyed one third of the city.

Montreal in the middle of the nineteenth century was also a city filled with narrow-minded individuals and rife with parochial attitudes. For two centuries the French represented a homogeneous cultural identity and had lived undisturbed on the island. Then, in 1760, the British arrived. Unlike Quebec City which had been captured by force of arms on the Plains of Abraham the previous year, Montreal dictated the terms of its capitulation to the British. As part of the treaty the British agreed to compensate members of the Sulpician fraternity of priests who had been Seigneurs of the Island of Montreal for 177 years. In 1853 Montreal was still very much a Sulpician town, largely run by the syndicate of Roman Catholic priests who continued to dictate the community's religious and social agenda.

Montreal's English-speaking community was Protestant, a world unto itself imbued with the imperial values imported from England. These Presbyterians, Methodists and Anglicans took root outside the city in the orchards and open fields along the slopes of Mount Royal where they were able to look down on the French and Irish Roman Catholics who inhabited the city beneath them. A sharp line divided those who were and were not Protestant, a line as sharp as between French and English, rich and poor. Protestants regarded Roman Catholics as superstitious, ignorant idolators; Catholics suspected Protestants of being gullible, uncommitted puritanical prudes. Montreal's Irish Catholics were caught in the middle and especially marginalized. Protestants avoided them because they were Catholic; French Catholics mistrusted them because they spoke English. But, to call either side bigoted would be overstating the case. Intolerance was a mutually accepted common denominator, the prevailing social code. Catholic or Protestant, very few doubted that sin was punished by a vengeful God who controlled all circumstances. Catholics might be accepted in Protestant circles, but they had to work at it. They had to prove themselves respectable. As Geoffrey Best put it in his study of mid-Victorian attitudes, respectability had the same cachet as being a good party man in a totalitarian state: "It signified at one and at the same time intrinsic virtue and social value."

Such respect did not come easily. If an English-speaking Catholic were to succeed in Montreal's Protestant circles he would need powerful and influential mentors, people who would vouch for his strength of character, work ethic, community spirit and social value. Into this society strode Hingston, born of Presbyterian and Roman Catholic parents and groomed to be a surgeon.

For a young doctor with a future, Hingston's medical office at the foot of McGill Street near Rue de la Commune was ideally located one block from the St. Lawrence River. Sloops and brigantines docked at the granite wharves nearby delivering a daily stream of merchant mariners and passengers who required medical attention after weeks at sea. Directly across the street from his office were the forbidding stone walls of the Hôpital Général de Montréal, founded in 1693 by the Grey Nuns. The Hôpital Général was a palliative care institution that housed the blind, the infirm, mental patients, prostitutes, epileptics, orphans and abandoned children. On what were then the outskirts of the city, the English Protestants had their own "General Hospital," a seventy-two-bed institution that opened in 1821. One block north of Hingston's office was a new, strange pagoda-shaped building that housed St. Anne's Market. West of the marketplace stood Collège de Montréal, the private Roman Catholic school Hingston had attended as a boy. Farther along the street beyond what was then called Commissioner's Square, and today is known as Victoria Square, could be seen the dramatic thrust of Hingston's parish church, St. Patrick's. Behind his office to the west lay the shanty dwellings of Griffintown, an impoverished industrial slum where wave after wave of dirt-poor famine Irish came to rest when they arrived in 1847. Unlike all but a few of the recently arrived Irish whom hunger had forced to leave, Hingston's father was pedigreed Anglo-Irish. According to *Burke's Landed Gentry for Ireland*, the name Hingston is derived from Hengist, a place in Devon, the suffix "ton" meaning a town or rural village. The family's coat of arms – a chevron between the heads of three leopards – has as its motto, *Deum Posui Adjutore*, or God can help. But God was not of much help to William's English ancestor, James Hingston, who chose Cromwell's side against Charles I during the English civil war. He fought with the "Roundheads" in the Parliamentary army and when the monarchy was restored in 1660, wisely set sail for Ireland from his home in Cambridgeshire and settled in Angish, County Cork. After that, the Hingston family tree is hard to trace. For generation after generation most of the males were named James, and six became Presbyterian ministers. One James Hingston was rector of Cobh, another James, a rector at Whitechurch, Cloyne, and a third, rector of Youghal.

Samuel James Hingston, whose father was a clergyman, may have been born in New Jersey in 1775, but taken back to Ireland when his parents, loyal to the Crown, fled the revolutionary war; he may also have been born in Cork, the records are not precise. When Sam was nineteen years old he enlisted in the Royal Irish Artillery. A handsome man, he caught the eye of Winifred Cavendish, the daughter of a prominent Roman Catholic Dublin family, and against her parents' wishes, they eloped. They were married in Dublin on February 21, 1801, and their first son, Thomas, was born there in June 1802. Two years later, Sam's regiment was disbanded and he was discharged with the rank of corporal. He then "served in and disciplined a corps of Yeoman infantry before signing up in 1804 with His Majesty's 100th Regiment of Foot," which was then shipped out to British North America to uphold the Empire. Sam Hingston arrived in Quebec City on November 14,

Portrait of Winifred's mother, Mrs. Cavendish, with deadly letter in hand.

1805. Two years later when the regiment moved to Montreal, his wife, Winifred, left Ireland and joined him. Her parents thereupon disowned her. To remind her daughter of how seriously she had disgraced the family name by taking up with a Protestant soldier, Winifred's mother had a portrait of herself painted which she dispatched not to her daughter, but to her son-in-law, Sam. From the canvas she casts a cold, disapproving gaze. In her hands she holds a note for all to see. It reads, "A prodigal daughter makes for an unhappy wife." The picture is still in the family.

On June 8, 1812, the president of the United States, James Madison, who believed "Canada was there for the marching," declared a "liberating invasion" of British North America. With war's outbreak Sam Hingston was made a lieutenant, the name of his company was changed to Prince Regent's County of Dublin Regiment, and off he went to fight. While he was away his wife, Winifred, died in Montreal on March 9, 1814, at the age of thirty-three. Her death certificate at Notre-Dame identifies her as Cavanaugh, not Cavendish.

Seeking a housekeeper for his three young children, Sam Hingston hired Eleanor McGrath, the twenty-three-year-old daughter of Owen McGrath and Margaret Carey who had emigrated to Canada from County Cork. Eleanor was Roman Catholic, born on January 25, 1791. She spoke fluent French and was a practical, no-nonsense woman who shared Sam's refined taste for leather-bound books, fine porcelain and crystal and for comfortable feather beds.

As the war continued, Sam Hingston saw action at Fort Erie, Sackett's Harbour, Black Rock and Plattsburgh. He took a bullet in the groin at the Battle of Chippewa, a ghastly engagement on the Niagara Peninsula on July 5, 1814 between the invading American forces under General Winfield Scott and the British forces under the command of Phineas Riall, a Tipperary Irishman. At the end of the day, 800 men, including Hingston's orderly, were killed, wounded or missing in action. Neither side had gained an inch. Hingston lost his kit in the battle and wasted no time in filing for fifty British pounds in damages. "I was severely wounded & my servant who had care of my baggage was killed in the same engagement," Hingston wrote to his superiors. "I was obliged to be conveyed to the rear as fast as I was able to be conveyed, & I call, sir, on you, to bear testimony of my not deviating in the smallest degree from orders. I was afterwards obliged to proceed to York [Toronto] for the recovery of my wound, by which I was deprived of any recourse to where my baggage was [before the action] by the advance of the enemy." The claim was paid.

When the war ended in August 1814, Hingston's regiment was disbanded and Sam retired on half pay. Eleanor McGrath was still present in his life, taking care of Thomas and Sarah, but their relationship had changed. On April 15, 1815, he married her "outside the rail," at the St. Gabriel Street Presbyterian Church, the Scottish kirk that used to stand at the western end of the Champs de Mars. At a time when women were expected to be subservient to their husbands, the marriage was anything but conventional. Sam's children from his first marriage would be brought up as Protestants, but Eleanor's would be raised Roman Catholic. They would have no children of their own until the children from his first marriage were self-

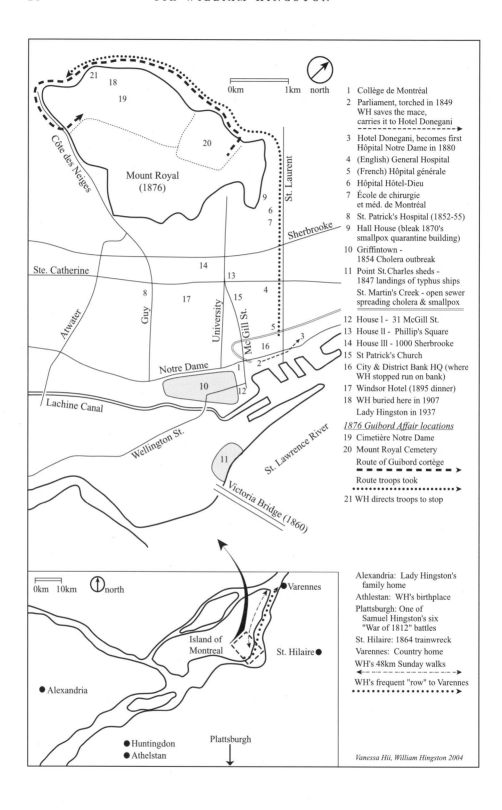

1 Collège de Montréal
2 Parliament, torched in 1849
   WH saves the mace,
   carries it to Hotel Donegani
3 Hotel Donegani, becomes first
   Hôpital Notre Dame in 1880
4 (English) General Hospital
5 (French) Hôpital générale
6 Hôpital Hôtel-Dieu
7 École de chirurgie
   et méd. de Montréal
8 St. Patrick's Hospital (1852-55)
9 Hall House (bleak 1870's
   smallpox quarantine building)
10 Griffintown -
   1854 Cholera outbreak
11 Point St.Charles sheds -
   1847 landings of typhus ships
   St. Martin's Creek - open sewer
   spreading cholera & smallpox

12 House l - 31 McGill St.
13 House ll - Phillip's Square
14 House lll - 1000 Sherbrooke
15 St Patrick's Church
16 City & District Bank HQ (where
   WH stopped run on bank)
17 Windsor Hotel (1895 dinner)
18 WH buried here in 1907
   Lady Hingston in 1937

1876 Guibord Affair locations
19 Cimetière Notre Dame
20 Mount Royal Cemetery
   Route of Guibord cortège

   Route troops took

21 WH directs troops to stop

Alexandria: Lady Hingston's
   family home
Athelstan: WH's birthplace
Plattsburgh: One of
   Samuel Hingston's six
   "War of 1812" battles
St. Hilaire: 1864 trainwreck
Varennes: Country home
WH's 48km Sunday walks

WH's frequent "row" to Varennes

Vanessa Hii, William Hingston 2004

sufficient and not until Sam had put the army behind him. In 1823, in recognition of Sam Hingston's service to king and country, he and his eldest son, Thomas, now twenty-one, were given title to two adjoining parcels of land, Lots 31 & 32 along the Chateauguay River in the fifth range of the Township of Hinchinbrooke, seventy-five kilometres southwest of Montreal. For the first time since they met, Sam and his wife had the stability she sought. Seven years after their marriage their first child, Mary Ann, was born in September 1822, but died shortly afterwards. A second daughter, Eleanor, was born in June 1825, and a third girl, Margaret, arrived in April 1827. Their first son was born on June 29, 1829, and since it was the feast of St. Peter when he was christened at Beauharnois, the priest baptized him William Peter Hales Hingston. He was named Hales after one of his uncles who had died in Ireland in 1823.

He never got to know his father.

Sam Hingston was an officer used to giving orders and having them obeyed, but he wasn't cut out for farming. The land was too wet to be cultivated, so he tried to make a living making potash. He walked with a limp, as the result of his war wounds, and according to one account, "he was rarely seen in his fields except on horseback," riding and hunting with his cronies and generally neglecting the property. He served as a local school trustee and organized a militia unit, the Fourth Battalion of the Beauharnois Regiment and became its lieutenant colonel. His rise through the military was quite unusual for a commoner at the time. He was elderly when he was made a lieutenant and that he continued to be promoted through the ranks was an indication of his ability.

One of Hingston's young farm hands, mistakenly identified in some accounts as his son, burned to death in 1826 when he accidentally fell into a kettle of hot lye used for making potash. The colonel went into a fit of depression as a result of the mishap. Early in November 1830, while stalking deer on his property, Hingston was thrown from his horse and injured. While he was recuperating, he caught the pneumonia that killed him on November 29, 1830. He died after what *The Gazette* described as "a short but painful illness which he bore with marked resignation." His obituary reported his death "without a struggle leaving his wife and five children to lament the loss of a kind husband and an indulgent parent." The swashbuckling officer was buried on his homestead with full military honours, coins on his eyes as was the custom. His grave, enclosed by a low stone wall, is still there on private property near the Chateauguay River, one kilometre west of Athelstan.

It was a critical moment for Eleanor to be widowed. Not only did she have three girls and a boy to look after but she was three months' pregnant with her second son, Sam James, who was born on June 28, 1831. There were now five children of her own to support and not enough money to go around. Eleanor was a proud, astringent woman, a model of hard work, common sense and discipline. In later years her sons would talk of her "firm belief in the adage found in the book of proverbs, *He that spareth the rod hateth his son*, always ready at hand was a birch rod." Her severity, they were quick to add, was strictly dictated by love. The only likeness of her known to exist is in Adam Sherriff Scott's painting, *Betrothal, 1846*, which depicts one of the more outstanding social events of the period. She is one of thirty-one figures in the painting, obviously a well-connected woman of important social standing. The painting shows the engagement of a young soldier, Major Melchior Alphonse de Salaberry to Marie-Amélie Guy, the daughter of Louis Guy, a member of the Legislative Council of Lower Canada. Eleanor stands off to the right of the canvas, a disciplined, dignified grey-haired woman, among the crowd of some of Montreal's most distinguished citizens. Her hands are clasped as if in prayer, and, considering the circumstances, the expression on her face is rather grave.

She sent her sons to a one-room country school in nearby Huntingdon,

Betrothal, 1846, by Adam Sherriff Scott. *Eleanor Hingston is the fourth figure from the right; Bishop Bourget is identified by his pectoral cross.*

where they were first taught by the local Anglican priest, a Rev. Mr. Williams, later by a brilliant young Scot with a promising career named John Rose. Rose was only eighteen years old, but he had already studied at Undy Academy Grammar School and at King's College, Aberdeen. Coming to Canada in 1836, his first job was to teach school in Huntingdon. At the time Rose was one of those "lighthearted and fairly irresponsible" teachers that students like, the kind of tutor who takes his work, but not himself, seriously. He was the first to recognize William Hingston's exceptional qualities, "a retentive memory, and a curious, clinical mind." Rose taught "Major Sam's boy" for two terms until the autumn of 1837 when he left his students behind to join the British volunteers in the fight against Canadian *Patriotes* and Irish rabble-rousers who had taken up arms, in the words of one leader, "to overthrow despicable British rule from the top of its branches to its roots." The rebellion, and its undercurrents of annexation by the United States, was poorly planned and quickly collapsed after much looting and burning by British volunteers. Once the uprising was crushed and its leaders captured and put on trial, Rose became the court clerk at the courts-martial. In the end, twelve of the *Patriotes* were executed for high treason.

Through all this Rose remembered his star pupil. It was Rose who encouraged Eleanor Hingston to have her son continue his education. Her options were limited; she could not afford to send him to Europe, there were no creditable English-language schools in Lower Canada. The only reputable schools that existed were private, French and Roman Catholic. Eleanor agreed to make sacrifices to send William, who was now twelve years old, to one of the best boarding schools on the continent, Collège de Montréal, more commonly known as the Petit Séminaire. The school had been founded in 1767 by a Sulpician, Jean-Baptiste Duratteau de la Blaserie, making it one of oldest classical colleges in North America. In those days the Collège de Montréal was not the sprawling structure that now stands on Sherbrooke Street, but a four-storey building hidden behind stone walls on the southwest corner of St. Paul and McGill Streets. Hingston was one of about 50 students in his class, and only one of perhaps a dozen who could speak English.

To understand the kind of man Hingston would become, it is important to know something of his teachers and of the Sulpician influences that shaped him. At their seminary in France, the Sulpicians began training priests to become businessmen and church administrators. They established their first mission in Montreal in 1657 and six years later were given title to the island as Seigneurs. In many ways they represented the nobility of the Roman Catholic priesthood. They were conservative monarchists and as such were among the early victims of the French Revolution in 1792. Not one Sulpician priest took the oath of office to the new French civil constitution and eighteen of them were guillotined. The names of those martyred are inscribed to this day on the wall outside the common room in the Sulpicians' Canadian headquarters on Place d'Armes. In the wake of the French Revolution, the best and brightest Sulpician minds quit France and came to Montreal to work. Brilliant men, they feared republican thinking and liberal ideas. During the 1837 *Patriote* rebellion they allied themselves with the British, preaching that it was "never permissible to revolt against legitimate authority or to violate the laws of the land." Discipline at their college was strict. Newspapers were banned as a corrupting influence. Boys woke at 6 a.m. and were required to attend Mass before breakfast. Students were responsible for their own laundry and were permitted a weekly bath.

Monseigneur Ignace Bourget

The curriculum featured Latin, French syntax, belles lettres, Greek, rhetoric, philosophy and elements of astronomy, physics, botany, and biology. Young Hingston was "quick and impetuous with a persuasive eloquence," which made him a leader among the other boys. He topped all of his classes, routinely winning prizes for excellence in every subject. One of his teachers, a priest by the name of Villeneuve, described him as "un grand farceur," willing to do anything "to create merriment or avoid a quarrel, but when a quarrel was forced upon him, never shrank from the issue, no matter how uncertain it might appear."

By the end of his second term Hingston was brought to the attention of the dynamic bishop of Montreal, Ignace Bourget, who had just embarked on an ambitious campaign to "Christianize society." Bourget was young, only forty-two, but already he was a prematurely grey, regal-looking autocrat, a man of secular ambition who was convinced that he spoke with the authority of the Almighty. He had already launched the first salvo in what would become an ecclesiastical skirmish between Ultramontanes and Gallicans. Bourget was an Ultramontane, with its emphasis on centralized church power and doctrine. He opposed the widespread Gallican brand of theology which was much more moderate and liberal. Anyone who crossed Bourget was threatened with excommunication. Anyone who refused to think as he did was branded a heretic. His scheme was to recruit and train priests as a bulwark against the rising tide of English indifference to French-Canadian interests in Lower Canada. Bourget was the architect of the Catholic nationalism that would endure for a century in Quebec. He built a state-within-a-state, in which legions of his priests administered and direct-ed every aspect of the religious, cultural, educational, linguistic, financial and social welfare of the Catholics in the diocese.

By now, Eleanor Hingston, struggling with family finances and hard pressed to pay her bills, learned that the church would pay for William's education if he would become a priest. With the church prepared to take the boy, Eleanor, who was no longer willing or able to support her son – the cir-cumstances are unclear – hectored William, telling him that if he wished to continue his schooling he would have no choice but to enter the priesthood. At fourteen, the boy had no sense of vocation and was bright enough to real-ize it. "I would be honoured if God was to call me to the priesthood, but I am too young to make that decision," he informed his mother, "but if you require a decisive answer, the answer is no."

He was on his own. Equipped with his breeding, his nature and his edu-cation, he took the next step and indentured himself as an apprentice to Rice W. Rexford, a chemist and apothecary with a shop at 29 McGill Street. Little is known about Rexford, other than that he was the son of United Empire Loyalists who settled in Magog after the American Revolution. Young William moved in with the Rexford family and worked long hours learning to cultivate medicinal plants and how to cap bottles and roll pills. He stud-ied the pharmacopeia, and became acquainted with contemporary treat-ments such as turpentine enemas and the application of leeches. He discovered how to administer proper dosages of popular cure-alls such as laudanum, quinine, opium and mercury. At night, after the rest of the house-hold had retired, he kept up with classical studies. But he had other advan-tages. Sympathetic teachers at the Petit Séminaire let him monitor their classes. His former teacher, John Rose, had become a rising commercial lawyer in Montreal and he continued to take an interest in William's progress. Even more importantly, Rexford, who admired the boy's industry, honesty and serious disposition, agreed to send him to McGill University in exchange for two years of labour.

Hingston was eighteen years old and preparing to enroll in pharmacology at McGill during the fateful summer of 1847 when sailing ships from Ireland dumped their cargoes of the living dead in Montreal. The nightmare began on June 7 when three merchant vessels, *Queen*, *Rolland Hill* and *Quebec* tied up at sheds near Point St. Charles and the first victims of the fiery typhus, their heads and faces hideously swollen, staggered to shore. By the end of the second week in June "a panic of almost incredible nature" swept through the city as the disease reached epidemic proportions. Immigrants died at the rate of fifty a day. Many of those who ministered to them, including the popular mayor of Montreal, John Easton Mills, nine Catholic and Anglican priests and a dozen nursing sisters were victims as well. Hingston delivered the quick lime to the mass graves and helped bury the dead. The stench was revolting, the sight obscene. Sick and dying were heaped together in agony like so much cordwood. It is estimated that 90,000 people driven from Ireland by famine set sail for Canada. Of that number, approximately 26,000 died – 6,000 at sea, as many as 8,000 at the quarantine station at Grosse-Isle, 6,000 in Quebec City and another 6,000 in Montreal. The experience had a profound effect on Hingston. If he would not fulfill his mother's wish that he become a priest and minister to spiritual pain, he could instead tend to human suffering. His youthful idealism gave him a desire to help those in need. By looking after the infirm he could serve God and at the same time satisfy what St. Augustine calls "that bond of human contact needed to lift one up to heaven." He could, like Christ, embrace their pain and become a wounded healer for others.

The famine Irish who survived in Montreal were not at all welcome. There was no work for them and no housing. Welfare and social assistance as we know it today did not exist. The French-language newspaper, *La Minerve*, proposed that the Irish be sent to the Caribbean to replace the slaves recently emancipated by their British plantation owners. The Legislative Assembly appealed to Queen Victoria to put an end to the invasion of Quebec by "the starving, the sick and the diseased." The Irish newcomers who crowded the fever sheds were a source of amusement for many Montrealers. "Sunday last, we understand troops of the idly curious were hanging about the immigrant sheds and hospitals throughout the day, to the great annoyance of those having charge of the sick. Between four and five in the afternoon, crowds were seen moving in that direction as if they expected to see a circus or raree-show gratis," *The Gazette* reported on June 28,

1847. "It is hoped that a sense of decency will turn the walk of these Sunday promenaders in some other direction."

In September 1847, Hingston enrolled in pharmacology at McGill University. The register identifies R. Rexford as his guardian. It also indicates that in an expression of youthful cheek or defiant pride, Hingston gave as his home address: The Church of Rome.

In his first term, Hingston discovered that he knew as much about pharmacy as his teachers. Out of boredom, he switched to medicine. The McGill of Hingston's day wasn't much of a university. The campus comprised "two blocks of unfinished and partly ruined buildings and a wilderness of excavator's and mason's rubbish overgrown with weeds, pastured at will by herds of cattle cropping grass, browning in shrubs, with the only access from town by a circuitous and ungraded cart track almost impassable at night." The professors of medicine were almost all graduates of the University of Edinburgh and the medical faculty at McGill was patterned after what they had learned at the Royal Infirmary in Edinburgh, which was the model for nascent medical schools in North America. Of the 200 or so doctors practising in British North America in the 1840s, at least seventy had an Edinburgh degree. At the time, acquiring surgical skills was like training to be an auto mechanic today. Some people learned on the job through trial and error; others were taught the nuts and bolts by demonstration. The doctors at McGill, however, knew little about pathology and brought nothing new to the faculty.

The dean of medicine, Andrew Fernando Holmes, was also treasurer, librarian and registrar. He taught chemistry and pharmacy, and although he kept abreast of the latest medical developments, students complained that his lectures were weak; his writings, they conceded, were vigorous and lucid. Other professors included Doctor James Crawford, assistant surgeon to the 24th Regiment, and Doctor George Campbell, an excellent teacher who proved to be a dexterous surgeon even though his right wrist was paralyzed.

Students paid three British pounds for a ticket to each course, and together they studied anatomy, materia medica, midwifery and what is today called homeopathy. Surgery was not part of the curriculum. In the days before anesthesia surgeons were not necessarily trained medical specialists, but tradesmen who engaged in bloodletting and performed operations that were really little more than human butchery. Surgery was so rarely performed in Montreal that medical students had to steal bodies from the morgue or dig up those freshly buried – a practice jokingly referred to as "resurrectioning" – so as to obtain cadavers with which to work. They dissected by candlelight in a room under the eaves, their sole company being "numerous rats which kept up a lively racket coursing over and below the floor and within the walls. The rattling produced by their rush over loose bones furnished a variety of sounds that would have been highly creditable to any old fashioned house."

It was a rigorous program. Students attended morning lectures on campus then went to the Montreal General Hospital at the corner of Dorchester Boulevard and St. Famille – at the time the only teaching hospital in North America open to medical students – for three hours of clinical lectures and hospital work. At two each afternoon they returned to McGill for another six hours of gruelling and monotonous lectures. Postmortems were occasionally performed at the General Hospital by generally incompetent, sawbone professors.

Nonetheless, 1849 was a dramatic time to be a university student in Montreal. In the five years since the city had become the capital of the United Canadas, political tensions between its French- and English-speaking residents had grown sharper. Hostilities between *Canadien* rebels and British loyalists, or Reformers and Tories – as they called themselves – had been smouldering for more than a decade. Britain exacerbated the problem in 1846 when it repealed the so-called Corn Laws, bringing an end to a preferential trade system that favoured Canadian agricultural and timber markets. The removal of the trade restrictions plunged Montreal into an economic depression. Then, on January 18, 1849, the government leader, Louis-Hippolyte Lafontaine, introduced a bill to compensate the 2,276 victims who had sustained damages when the British militia looted, burned and expropriated their property during the 1837 uprising. What stuck in the craw of the English-speaking Tories was the fact that one of the leaders of the rebellion, Louis-Joseph Papineau, who had been granted amnesty and now sat as a member in the legislative assembly, was eligible for compensation. *The Gazette*, the mouthpiece for Montreal's English-speaking merchant class, was especially incensed. "We have said yes, and we will not hereafter cease to say it: One race or the other must assert its supremacy. Which shall it be?" the paper thundered in one of its editorials. "The Anglo-Saxon which, like the roll of a mighty ocean, is sweeping over the continent? Is it that energetic, powerful and sleepless race that is to pale before the rushlight of an insignificant French nationality in a corner of Canada?"

The contentious bill passed, and on April 25, 1849 the governor-general, Lord Elgin, gave it royal assent. *The Gazette* continued to inflame public opinion and goaded those who opposed concessions for the French to take the law into their own hands. "Anglo-Saxons, live for the future. Your blood and your race will be supreme," began another incendiary editorial suggesting the time was ripe for anarchy. "Anglo-Saxons to the struggle. Now is your time."

Filled with anger and seething with frustration at British indifference to their colonial grievances, thousands of English-speaking protesters heeded the call. Hingston, who lived one block south of Parliament House on St. Anne's Square, was there as the mob rallied in the Champs de Mars and then descended upon the legislature. The house was sitting when demonstrators reached the building and swarmed up the main staircase inside to the House of Assembly. A hotel bookkeeper by the name of William Courtney seized the speaker's chair and, "in the name of the people of Montreal," declared the session dissolved. The building was set on fire and the square was soon engulfed in a hell of flames. The firefighters, led by one Alfred Perry, refused to extinguish the blaze and in fact joined in the pillage. Parliament House burned to the ground and with it the government archives containing all of the records of British North America. The next day *The Gazette* described the blaze as "an awfully and magnificently beautiful sight," and reported that during the looting, "some scoundrels made off with that bauble, the mace," as well as a gilt-framed portrait of Queen Victoria. Had *The Gazette* bothered to investigate, it would have learned that the scoundrels were none other than William Hingston and Sandford Fleming, a twenty-two-year-old immigrant Scots civil engineer who would one day devise the international system of time zones.

In this engraving Hingston may be seen running with the mace beside firemen.

As Hingston was swept along with the insurgents, he saw looters spoiling for action. As he watched, someone darted away with the mace, Parliament's symbol of authority, and tossed it into an open carriage. Hingston took after the thief, wrestled with him, grabbed the mace and ran with it to the Donegani Hotel at the corner of Notre Dame and Bonsecours Streets where he delivered the precious silver booty – worth 600 British pounds – to Sir Alan McNab for safekeeping. McNab was the Tory member for Hamilton who had served with Hingston's father at Sackett's Harbour and Plattsburgh during the War of 1812. Although a Tory, McNab did not condone the torching of Parliament. The next day when the chastened members of the Legislative Council resumed their session in Trinity Anglican Church, the mace was there to usher them in. Young Hingston would long be remembered as the gallant trooper who saved the mace. It would continue to be used in every Canadian parliamentary session until it melted in the fire that ripped through the House of Commons in Ottawa in 1916. The silver was recovered from the ruins and used to recast an almost identical mace that is paraded into Parliament to this day.

What is still uncertain is whether Hingston was swimming with the stream in the uprising, defending the urgent interests of the English-speaking community, or whether he was an innocent bystander who acted only when the protest spun out of control. After the mob burned Parliament it sacked the home of Prime Minister Lafontaine, and then threatened to march on St. Patrick's Church. Hingston found himself standing on Beaver Hall Hill one night guarding the church from an attack by many of the same people in the very crowd that he had run with the night before.

Hingston came of age when the fate of the country was at stake and the air filled with contradictory allegiances. If he is to be judged by the company he kept at the time, he would have considered himself an English Montrealer. He belonged to a circle that included John Rose, who had signed a manifesto supporting annexation by the United States, and as an adolescent upstart Hingston probably shared those sentiments. Young Hingston could not identify with the tribalism of the French Canadians, nor could he be expected to relate to the oppression in distant Ireland, for he had never been there. Because of his Roman Catholic faith he had little sympathy for British colonials.

He wasn't easily intimidated by the cruelty in ethnicity and religion, but he needed to confront his heritage if he was to forge a new destiny from its ashes.

Hingston graduated from McGill on May 8, 1851. *The Gazette* took note of the convocation, and reported that William H. Hingston of Huntingdon, was one of eleven gentlemen "to have passed through the course of study imposed by the Statutes of the medical faculty, and having successfully undergone the different examinations required of them, who had received the degree of Doctor in Medicine and Surgery. The convocation was fully attended and we were happy to see the seats for the public more than filled by our fellow citizens, and their wives and daughters. Dr. Campbell delivered an excellent valedictory address to the graduates." Among his fellow graduates were John William Mount, who despite his name and British ancestry was a francophone who would become a Montreal alderman active in the St. Jean Baptiste Society, and Charles Eusèbe Casgrain, the first Franco-Ontarian to be appointed to the Canadian Senate. As is still the custom, Hingston took the Hippocratic oath and pledged to administer "no deadly medicine... not to give a woman a pesky to produce an abortion," and promised "to impart a knowledge of the art of medicine to my own sons..."

He was not a man to take an oath lightly nor to take an oath he could not keep. He would indeed, one day, pass on his knowledge of medicine to one of his sons.

It is as difficult for a boy to be a surgeon as it is to educate them to be a bishop...

James Syme, dean of medicine,
Edinburgh University

CHAPTER TWO

EDINBURGH, PARIS, BERLIN AND MEDICINE

Hingston had his diploma but that didn't give him a licence to practise. The College of Physicians and Surgeons of Lower Canada,
such as it was, required even those with diplomas in medicine to
obtain a licence. The only way a McGill graduate could do that was either
to serve an eighteen-month apprenticeship as a dresser to another doctor or
complete a six-month internship at the Montreal General Hospital, and only
at the General. James Crawford was both head of clinical medicine and surgery at McGill and chief of the College of Physicians and Surgeons, and he
blocked both those avenues to Hingston's future.

The awarding of these licences appears to have been an arbitrary procedure. Only doctors at the Montreal General could sit on the board of examiners. In other words, students wanting to go on to practise medicine had to
impress the same learned McGill professors who had taught them. One of
Hingston's classmates, Doctor Duncan C. MacCallum, writes that "the
examinations for the degree of the university were conducted orally, ten
minutes being allowed to each examiner. Immediately on the termination of
the examination, the professors met, and decided then and there the fate of
the candidates."

For whatever reason, they would not give Hingston his licence. Hingston
believed, in fact, that he was turned down simply because he was a Roman
Catholic. For the rest of his life he nurtured a resentment towards McGill
and his examiners. He may have been right. The stated aim of the university
was, after all, to "by degree induce Catholics to embrace the Protestant religion." Anti-Catholic sentiment was rife on campus, fuelled no doubt in part
by memories of Edmund Bailey O'Callaghan, an Irish Catholic firebrand
who had been engaged as the first head of the General Hospital in 1826,
then turned his back on the institution by joining the 1837 *Patriote* rebellion,
becoming one of the uprising's most zealous supporters.

On the other hand, Hingston may have been rejected because of his attitude. He was anything but a docile student. Crawford may simply have judged him as immature.

Unable to work in Montreal, Hingston had no choice but to go to Europe to hone his skills. He left in July 1851, to do post-graduate work in Edinburgh. On the way he planned to spend three weeks in Ireland visiting his ancestral homeland. A cousin, Reverend George Cotter Hingston, the rector of Queenstown, had invited him, but when he got there, Hingston received a rude reception. As soon as the clergyman learned that Hingston was Roman Catholic, he sent him packing.

After that unfortunate start, Hingston was pleasantly surprised by the congenial student atmosphere in Edinburgh. When he arrived the city was an amazing place, a world capital of learning and scientific culture known as "The Athens of the North." Its university, founded in 1726, was an integral part of the city. The medical school on George Square was renowned, the finest in Europe. One of its principal advantages was that it was one of the few schools to include chemistry and botany in its curriculum as well as practical courses in extirpative surgery, with a focus on amputations, and offered students a hands-on clinical experience. An inscription above the portal of one of the monumental university buildings caught Hingston's eye: "On Earth there is nothing great but man; in man there is nothing great but mind."

It became his lifelong mantra.

Hingston's decision to study dissection was unusual for the time. Surgeons were not considered to be medical specialists. Beginning with the Renaissance, dissection was something artists and sculptors needed to know about, not doctors. Surgeons were really tradesmen unto themselves, like barbers, whose job it was to chop off limbs.

The dean of Edinburgh's medical faculty was James Syme, a fearless doctor who was difficult and querulous, but who had, nevertheless, few peers in his field. Syme took a cold-blooded approach to surgery. He taught that surgeons must focus on the act itself, not on the incidental pain or the consequences of their operating procedures. According to the course prospectus, Symes taught "the discrimination of surgical diseases by pointing out their distinctive characters in the living body. All the patients whose cases come under consideration are placed before the students in the theatre of the hospital, when, with due regard to their feelings, the opinions entertained as to the seat and nature of the malady are freely expressed and the means of remedy deemed requisite are administered."

Hingston was taught by a number of leading lights of nineteenth-century medicine. Another of his professors was Doctor James Simpson who taught a course on Midwifery and Diseases of Women and Children. Simpson was a linguist, philologist and a biblical scholar. His course in midwifery was an innovation. Men were only beginning to get involved in the birthing process; fashionable women in Britain had for some time thought it was safer to employ a man as a midwife, but everywhere else women – especially nuns and nursing sisters, who could not be licensed as doctors – attended births, studied female anatomy and had the general responsibility for dealing with pregnancies. The only time men were called to assist was in case of a difficult birth where they were needed to perform a caesarean section with blades, or to remove a stillborn fetus from the womb using instruments that resembled fish hooks.

Simpson's enduring preoccupation was the alleviation of pain and suffering on the operating table. He had recently pioneered the use of chloroform as a clinical anesthetic making the delivery process relatively painless. He was especially obsessed with finding the means of putting patients to sleep in order to avoid the worst agonies of childbirth. Chloroform, however, is potent, highly poisonous and tricky to administer. In inexperienced hands it can be fatal. Initially, Simpson's reliance on chloroform was opposed on both medical and theological grounds. Religious fundamentalists argued against its use citing chapter and verse in Genesis, "In pain you shall bring forth children." In Simpson's view, the word "pain" was simply a bad translation of the Greek word for contraction. The controversy raged until 1853 when chloroform was administered to Queen Victoria during the birth of her sixth child, Prince Leopold.

Most of Hingston's classmates at Edinburgh were rowdy exhibitionists. Charles Dickens described medical students of the period as "young gentlemen who smoke in the streets by day, shout and scream in the same by night, call waiters by their Christian names, and do various other acts and deeds of a facetious description." Even if Hingston had wanted to join his fellow students in hard drinking and partying, he couldn't afford to. He had 200 pounds to live on during his two years of study, the equivalent of about $16,000 today. This was all his mother could afford to provide. He worked unbelievably hard at Edinburgh, often subsisting on little more than bread and water, although "when in the company of others, he never gave the impression that he was short of funds." While he was short of cash, he was never short of friends. Among those he counted Alexander Burns Shand, who became Lord Shand of Edinburgh, one of the forbears of Diana

Spencer, Princess of Wales. He also befriended George Drummond, a young Scot from a well-to-do family, who was studying chemistry. The friendship would endure and prove mutually beneficial, since Drummond's sister was John Redpath's second wife and Redpath had moved to Montreal to open a sugar refinery. Drummond too would immigrate to Montreal and eventually help Hingston's fortunes along.

Because German doctors were at the forefront of clinical teaching, Hingston decided to continue his internship in Prussia after a year in Edinburgh. He travelled to Berlin in the autumn of 1852. Fragments of the journal he kept while there reveal a serious young mind intent on piety but not altogether unfamiliar with the carnal. He went first to the Bethanian Hospital, run by the Protestant Sisters of Charity ("unlike the Roman sisterhood they pledge themselves to celibacy but for five years," he observed, "at the end of which, if providence should have thrown in their way some LIKELY fellow, they can doff the modest grey and white to marry.") Hingston was impressed by the Teutonic passion for order and authority, and especially taken with the way the Kinder Hospital for children was run. He could, however, understand nothing the doctor in charge, Johann Lukas Schoenlein, said – either in German or English. Schoenlin was thought to have the largest practice in Prussia, but as far as Hingston was concerned, he laboured "under edema glottides, his voice is hoarse and guttural. His therapeutics, however, are excellent."

On January 6, 1853, Hingston was present during an eye operation at a university clinic in Ziegle Strasse when the patient, a fifty-eight-year-old woman, died. From what Hingston had learned under James Simpson, he was certain the woman had died of a chloroform overdose. Nonetheless, the attending physician, a Doctor Juenken, attributed the death to a shock to the woman's nervous system. Hingston vehemently disagreed. In his journal, Hingston wrote:

"Juenken strenuously, and I fear unsuccessfully, endeavoured to show that death can never take place in any patient from the inhalation of chloroform in any quantity. It might be supposed that the loss of a half a dozen patients in his hospital when in a state of anesthesia might lead him to suspect that chloroform is NOT perfectly harmless. Yet he has attributed those deaths not to chloroform, but to the shock of the operation. It is unfortunate that a man should hold such views as it causes him to pay less attention to his patients."

Hingston was fortunate to have as another of his teachers, Bernard Rudolf Konrad von Langenbeck, one of the fathers of formal surgical techniques who made important contributions to the treatment of ankylosis, the stiffening of elbow and knee joints by eliminating fibrous or bony tissues. Langenbeck was also the first to describe the use of mucoperiosteal flaps to close cleft palates.

From Berlin, Hingston went on to Heidelberg, Wiesbaden and then to Vienna where he gained admission to the Imperial Leopold Academy. During this period he picked up enough German to be able to communicate, and while at the Academy he discovered the theories of one, Herman Brahma. Brahma was a Bavarian physician who swore by clean, fresh air and good food as a cure-all, theories that Hingston would take to heart and later champion in Canada.

He had still not entirely abandoned the notion of becoming a priest, and studied some philosophy. In Germany he discovered "only one of thirty physicians who believed in God.

"The atheists denied the existence of God, but not aggressively but subtly," he wrote, "but the agnostics who pretended to know nothing about it, act and speak and argue as though they knew everything about it, and that was the difference between them. We teach physiology and all of the other 'ologies', but nothing of theology. God is kept in the background."

Hingston had not planned to return to Canada. Doctor Simpson wanted him as his assistant in Edinburgh and as the final step in the qualification process Hingston went to London. There he obtained his College licence allowing him to practise medicine anywhere in the British Empire, including, of course, Montreal!

He was on the verge of joining James Simpson, but his mother vetoed the idea. A forceful personality who tempered her love with a good dose of guilt, she insisted that her son's first responsibility was to her, and if he really wished to be of service, Montreal was where he was most needed. Hingston would remain steadfastly devoted to his mother as long as she lived and in the spring of 1853 he returned. During his absence the city had burned, and one-quarter of its population in the east end had been left homeless. A visitor from Boston at the time remarked, "Montreal wears a dismal aspect, the population has decreased and the removal of government has caused some four thousand to leave. Every third store seems to want an occupant and empty houses groan for tenants. The fate of Sodom and Gomorra appears to hang over the city... its citizens poke about in the dark."

At the age of twenty-three Hingston had travelled through more countries than most Montrealers would ever see. He had fresh ideas about the practice of medicine and as soon as he got home, let it be known that he was qualified to act as an *accoucheur* or male midwife, ready to attend women in town who could afford his services. His first office at 31 McGill Street was small and, as a neophyte general practitioner, Hingston only examined and diagnosed patients. He dealt with diarrhea, dyspepsia, typhus, cholera, frost-bite, tuberculosis, burns, headache, rheumatism and, with the waterfront almost next door, he treated sailors for venereal diseases such as syphilis.

He had not been in town long when he was approached by Doctor Aaron Hart David, attending physician at a new Catholic hospital, to become the institution's chief surgeon and apothecary. St. Patrick's was a seventy-bed hospital at the bottom rung of the medical ladder. It had begun as a charitable institution founded in 1852 by Bishop Bourget for "the principal purpose of providing for the Irish and English Catholics who have no homes, and for those unfortunates who could not be assisted in their homes with English-speaking physicians and sisters." In the middle of the ninteenth century, those who could afford medical care, including surgery, were privately treated at home. Hospitals were for the indigent. The issue that contributed most to the opening of St. Patrick's were the repeated complaints from Protestants who objected to priests bringing the Viaticum so that dying Catholics could receive Holy Communion.

St. Patrick's was financed, in part, with the coins taken from the bodies of the Irish immigrants who had died during the 1847 typhus epidemic. The first St. Patrick's burned in the fire that destroyed much of the city in 1852 and was relocated in a run-down Methodist school at the southwest corner of Guy Street just below what is today René Lévesque Boulevard. It was a draughty hospital from the medical Middle Ages. Patients slept on straw mattresses. St. Patrick's was run as an annex for English-speaking patients by Les Hospitalières de Saint-Joseph, a nursing order of French-speaking nuns. The nuns had been recruited to run Montreal's Hôtel-Dieu Hospital, an institution as old as the city itself, having been founded in 1642 by Jeanne Mance, the French nurse who accompanied Paul de Chomedey de Maisonneuve to the religious colony he founded that year on the island, Ville-Marie de Montréal.

Hingston went to work at St. Patrick's because he needed the salary of 50 pounds a year. It was an unusual trio of doctors that Les Hospitalières had engaged. Doctor David was an observant Jew, one of about only 150 living in Lower Canada at the time. Like Hingston, Doctor David had attended the University of Edinburgh, where he had placed 24th of 117 in his 1835 graduating class. During the 1837 Rebellion, David gained practical experience as assistant surgeon with the Montreal Field Rifles. A highly strung, but determined little man with large ambitions, he had helped to open the private St. Lawrence School of Medicine in 1851. It survived less than a year because the examiners of the College of Physicians and Surgeons, all McGill doctors, ignored David and his students, forcing it to close. Henry Howard, the other staff doctor at St. Patrick's, was a genial and popular man, heavily involved in the politics of the Irish community. He had studied medicine in Dublin and came to Canada in 1842 when he was twenty-six, working first in Kingston, then in Montreal. Howard was the author of *The Anatomy, Physiology and Pathology of the Eye*, and a pioneer in the treatment of mental illness.

Working at St. Patrick's gave Hingston his first brush with administrative responsibility, and he excelled at it. But more importantly, soon after joining the staff he performed his first successful operation. In December 1853 he removed a tumour "about the size of a walnut" from a twenty-year-old patient. Inexperienced surgeons were generally assigned younger patients; in case anything went wrong, nature's recuperative powers could be counted on to bolster the patients' chances of recovery. Hingston tells us that he began the operation cutting a thirty-one-inch incision into the left side of the man's lower jaw, and the tumour, "of a whitish colour, very hard, creaked under the knife" when he removed it. Hingston also lectured, which is something professionals did in those days to augment their salaries. Early in January 1854, *The Gazette* reported at length on a talk about acoustics that Hingston gave "to the largest audience we have ever seen at any meeting" of the Natural History Society.

Like many city doctors, Hingston was concerned about growing unsanitary conditions in Montreal. Newspapers drew increasing attention to the problems. In the spring of 1854 there were stories of stagnant swamps and pools of water, "nests of pestilence and disease in the heart of town" and of "filth and dirt hanging in clouds, resembling a dense fog over these hotbeds of death. There are alongside these frog ponds, butcheries conducted in the most slovenly manner and which assuredly, should not be allowed to poison a valuable neighbourhood."

The conditions undoubtedly contributed to the outbreak of an Asiatic cholera on June 24, 1854. During the first week of the epidemic, 400 died in Montreal. Untreated, a cholera patient can discharge up to seven gallons of diarrhea fluid a day; the waste from homes and hospitals was thrown into St. Martin Creek, which ran along what is now St. Antoine Street. From there, the wastes were carried to the town's water supply where they infected new victims. Throughout the epidemic Hingston was on call twenty-four hours a day. He spent all his time looking after patients in Griffintown, a hodge-podge of tenements, breweries, brickyards, livery stables, foundries and tanneries a stone's throw behind his McGill Street office. It was generally supposed that cholera was caused by "swamp gas," invisible clouds that floated two or three feet above the ground, and that if people slept on the floor the infectious cloud would drift harmlessly by.

Hingston was known to work thirty hours at a stretch without sleep. When exhausted, he would rest on horseback or catch a few winks napping on the floor beside a cholera patient. "He invariably declined to accept fees where appearances seemed to indicate anything like poverty," *The Canadian Illustrated News* noted. It was, he would later recall, the most difficult yet most rewarding and memorable period of his career. "A labour of love," he would say, "the esteem and affection of my patients was ample payment. If I live to be one hundred years old, my efforts in Griffintown will be remembered with the greatest love."

In 1854, Les Hospitalières began to look for ways to consolidate its services and move several buildings, including the Hôtel-Dieu and St. Patrick's hospitals, under one roof. Hingston was sent to France to look into the management of hospitals in Paris. He left for Europe in September and toyed with the idea of going on to the Crimea, where Britain and France had joined Turkey in its war with Russia over the protection of Orthodox Christians in the Ottoman Empire. Once again, his mother intervened and Hingston remained in Paris for three months investigating hospitals. He found the French capital "artificial" and its medical community "superficial and abstract."

Principles of modern surgery were just being developed, and impatient to learn, Hingston had a low opinion of French doctors who, he felt, spent more time debating theory than they did conducting medical experiments. "The French physician possesses an eminent degree of verbiage oft times substituted for argument," he wrote. "An hour is with ease occupied discussing questions of trivial importance. For awhile, the auditor may be well satisfied, but a retrospective glance shows him that there has been nothing."

Hingston's clever account of his sojourn, *The Medical Institutions of Paris*, was published in *The Canadian Medical Journal* on January 22, 1855. Summarizing conditions in two dozen French hospitals, it reveals a decent mind working through administrative quandaries as it follows the so-called seven ages of a patient, beginning with a maternity hospital, L'Hospice de la Maternité, "in which an infant first draws the breath of life," and ending at L'Aile de la Providence, "a refuge for the aged and the infirm." Hingston denounced French hospitals as overcrowded and inferior to those in Germany and Great Britain. He also censured their "direct infringement of Hygienic law, by which 80, 90 or 100 sick persons are confined in not over cheerful or too well ventilated rooms." He was critical of the operating techniques, especially those of one doctor, Jobber de Lamellae: "The rudeness of his manner renders him unpopular, and his clinic is very thinly attended. I first saw him completely enveloped in smoke, which, with the stench arising from the application of the coterie to diseased mouths and necks was almost intolerable. Seven or eight women are operated upon in a morning. A three bladed speculum is introduced up to the os [bone] and through it a red hot iron is applied to the diseased structure. These manipulations necessarily indelicate are rendered still more repugnant to their feelings by the rude and disgusting manner in which they are performed. Their persons are uncovered even to their waists and are exposed to the gaze of the assembled. One word of comfort or encouragement I have never heard to escape his lips. He still adheres to the old practice of enveloping recently cut stumps with linen, is a very indifferent lecturer, but manages to fill up the hour administering rebukes to his assistants." Hingston's observations aren't, however, without a wry sense of humour. He reports, for instance, that of 19,000 patients housed in Parisian insane asylums, 450 had been committed for excessive masturbation, a vice reviled as a dangerous practice because it was thought to result in organic brain damage. "Comparing this to the statistics in the *American Journal of Insanity*, half the cases of insanity in the United States were traceable to this solitary vice." Why, Hingston wondered, "is masturbation so much less frequent in France?"

"The remarks of a French gentleman, to whom I mentioned the circumstance may explain it: 'In France, we don't need to stimulate ourselves by hand. Women of easy virtue aren't as rare here as they are in America, and at the same time we can cheerfully engage in as much debauchery as the law permits'." He was most impressed with what he saw at the Hôpital Beaujon in the Faubourg Saint-Honoré, "an unassuming, and at the same time, most comfortable hospital."

"On entering, our nasal organs do not receive that disagreeable evidence of the vicinity of sick wards that they are accustomed to receive in such localities," he wrote. "The air is as pure within as it is without. A process of removing tainted air and introducing fresh air is constantly going on."

Hingston headed home in January 1856 armed with even more references from many of the continent's leading physicians and surgeons. Typical was this recommendation from Johann Ferdinand Heyfelder, a former surgeon general to the Russian Army. Heyfelder described Hingston as "a physician rich in knowledge and a gentleman.

"I know him to be a gentleman of excellent education and much informed in all departments of his profession. His contributions to the medical journal display considerable research and medical knowledge of no ordinary kind."

Christian Gottfried Daniel Knees von Esenbeck, who had been with the Imperial Leopold Academy, a scholarly society devoted to the healing arts, recorded that Hingston's leave-taking from Paris "was the object of uncommon interest and attention. All the members of the society are anxious to express their sincere wish that Dr. Hingston, may in his fatherland, Canada, meet with the same esteem and the attachment which we have been desirous of bestowing upon him here, regretting deeply that it was only for so short a period."

The Crimean War ended in 1856 and with it, so too did the European demand for Canadian farm produce as Russian grain came back on the market. In the spring of 1857, Hingston's mother, tired of making ends meet, sold the property with its "stone house, barn, stables and other buildings" for 800 pounds. The new owner was Daniel Brims, an American from Jamaica Plains, near Boston. Under the Civil Code, Eleanor did not have full right of ownership to her property, and had to share the proceeds of the sale with her four children: Margaret, who had married John Davidson in 1846, Eleanor, who had married Richard Pierce-Smith in 1847, and her two sons, William and Sam. With his share, Sam moved to Kansas City, Missouri, where he opened a dry goods store and married Rebecca Turney. William and his mother moved to new offices a few doors up the street at 88 McGill, where he soon built a tidy private obstetrical and general practice.

His approach was respectful and pragmatic, and the wives of some of the city's most prominent leaders were grateful for his early use of chloroform in the birthing process. They also acknowledged him as one of the best specialists in the treatment of breast disease. "For this sickness, the most serious diagnostic element resides in the sense of touch," he wrote, "for the education of which, an entire life is not too much."

Hingston was now a property owner, and as such eligible to vote. He was not a politician; principles would always be more important than partisan ideology and efficient administration would always interest him. His introduction to the political process came during the 1857 election when a spellbinding newcomer to Montreal, Thomas D'Arcy McGee, was picked by the city's Irish businessmen to contest a seat in the House of Assembly. Also running for election was Hingston's former grade-school teacher, John Rose, who by now was the Solicitor General for Lower Canada.

McGee, a former Irish rebel, had arrived in Montreal from New York a mere eight months previously to start a newspaper, *The New Era*. The idea of combining all of Britain's North American colonies into one federal union was beginning to take hold, and McGee, who had found the United States less than hospitable to Irish immigrants, campaigned for what he called "the new nationality ... a Canadian nationality yet undreamt of along these shores." Bishop Ignace Bourget, worried that Quebec would surrender its political and demographic advantage in a confederation combining four jurisdictions instead of two, opposed McGee as a candidate. Hingston, too, was similarly irritated by McGee's presumption. "He is clever but not very sensible," Hingston said of the Irishman. "Unpleasant and severe, and he brushes everybody's hair the wrong way."

On election day in Montreal, December 18, 1857, Hingston turned up at the public election forum on the Champs de Mars where he voted for Rose. There was no secret ballot; votes were recorded verbally. Rose won in Montreal Centre; McGee won in Montreal West.

In that election, which started Canada on the road to autonomy, John A. Macdonald and Sir George Étienne Cartier became joint premiers of the British colonial Province of Canada, and the government appointed Rose as Minister of Public Works responsible for the construction of buildings to house a new Parliament in Ottawa.

In the spring of 1858, Hingston was put in charge of looking after the Roman Catholic soldiers assigned to H Battery of the Fourth Battalion, Royal Artillery. As a result he came into contact with one of the most unusual and knowledgeable doctors he would ever meet, the highly eccentric James Barry. Stationed in Montreal that winter, Doctor Barry was inspector general of Her Majesty's Army Hospitals. Before and after his Canadian postings he had major medical responsibilities in other British colonies. Barry was an effeminate character who had, to the amazement of all who met him, achieved the highest rank a military doctor could attain. He was not only an expert in the sciences of anatomy and dissection, but a pioneer in improving the process of childbirth as well as an authority on the treatment of all things sexually, genitally and reproductively related. We know Barry and Hingston discussed such matters as ovariotomies and lithotomies but nowhere is there any record of what Hingston thought of Doctor Barry – which is a pity. Barry cut a magnificent swath through Montreal, where he was often seen wrapped in his musk-ox robes as he drove through town in a splendid sleigh accompanied by two handsome footmen. It was nine years later, only after he died, that the world learned Doctor James Barry may have been a woman.

Doctors differ. We do not all see through the same medium, otherwise we would all be of one mind.

WILLIAM HALES HINGSTON

CHAPTER THREE

PRIVATE PRACTICE, PUBLIC SERVICE

The patient was pregnant and she had been badly beaten. On May 23, 1859, Hingston was called to a house on Wellington Street to attend Sarah Nolan, a tavern keeper's wife who had been assaulted by her husband, James Connell, in a fight over family finances. When Hingston arrived, Sarah was writhing in pain, unable to speak. To relieve her agony, Hingston gave her a shot of opium. He returned the next day to find Nolan unconscious. "Dr. Hingston with his usual alacrity was on the spot, and performed the Caesarean," noted *The Gazette*, "but the child did not live. It expired in a few minutes." Shortly afterwards, Sarah, too, died.

Hingston conducted an autopsy on a body "black and blue all over," and concluded that Nolan had been beaten to death.

"A bruise in the centre of the forehead, another higher up; one over the right eye, one over each ear, an abrasion on the right side of the larynx, an ecchymosis of upper end of breast bone; an abrasion of considerable extent over the right shoulder, three bruises on the right side of chest near the mamma [breast]; four on the left arm, three on the right thigh, an abrasion of left knee, another of left leg. In addition there were numerous bruises of longer date on different parts of the body too numerous to count."

Hingston's opinion was supported by a second doctor, Robert Palmer Howard, who helped conduct the postmortem. Howard, too, concluded that Nolan had died as the result of "external violence, causing a series of shocks to the nervous system."

Connell was charged with murder.

Hingston took the stand at the trial which opened at the Montreal courthouse on January 13, 1860. He was not, however, the only medical expert to testify. Six other doctors, none of whom had seen the body, were recruited by the defence to offer medical evidence on Connell's behalf. One of them,

Doctor Archibald Hall, who lectured at McGill on midwifery, told the court that Hingston might have been guilty of malpractice by giving opium to the beaten woman. Hall suggested "epilepsy produced by the irritation of the stomach" could have killed Nolan. Another doctor, Robert Craik, still a young house physician at the Montreal General Hospital, testified that a beating could not have done Sarah Nolan much harm, "since she was used to it." Yet another learned doctor, Hector Peltier, chief instructor at the Hôtel-Dieu Hospital, suggested death could have resulted from complications in the woman's pregnancy.

The trial judge, Thomas Cushing Aylwin, was angered by so many conflicting, "expert," medical opinions:

"The theories of the medical men amount to absolutely nothing," he told the jury. "It is much to be regretted that medical science has not attained a greater degree of precision, than, judging by its votaries latterly in criminal courts, it seems to have attained where technicalities and sophisms are indulged in to the exclusion of common sense. Medical evidence of a proper character is of the highest value, and being of such value its legitimate limits should be well defined. Medical men should not become prisoners' advocates. If courts of law do not censure the unjust interference with the purity of medical evidence, the results to society would be terrible."

Connell was found guilty on a reduced charge of manslaughter and sentenced to ten years in jail.

Angered and devastated by the experience, Hingston wrote and published a critical paper, *Hingston on Medical Evidence*, that denounced professional jealousy and infighting.

"No remark of mine will be penned in a spirit of harshness, ill nature or disrespect," he began. He then proceeded to savage those doctors who offered testimony without knowing what they were talking about. Hingston ridiculed Robert Craik's claim that Nolan could be immune to a beating and suggested that his former classmate might, in the interests of science, "temporarily martyrize himself by submitting to a thrice daily or hourly flagellation or pounding in order to ascertain just how many bruises a man may bear [being duly accustomed to them] without their 'doing any harm'."

He urged doctors who were proud of their profession not to make fools of themselves, at least not in public.

"When two or more medical gentlemen of the faculty are to offer their opinion it would sometimes obviate contrariety if they were to confer freely with each other before their public examination," he wrote. "Intelligent and honest men, fully acquainted with their respective means of information are much less likely to differ when communication has previously taken place. And who can doubt the correctness of this principle who is willing to admit medical gentlemen are, and should be responsible for, and, to a certain extent, the guardians of the honour of each other?"

This was to be one of the first steps in Hingston's efforts to rid doctors of their sawbones image and have them respected as healing arts professionals. He was also one of the first doctors in Montreal to suggest that, as in England, pathology tables be required by law to list the cause of death: "So much useful information might be furnished to the profession which they might render available for the public."

By now, Hingston was doing very well for himself in Montreal. He could lay claim to the military and Protestant inheritance on his father's side, while his mother enjoyed a wide circle of influence in French-Catholic circles. He attended the levee for Edward, Prince of Wales when His Royal Highness came to Montreal to open the Victoria Bridge in 1860. As a member of the Medico-Chirurgical Society, an association of English-speaking doctors, Hingston was also present when the College of Physicians and Surgeons presented its address to the prince, who would later become King Edward VII.

But there was more to his life than medicine. From early youth until late in life, he loved outdoor activity. As a young boy he had a horse of his own in the country. Now, as an increasingly prominent Montrealer, he rode to hounds with the Montreal Hunt Club. He rode so well in fact that he won by two lengths the Hunt's sterling silver steeple chase trophy now on permanent display at Montreal's McCord Museum and the $250 first prize that went with it. He joined the Montreal Athletic Social Club and in winter skated at Victoria Rink and tramped around the island on snowshoes. He also helped organize the McGill University Alumni Society. Most Sundays after Mass and weather permitting, Hingston would take meditative twenty-two-kilometre walks from his house to Bout de l'Isle on the east-

Hingston can be seen in the centre frame watching a curling match

ern tip of the Island and back, a habit he followed well into his sixties. He was physically fit, a great believer in the recuperative power of fresh air and exercise. His only social limitation was that he was thirty-years-old and still a bachelor. Or as *The Canadian Illustrated News* would put it: "No fair one bears his name, and no little ones – except the citizens generally call him Father."

All of his adult life Hingston would be drawn to strong, independent women who in one way or another resembled his mother. In the spring of 1860, St. Patrick's Hospital was absorbed into the Hôtel-Dieu and he found himself reporting to one of those tough, extraordinary women lost to history simply because she was a nun living in a man's world. Her name was Marie Pagé, and she was Superior of Les Hospitalières.

Pagé was a farmer's daughter, born in St. Philippe on Christmas Day, 1811. She entered the religious order at twenty-two, only after she had had, according to one biographer, "a taste of the real world and had experienced its futile pleasures." Pagé proved to be a determined nun who often fortified her resolve with a glass of milk laced with brandy and who never allowed rejection to dash her spirits. She was an intuitive judge of character. Just before she invited Hingston to become a surgeon at the Hôtel-Dieu, she suspected that he might be happier as a priest. "If I were to become a priest, I would belong to God and be a priest forever. I became a doctor, not for God, but for myself," Hingston told her. Yet evidently he still harboured guilt for not following his mother's ambitions for him. Years later Hingston's daughter would write a short story, *Père Jean*, a piece of fiction obviously influenced by her father's struggle with his conscience. *Père Jean* is about two boyhood friends – one who becomes a celebrated doctor, the other, a simple rural priest. In the story, the one who chooses medicine visits Bishop Ignace Bourget beforehand to determine whether he is making the right decision.

"My son, the priesthood is not the life intended for you," the bishop tells him. "God has chosen you for a different work, none the less His because it is different. I have many excellent priests, but few outstanding laymen. You be one of these, that is your vocation."

Pagé was responsible for the Hôtel-Dieu Hospital, but medical control was, by notarial deed, entrusted to l'École de médecine et de chirurgie de Montréal, the hospital's clinical training centre. Inaugurated in 1845, the school was the brainchild of Pierre Antoine Confrey Munro, an assimilated Scot who had been at the hospital for ten years. Initially, the school was designed to teach medicine to students whom McGill had not accepted, either because they spoke only French or were Catholic by religion. A melancholy fifty-year-old anatomist, Munro had learned his medicine from his United Empire Loyalist father who had also been a doctor in New York before losing his practice during the Revolutionary War and moving to Canada. Pierre Munro's school was autonomous. The professors, all doctors at the Hôtel-Dieu, made their money from teaching; their salaries were paid by the school, not the hospital. Only those who taught at the École could get privileges at the Hôtel-Dieu. Since Hingston was not qualified as a teacher, and because Pagé keenly wanted him in her hospital, she bent the rules and had Munro hire him as a teaching assistant.

There were now going to be new and different medical influences in his life; some competent, others less so. His overseas experience had trained him well for the challenge. Besides Munro, one of the key players at the École was Doctor Hector Peltier, who had testified at the Connell trial. Born in Montreal, Peltier had received his medical training in France, studying philosophy at Collège Henri IV and medicine at the Faculté de médecine de Paris. He returned to Montreal in 1847 where he was hired as chief instructor at l'École de médecine et de chirurgie de Montréal. In Hingston's estimation, Munro was the more practical of the two; Peltier, by contrast, all theory. Even more troublesome to Hingston was Doctor Joseph Émery-Coderre, an overbearing character who owed his authority to the fact that he had been jailed as a member of l' Association des fils de la liberté during the rebellion of 1837. That in itself was enough to make him a folk hero in nationalist French-Canadian circles. What little Émery-Coderre knew about medicine, he had taught himself. He had been licensed in 1844, three years before the practice of medicine was officially recognized by the Canadian Parliament. Coderre taught botany at l'École de médecine et de chirurgie, but considered keeping abreast of the latest medical techniques a waste of his time. Like Coderre, another doctor on staff, Edmond d'Odet d'Orsonnens was also self-taught. The forty-one-year-old d'Orsonnens was the son of Swiss immigrant parents and was licensed in 1841. Implacable and blunt spoken, he began practising in Joliette, working there for nine years until he was hired to teach obstetrics at the Hôtel-Dieu, where he also specialized in women's and children's diseases.

Hingston's first patients in the new facility were Catherine Lynch, a "healthy looking twenty-three-year-old girl" suffering from a diseased elbow, and Patrick Carey, "a robust sixty-year-old admitted for cancer of the jaw." Surgery on both patients was successful, and both made rapid recoveries.

The kind of diagnostic aid we take for granted today simply didn't exist.

Hingston was learning to rely upon his own direct perception and judgment. He maintained that if a surgeon really has a patient's interest at heart, "he'll find a way to get around any handicap." He especially admired Doctor Munro's ingenuity, and the two men worked well together. Hingston often told the story of Munro attending a rural patient who had difficulty urinating. Munro didn't have a catheter with him and there was no chance of finding one. "Munro looked around the cabin to see if there was anything he could use as a substitute, and noticed that the floor had been swept clean. Such a good job required a broom, so he asked for a broom. One was brought to him, and he used it. How you may ask? With the bristles? No. He noticed the bristles were bound to the handle with wire. He took a piece of the wire, bent it, and gently inserted it into the bladder."

Primitive, but it worked.

The profession of medicine is a liberal one, not mean, or narrow or selfish. Science requires and humanity demands unfettered complaisance and civility.

WILLIAM HALES HINGSTON

CHAPTER FOUR

MAKING BETTER MEN
AND MEN BETTER

Mechanics' Hall Institute, a three-storey building on the southwest corner of St. James and St. Peter Streets, had been established in 1828 as an adult education centre for Protestant blue-collar workers. Its stated objective was "to make man a better mechanic and the mechanic a better man." Here people met to mull over and debate the burning issues of the day. In January 1861 the burning issue in Canada was the John Anderson affair. Everyone was talking about Anderson, a slave who in 1853 had killed a man in Missouri as he was making a break for freedom, heading north to Canada. He reached his goal, but seven years later, early in 1860, authorities in the United States demanded Anderson's extradition. Anderson was jailed pending the extradition hearings and Canadians were outraged at American interference in their justice system.

Protest meetings in Anderson's support were held throughout the country. Hingston, already working his way up the social ladder, was present as a recording secretary at a meeting held in Mechanics' Hall on January 17 to petition the authorities to allow Anderson to remain in Canada.

It was an impressive gathering. Ignoring his doctor's orders, the mayor of Montreal, Séraphin Rodier, had left his sickbed to attend. An Anglican clergyman, William Bennett Bond, was there, as was Hingston's old friend from Edinburgh, George Drummond, on his way to becoming a leader of Montreal's business community by virtue of his recent marriage to Helen Redpath, sugar baron John Redpath's daughter from his first marriage. (George Drummond's sister was Redpath's second wife.)

Antoine-Aimé Dorion, a future chief justice of Quebec, argued in Anderson's favour. "Is this man who committed no crime according to the common understanding of moral obligations [...] to be delivered up to the authorities of the United States? Now, sir, I maintain that it would be a crime on the part of our authorities – on the part of the people of Canada –

to render this man up." The extradition treaty, he reminded the cheering audience, was not intended to apply to political crimes or to those fleeing from slavery. Another speaker electrified the hall when he held up a heavy chain like those used to fetter slaves. It was Hingston who framed the four resolutions demanding the "immediate liberation of the prisoner," and failing that, urged that "the case be appealed to the Privy Council in England." The evening's significance showed that Hingston was prepared to venture beyond the confines of medicine to take on civic responsibilities. One month after that meeting in Montreal the Court of Common Pleas in Toronto ruled in Anderson's favour and ordered him released. Hingston met Anderson in March when the freed slave passed through the city "to return thanks for the manner in which Montrealers stood by him." In June Anderson sailed for England, thence to Liberia, and was never heard from again.

By that time, civil war had engulfed the United States. While most Montrealers were opposed to slavery, they subscribed to the view that states had the right to self-government, and the widespread opinion in the city was that the Confederates would win. A *Gazette* editorial was typical of prevailing public opinion:

"For ourselves we condemn the principle of slavery entirely, but in practice, we are free to confess that it has necessarily no absolutely repugnant features. Practically, we are all slaves, more or less and the mildest form of the condition is perhaps that of the slave with a reasonably benevolent master. A great deal of humbug is mixed up with this question as with all others... if accounts are to be relied upon, all of the outrageous crimes and two thirds of the minor ones are perpetrated by the coloured people. Let every man in Lower Canada take his experience of them. Respectable men ought to be made welcome, whatever may be the colour of their skins, but the idle and vicious are unworthy of consideration. What have we to do with the institution of slavery in the United States? It does not affect us."

Hingston had now been in practice for more than ten years. He had become an important presence not only in the community, but in the lives of women who depended on him to deliver their babies, care for postpartum disorders, and treat their gynecological problems. He was also building on his growing and varied surgical experience and had started to experiment with skin grafts. ("The size of the graft is of no importance. The skin alone, and no adherent fat should be grafted.") His rise was rapid because he was whip-smart and because he drove himself. The Grand Trunk Railway paid him a retainer to provide medical attention for the men working on the construction of the Victoria Bridge. When the Hôtel-Dieu consolidated all of its pavilions including St. Patrick's Hospital under one roof in its new super hospital – Pensionnat du Mont Sainte-Marie, which opened at the corner of St. Famille and Pine Avenue – Hingston alone of the three doctors from St. Patrick's Hospital was retained. Aaron Hart David left to become an army doctor with the Sixth Battalion; Henry Howard was appointed superintendent of provincial lunatic asylums. Hingston was promoted to chief of surgery in charge of English-speaking patients in the St. Patrick's wing of the splendid new hospital. Pagé guaranteed him his "Medicine Permanence," or tenure, at the hospital.

He moved into one of three stone terrace houses in an emerging residential district on the north side of Phillips Square. The houses had been built by John Honey from stones that he salvaged from the Parliament buildings after they were torched in 1849. Hingston had his offices on the southeast corner; Mrs. Robert Lovell conducted a girls' school on the other. Although Hingston's house was three storeys tall, it was crowded. The 1861 census shows "eight people, one horse and one cow," on the property. In addition to his seventy-year-old mother, Hingston was living with his eldest sister, Sarah Davidson, and looking after his niece and nephew, fourteen-year-old Ellen, and thirteen-year-old Richard H. W. Smith, whose parents were in Sault Ste. Marie, Ontario. There were also three servants, including Hingston's groom, his mother's personal maid and a cook.

The bay window to the right identifies Hingston's office and residence in this building on Phillips Square

Hingston went back to Europe in 1863 where his old Edinburgh friend and mentor James Simpson invited him to perform an operation. He returned to Canada rejuvenated. During the trip he became aware of Augustin Grisolle's *Pratique de Pathologie Interne*, which he rated "as among the greatest productions of a genius."

During the course of the American Civil War, medical men were recruited in Canada. Wars, after all, tend to advance the bounds of medical science. Coming as it did on the heels of the slaughter in the Crimea, the Civil War was no exception. More soldiers died of infected wounds, or operative sepsis – then called "hospital infection" – than they did in action. A Hungarian doctor, Ignac Semmelweis, an obstetrician at a Viennese hospital in the 1850s, was the first to be convinced that germs were responsible for spreading disease, but he couldn't persuade his peers to accept his theory of medical microbiology. It took another ten years before Joseph Lister, a surgeon at the Glasgow Royal Infirmary, began to experiment with ways of helping amputees to recover from their operations, with little or no success. Lister believed that stagnant hospital air wasn't responsible for patient mortality, but rather invisible pollen-like particles that infected their putrefied wounds. At the same time, Louis Pasteur in Paris went one step further and suggested that the pollen-like dust Lister was talking about might be a chemical process that involved living organisms, or microbes. Lister advanced his "germ theory" and recommended that carbolic acid be used to rid operating rooms of the microbes. In short, his theory proposed that minute living organisms invaded the body, multiplied and caused disease and that minute particles caused specific diseases.

Hingston was a surgeon, not a scientist. He remained stubbornly unconvinced by the germ hypothesis. He subscribed to the miasma theory which taught that disease was caused by "bad air" – noxious fumes from decaying fecal matter or some kind of putrefaction in the atmosphere. Fresh air, he argued, was healthy because it "sets particles in motion, and particles when in motion sterilize matter that is peccant. Cold days, as they are the clearest, are also the purest. I have fresh air, I have pure water, that's all that's needed to mock microbes."

Surgeons, however, develop their medical skills not by debating theories, but by operating. The more patients they have, the more experiences, the more proficient they become. Often, their most important lesson comes in the form of crisis surgery. By tragic happenstance, Hingston did not need to be standing on a Civil War battlefield treating wounded soldiers in order to encounter mass trauma. On June 29, 1864, a great black Grand Trunk train

The Grand Trunk accident June 29, 1864

locomotive, its throttle wide open, failed to stop for a swing bridge over the Richelieu River near St. Hilaire, fifty kilometres southeast of Montreal. The engine plunged into the water, crashed into a barge and then exploded. Aboard the train were 458 passengers, most of them German and Polish immigrants. Hingston was the first of three doctors rushed to the scene to separate the dead from the living, and to lift those still breathing out of the wreckage. Ninety-nine people died and more than 100 were injured. Hingston's knowledge of German served him well; he was able to direct and comfort many of the injured in their own language. He performed so capably that the president of the Grand Trunk Railway invited him to work for the company full time. The notion of being a corporate doctor wasn't something Hingston envisioned for himself, however.

The American Civil War ended in April, 1865. In May, Hingston's next-door neighbour, Mrs. Robert Lovell, rented rooms to an intriguing lodger. The lodger's name was Margaret Howell; her daughter, Varina, was married to Jefferson Davis, president of the Confederacy. Davis had been arrested in May and jailed in Fort Munroe, Virginia. He had sent his mother-in-law to Canada with three of his four children, Margaret, Billy, and Jefferson Jr. Margaret Howell lived with the Lovell family and became one of Hingston's patients until her death in November 1867.

One of the consequences of the recruitment of doctors in Canada during the American Civil War was the exposure of difficulties in McGill University's Medical school. Again there was talk of starting an "opposition school of medicine." One leading exponent of a new school was Doctor Francis Wayland Campbell. A man of "powerful physique and dauntless courage," Campbell was still in his twenties, a headstrong military surgeon with the Prince of Wales Rifles. Like Hingston, Campbell had studied medicine at McGill, and obtained his degree; but he, too, had been refused a licence by the doctors who taught him, and also like Hingston had to go to London for his College licence. Returning to Montreal, he helped start the *Canadian Medical Journal*, and "found among many a feeling of the necessity for an opposition school of medicine." Campbell believed the time had come round once again to put an end to McGill's monopoly. The university's instructors, he insisted, were behind the times, "running in the groove which they had long followed." McGill's faculty, he argued, was no longer keeping abreast of medical advances and what was needed now was "an up-to-date school that would teach subjects taught in the United States not yet having been added to the McGill Curriculum." Even Joseph Hanway and Richard Cruess, authors of a 1996 history of medicine at McGill, concede that despite McGill's reputation, its medical school had reached a low point by the 1860s. "The faculty, with few exceptions, were non-progressive practitioners and there was little hope that the existing staff could make the effort to break from tradition," they write.

Hingston shared the view that another medical college was needed, and that the logical venue was at the Hôtel-Dieu, which had its own internal teaching faculty, l'École de médecine et de chirurgie. Established as a proprietary school by the doctors who taught there, it had been in operation for almost twenty years. The École was something of an anomaly, part of, but not owned entirely by the hospital. Initially lectures were given both in French and English. But the bilingual courses didn't prove satisfactory and it became a centre for French-speaking students. The Hôtel-Dieu had twice applied for accreditation to Université Laval, in 1861 and again in 1864, but the application had been rejected on both occasions. Laval was trying to get its new university off the ground in Quebec City, and wanted to cap enrollment in its faculties of medicine and law. So, out of frustration, the Hôtel-Dieu turned to Victoria University in Cobourg, Ontario, which in 1866 agreed to award medical degrees to the École's graduates. Victoria University had been established in 1836 as a centre for Wesleyan Methodists. Affiliation with a secular university was a notion alien to the Roman Catholic mind-set in Canada at the the time, and co-operating with a Methodist institution was considered unconventional, if not downright heretical. Victoria University had been poorly funded and was in danger of closing. It needed the revenue new students would bring. The Hôtel-Dieu wanted its school's matriculating students certified as doctors. It was an uneasy alliance. In Montreal, many Catholics felt tainted by the association and thought that the faith of French-Canadian medical students had somehow been compromised, even though all of their instructors were Catholics and students didn't have to leave Quebec, or even show up in Cobourg, to pick up their degrees. The first graduating class, numbering eighteen, were awarded diplomas in May 1867. Among them was Jean-Philippe Trefflé-Rottot, who would go on to assist Hingston and play a major role at the Hôtel-Dieu.

Hingston's mother died on October 3, 1866. She was seventy-five. He was thirty-six. While she was alive he had remained steadfastly devoted, and everything he did revolved around her. She had supported, nagged and encouraged him. Now she was gone. Her funeral was at St. Patrick's Church and she was buried in Notre-Dame-des-Neiges Cemetery. No one today knows exactly where the grave is. Cemetery records for that year no longer exist, and if a tombstone was erected, it has long since disappeared. Her death appears to have liberated Hingston. "It was only after my mother was gone that I was able to grow up," he admitted years later.

The following February, Hingston sailed for a sabbatical in England, once again at the invitation of his old mentor, the recently knighted Sir James Simpson. The Atlantic crossing was rough. Hingston was distressingly seasick and vowed never again to return to Canada if it meant boarding another vessel. He was in Glasgow on July 1, 1867 when Canada became a country. Hingston was not overly optimistic about the future of the new nation. That same year doctors in Upper and Lower Canada formed the Canadian Medical Association, and Hector Peltier, one of Hingston's colleagues at the Hôtel-Dieu was elected Quebec vice-president. In absentia, Hingston was elected the CMA's Quebec secretary. From the outset, he was determined to champion the British model in Canada, so that "a practitioner in one part of the Dominion could be a practitioner in all."

Having reconsidered his vow, the first thing Hingston did when he returned to the Hôtel-Dieu was to adopt the British practice of making operating-room reports mandatory. The field of bacteriology was still unheard of. Surgeons and medical students went into operations without so much as washing their hands. If disinfectants were used, it was to disguise the smell. As medical historian Julie Fenster observes, nineteenth-century doctors "regarded spatters and smears of blood as badges of honour, the way a gardener today takes pride in hands that are caked in earth." Still, the Hôtel-Dieu was internationally recognized for its high hygienic standards. As one visiting doctor remarked, the hospital was remarkably well ventilated, "one of those rare establishments that astonished European doctors as perhaps the only healthy hospital in Montreal." Wards were spacious, and each bed was surrounded by white drapes giving patients a modicum of privacy. Each of the beds was dedicated to a specific saint; for example, #32 was known as St. Joachim's bed. There were private rooms for patients who could afford them complete with a bed, two armchairs, an armoire, and elegant carpets. Hingston, however, disapproved of carpeting; he thought it was unhealthy and had the carpets removed from the rooms of patients in his care.

In 1868, Hingston's surgical experience grew. He started doing plastic surgery. Records show his first patient was a twenty-two-year old male from Middelboro, Massachusetts. That same year he became the first surgeon on the continent to attempt to remove part of a kidney, the organ that removes wastes from the bloodstream. The operation gave rise to the prospect of a new field of surgery, the organ transplant. But because the patient, a woman named Moreau, died during the procedure, the credit for the first successful kidney operation – known as a nephrectomy – went to a German urologist, Gustav Simon of Heidelberg, who performed it the following year. It wasn't until 1902, however, that kidney transplants were attempted.

Hingston was also one of the first surgeons in Canada to experiment with skin grafts. No matter how innovative doctors may be, they don't always just treat illness, sometimes they contribute to it. Hingston, too, made occasional mistakes in the operating room. After performing one ovariectomy, he discovered that one of the twelve sponges he had used in the procedure was missing.

"The students present said they had seen me, with their own eyes, remove every one of the sponges and suggested one must have been thrown out with the water we used," Hingston recalled. "The patient was still asleep on the operating table. I intuitively felt that everyone was mistaken. After everyone left the room, I asked another doctor to help me do the operation all over again. I opened her up, and I found my missing sponge in her abdomen. I can tell you that the woman, who had been operated on twice, recovered rapidly. Today she's in perfect health. Ah, those French-Canadian women of ours are solidly built."

Medicine is a God-like profession. I am a member of a God-like calling whose function it is not to check life, but to save it.

WILLIAM HALES HINGSTON

CHAPTER FIVE
THE BISHOP'S GAMBLE

What was to become notorious as the Guibord affair began on November 21, 1869. That was the day when Bishop Ignace Bourget first refused to allow the body of Joseph Guibord, an obscure, sixty-year-old typesetter, to be buried in ground blessed and considered holy in Notre-Dame-des-Neiges Cemetery. Guibord had died five days earlier and had been refused the last rites of his church because, in Bourget's judgment, Guibord had committed the unforgivable mortal sin of printing *L'Annuaire de l'Institut Canadien*, the literary review of a left-wing liberal organization called the Institut Canadien. Bishop Bourget, who was opposed to unbridled freedom of thought, expression, and individual rights, had already denounced the Institut and its roughly 200 members as "liberal children of Protestantism, and the most formidable of modern heretics because they are the best disguised."

There is no evidence Hingston had ever been a member, but he certainly knew individuals who were: Doctor Joseph Émery-Coderre, for one, had been president of the Institut in the 1850s; Wilfrid Laurier, the future prime minister, for another, had been a vice-president earlier in the 1860s. The Institut dug in its heels and filed for a *mandamus* ordering the church to abide by the law as written and permit Guibord a civil burial in the Catholic cemetery. As the courts considered the arguments, Guibord's body was temporarily stored in a vault in Mount Royal Protestant Cemetery. No one in Quebec had ever challenged the authority of the church. What followed was the first epic struggle in Canada between church and state. The issue took on a life of its own and gained international attention as lawyers quickly digressed from the issue of Guibord's funeral. The Quebec Superior Court ruled in Guibord's favour, and declared that Bourget had abused his power. The church appealed and a court of revision reversed the initial ruling, saying civil courts had no jurisdiction in ecclesiastical affairs. With that, the Institut Canadien launched an appeal to the Judicial Committee of the Privy Council in England. The case would drag on for six years and have far-reaching consequences that would eventually ensnare Hingston, test his patience and intelligence – even his faith.

In the spring of 1870, Hingston bought a 144-year-old fieldstone house in Varennes, twenty kilometres downstream from Montreal on the south shore of the St. Lawrence River. Known as Domaine du Cap Saint-Michel, the property had once been owned by Jacques Le Moyne, Sieur de Martigny and Seigneur de La Trinité, an uncle of the first Baron Longueuil. Hingston thought the high elevation and clean country air was healthier than the swamplike conditions that prevailed in Montreal during the summer months. He dubbed the property The Cape, and for the rest of his life it would be his real home, a bucolic sanctuary away from the professional demands on his time where he could "breathe cool air, charged with the perfume of fern and seaweed," which always invigorated him. "The air there is in the highest degree stimulating," he would write of his country residence, where each year he would faithfully record the "movements of many birds which hibernate not with us; and the regularity of their advent and of their departure."

Domaine du Cap Saint-Michel at Varennes, painted by Georges Delfosse.

On January 31, 1871, Doctor Aaron Hart David invited Hingston to a meeting to discuss the audacious notion of founding a new medical college for English-speaking students, this one based in Montreal. The idea was to approach Bishop's University, an Anglican college in Lennoxville in Quebec's Eastern Townships, which had received a royal charter to grant degrees in 1853, and see if it would agree to accredit the proposed medical school's graduates. Three other doctors were present: Francis Wayland

Campbell, whose idea it had originally been; Doctor Edward Trenholme, an obstetrician and gynecologist who came from the nearby town of Trenholm, and who had both medical and law degrees from McGill, and Doctor Charles Smallwood, a Birmingham physician who had come to Canada in 1833 and was a highly respected professor of meteorology at McGill. Following the meeting, Hingston sent a telegram to Thomas Edmond Campbell, a member of Bishop's Board of Trustees (and no relation to Francis Wayland) soliciting his support. Bishop's was clearly interested:

"MORE PARTICULARS OF MEDICAL CORP REQUIRED. GIVE THEM IN PERSON: WILL HASTEN MATTERS," Campbell wired Hingston the next day. Hingston and Doctor David took the train to Lennoxville where the proposal was accepted. A School of Medicine affiliated with Bishop's University would open in Montreal in October.

Charles Smallwood was appointed dean of the faculty, but abruptly resigned in June to join the the U.S. War Department in Washington as a medical officer. Hingston was elected to replace him. Although the Bishop's medical school was supposed to open in four months, on October 4, it still had no building, no lecture halls and no affiliated hospital. Hingston had hoped the students could attend clinical lectures at the Hôtel-Dieu's school on a temporary basis. He also believed that since the Bishop's school would cater to Protestant students, the Montreal General Hospital would be accommodating. He was wrong on both counts.

Doctor Craik, now head of the Montreal General, who may still not have forgiven Hingston for questioning his competence at the Connell murder trial, refused to allow Bishop's medical students to use the General's facilities. And the École de Médecine et de Chirurgie de Montréal was not eager to share its own premises with a new school either. Marie Pagé questioned the ethics of a Catholic doctor working for a competitor. Hector Peltier, secretary of the École's medical department, delivered an ultimatum: Hingston must either resign as dean of Bishop's or leave the Hôtel-Dieu. He was given until August 7 to make up his mind. Hingston argued that Pagé had guaranteed him his "Medicine Permanence" when she hired him. Peltier reminded Hingston that Pagé had no jurisdiction over the Hôtel-Dieu's medical school, and that the same authority that had given him the guarantee could just as easily rescind it.

Believing it to be "madness to go on with a school without a hospital," Hingston resigned both as dean and as a professor at Bishop's fledgling medical school on August 12. He had been dean for sixty days.

He negotiated his return to the Hôtel-Dieu, this time on his own terms.

He would accept his appointment directly from the nuns and be free to deliver clinical lectures at the École as an independent doctor.

He began experimenting with acupuncture. There were also new methods of skin grafts to treat intractable ulcers. The procedure was devised in France, and initially Hingston was skeptical because "so much had already been written on the treatment of ulcers that it seemed unlikely a new method of treatment, differing from every other one which preceded it should thus suddenly be ushered into existence."

Hingston had two elderly patients, one an "ex-sanguine old man of seventy-two"; the other, a fifty-nine-year-old who had been suffering from an eczematous ulcer over the right tibia for more than six years. He used skin grafts to treat the ulcers, and it worked. "In both cases it was most interesting to see the small, shining islands of skin increase day by day, the rapidity of the cure was marvellous," he wrote in the *Canadian Medical Journal*. "I have never seen anything in surgery which interested me more." Some staff doctors resented Hingston's unorthodox methods. For example, while removing a nasopharyngeal polyp, the patient began hemorrhaging under the influence of chloroform. Hingston had four orderlies manhandle the patient from the operating table and suspend him by his feet as he continued the surgery. Because the patient's head was against the floor, blood rushed to his brain and the hemorrhaging stopped.

Nothing made Hingston happier than teaching, standing in a lecture hall surrounded by his students. His method of instruction was similar to that practised in Bavaria. He would call on students to diagnose a case, discuss each diagnosis in detail, then give his expert opinion. He insisted above all that his students develop their medical skills by trusting their eyes and their sense of touch. He hired as his assistant a young medical resident with a booming voice, Joseph-Antoine Stanislas Brunelle, who would become a brilliant surgeon in his own right, a physician who believed that putting a patient under the knife wasn't as important as the post-operative care they received.

Later that year, on September 26, Hingston pioneered another surgical technique when he operated on a sixty-nine-year-old Irish-born tradesman from Lacolle who had been diagnosed with cancer. Hingston removed the man's tongue and the lower jaw at the same time. Later he remarked he had never in his practice witnessed so feisty a patient. Warned of the risk involved, the patient declared, "If I live, I will be better off without my tongue, which has gotten me into enough trouble in my life. If I die on the table, thank God, I am prepared for that too." The operation was successful, and Hingston devised a crude gastric tube to feed the patient during recovery. Hingston triumphed because of his skill with a scapula, cutting nimbly through diseased tissue, excising tumours and knotting the wound. He dared to perform operations that many of his peers considered foolhardy. Some of his colleagues viewed him as a man who took unnecessary risks, complaining that he exploited his patient's misery and should never have performed such an operation in the first place. Hingston defended his actions, saying he would never have attempted so risky a procedure had it not been for the patient's attitude. "Among the conditions necessary for a successful operation, at the top of the list is the patient's acceptance and willingness to go under the knife," he said. "Because of his attitude, this man was able to survive, I am certain, a mutilation that would have been fatal to anyone else his age." The patient recovered, lived another eleven years, and even regained his ability to speak without his tongue. Hingston also started performing hysterectomies, which some of his peers considered an audacious operation at the time. He was also extremely proud of the fact that he had removed twenty-six gall stones, "without the loss of a single life."

On October 29, 1872, Hingston attended celebrations, including High Mass and a civic dinner at City Hall, marking Bishop Bourget's fiftieth anniversary as a priest. The city that night was aglow with light. "As one passed through the streets, the only surprise was to see just how many people had been found ready to spend the money and the time to illuminate their homes with lanterns to do honour to their bishop," *The Gazette* observed. Bourget used the occasion to announce that his crowning achievement would be the establishment of a Catholic university in Montreal. At the time Catholics who wished to train for law or medicine had no choice but to enroll in McGill or go to Quebec City to study at Laval. This made Bourget impatient and he planned to ask the Vatican to intervene and grant Montreal's Jesuit school, Collège St. Marie, a university charter.

During the jubilee Mass, a Jesuit priest, Antoine-Nicolas Braun, signalled Bishop Bourget's intention to take control of higher education in Montreal, including the appointment of professors. In his sermon, the priest echoed Bourget: "Civil authority is subordinate to the Vatican, and if civil decrees were given any authority at all, it is due to the leniency of the church. The church alone has the authority to make laws, and merely employs the state to implement them."

The new bishop of Quebec City, Elzéar Alexandre Taschereau, an independent and intellectual moral philosopher, a man who was everything Bourget was not, held a different view. For ten years, Taschereau had hoped to expand Université Laval by opening a branch campus in Montreal, and for ten years he and Bourget sparred over the plan. Taschereau didn't believe that Quebec's population was numerous enough to support two Roman Catholic French-speaking universities. He wanted Bourget to yield to his wishes. Since Laval's branch campus would be in Montreal, Taschereau expected Bourget to absorb the cost of running it, but because the Montreal diocese was still subordinate to the Quebec archdiocese, Taschereau would continue to maintain control over the Montreal institution. That, of course, was totally unacceptable to Bishop Bourget.

In 1875 the École at last moved into its new premises across the street from the Hôtel-Dieu. It was a state of the art building for the nucleus of an independent university in Montreal, and, despite Taschereau's warnings, Bourget wasted no time setting his designs on the Hôtel-Dieu's new school of medicine. Marie Pagé was not prepared to let either Bourget or Taschereau interfere with her hospital and she took steps to safeguard the autonomy of both the Hôtel-Dieu and its École. She required each teaching professor to guarantee a $25,000 loan, in effect making the doctors joint owners of the school with the Hospitalières, making it at once an independent institution, out of reach of the church but at the same time run by the Hospitalières. Its director, Doctor Munro, was appointed by the Hospitalières but, as one of the École's owners, took orders from no one. Eventually, though, Hingston, Munro and the other doctors involved would discover that when it came to ecclesiastical politics, nothing could be more vicious than a struggle between duelling bishops.

Hôtel-Dieu in 1860

No one should seek political office, but if the office seeks you, you would be a fool to decline.

WILLIAM HALES HINGSTON

CHAPTER SIX

FRIENDS IN HIGH PLACES

No one in Montreal, least of all William Hingston, knew what to expect when Frederick Temple Blackwood, fifth baron and first Earl of Dufferin, and his consort Harriot Rowan Hamilton arrived at the St. Lawrence Hall Hotel on January 5, 1873 for a one-month stay. Dufferin had been Canada's governor-general for only eight months, but already he had made a dashing impression. He was the first governor-general to enjoy the job, the posting, and the people – especially the French Canadians. The feeling was reciprocal. Dufferin wasn't a dull, aloof, bureaucrat who stood on ceremony. He was the ceremony. He and his young family struck a chord with Canadians.

Dufferin's young wife, Harriot, was five months' pregnant. Before the vice-regal party left Ottawa the governor-general's personal physician, James Grant, referred Lady Dufferin to Hingston while she was in Montreal. Grant and Hingston had been classmates at McGill and had a high regard for each other. So it was, as the vice-regal physician in Montreal, that Hingston found himself at a dinner on Thursday, January 16 given for the Dufferins by Sir Francis Hincks. Hincks was a man of unusual influence in Montreal, a member of the city's ruling class. A former prime minister of the United Canadas, Hincks had retired from politics in 1854 to become governor-general of Barbados and later of British Guiana. He came back to Canada in 1869 to become minister of finance in Sir John A. Macdonald's administration and stayed for four years. Hincks had cemented an alliance between French and English in Montreal, and worked with Louis-Hippolyte Lafontaine in the campaign for responsible government. He was still very much a political power broker.

It started out to be a dull party – "I fear it was not lively," Lady Dufferin complained afterwards. "What can one do in a small room with thirty strangers?" But for Hingston, it was a momentous gathering. Among those present that night was Margaret Macdonald, the second daughter of Donald Alexander Macdonald, then Canada's postmaster general, and one of the richest men in rural Ontario. At the age of twenty-six, he had established a grist and saw mill at Alexandria and through his connections, built an aqueduct in Montreal. He then went on to make a fortune building railroads. His brother, Margaret's uncle, John Sandfield Macdonald, had been prime minister of the United Province of Canada between 1862 and 1864; after Confederation in 1867, he became the first premier of Ontario.

The Macdonalds were Scottish Catholics who had settled in Glengarry County near Cornwall. Margaret and her eldest sister, Annie, had been befriended by the governor-general's wife and were travelling with the Dufferins. It is likely that Hingston met Margaret for the first time at that January dinner. Soon they spent a lot of time skating together at the Victoria Rink. Although Margaret was fourteen years his junior, she was no stranger to the expectations of older men. Margaret was just fourteen years old when her mother, Catherine Fraser, died, leaving Margaret and two of her three sisters, Annie and Ida, to act as their father's hostesses and entertain his many guests. She was a lissome woman, animated, clever and self-confident. Above all, she was, like Hingston, an ardent Roman Catholic. Margaret had taken as her role model St. Elizabeth of Hungary, the daughter of a thirteenth-century Hungarian king who renounced a life of privilege and devoted herself to the care of the underprivileged.

Lord Dufferin   *Harriot Dufferin*

Visitors to Montreal in the 1870s could easily be forgiven for believing mistakenly that it was a prosperous, progressive city. "Buildings are sprouting up around us as if by magic," boasted Mayor Charles Coursol, and indeed they were. Ornate Second Empire facades, like that of the new City Hall and Post Office were beginning to decorate the streets. The cornerstone of the new Roman Catholic cathedral – a replica of St. Peter's in Rome, no less – had been laid by Bishop Bourget in the heart of the English-speaking Protestant neighbourhood and the handsome headquarters for the Life Association of Scotland was rising on Place d'Armes. Writing of this period, a tourist from Burlington, Ontario, who had not been in Montreal for twenty years, described it as "a very different place from what it once was. What was then field and forest is now covered with splendid stone palaces, the residences of the merchant princes of the city. Streets which were then of the narrowest dimensions are no more, while large and elegant new structures are to be found in all quarters for Divine worship. The public buildings have also kept pace with general progress." In spite of the building boom, Montreal was the unhealthiest place on the continent.

More than 120,000 people teemed through its streets. But humans made up only a small fraction of the city's inhabitants. Livestock still roamed freely around Place Victoria; rats and mice, insects and bacteria infested many of the dwellings. There were open sewers, and each year, thirty-seven out of every one thousand Montreal residents died – the highest mortality rate of any city in the Western world. One reason was that Montreal was a self-contained island with a densely quartered population, an ideal breeding ground for disease. Another reason had to do with the way the city was administered. Montreal was divided into five separate and unequal wards or districts. The richest of these, St. Antoine Ward, was an English-speaking enclave in the west end on the slopes of Mount Royal. The poorest, St. Marie, was an industrial, French-speaking, blue-collar district in the east end. In addition to the wards, Montreal was circled by hamlets, towns, and *paroisses*, each with their own administrations: places no longer on the map such as Tanneries, St. Jean Baptiste, Petit-Côte-de-la-Visitation and Abord-à-Plouffe.

Montreal was a city without a cohesive public spirit. People in each of the wards kept strictly to themselves and looked after their own interests. St. Antoine Ward, five times richer than St. Marie, could afford to spend money on public works and other municipal improvement programs. Districts like St. Marie, or St. Ann's Ward, on the city's southwest fringe where the Irish congregated, had no such luck. For example, when a special assessment was levied on the taxpayers of St. Antoine Ward in order to expropriate the old downtown cemetery to create Dominion Square, the residents balked, and "were not willing to be taxed for a park to which children and citizens from every other part of the city had access."

Montreal's operating budget in 1873 was one million dollars and the city was five million dollars in debt. Less than two percent of the budget – $16,000 – was spent on public health. It was generally believed that fresh air and water would help defuse the ongoing public health crisis, so the city began expropriating land for a park on Mount Royal. In 1871 Mayor Coursol had also embarked on a scheme to build drinking fountains for the public "separate from the ones for the use of animals." Clearly, something had to be done to improve public health. It was a cry heard everywhere. A clique of three so-called "public bodies" – the Board of Trade, the Corn Exchange and the Chambre de Commerce – a network of interests and family connections that ran Montreal as an oligarchy, spoke out. They wanted conditions improved. They harboured suspicions that the influx of Irish immigrants were responsible for the spread of disease. If that were true, they asked, could not an Irishman – one of their own to be sure – best deal with the situation? Francis Cassidy, a trial lawyer who represented the Roman Catholic church in the ongoing Guibord affair, was chosen. Cassidy was an ideal candidate – a member of the Quebec legislature and president of the St. Patrick's Society who promised "to stop the running of the pigs" and other livestock through Montreal's streets. He was elected in February 1873, and turned out to be one of the most delightful mayors Montreal has ever encountered. "He was," as Laurent-Olivier David described him, "a little Irish redhead with a merry eye, a sprightly air, a precocious mind and lively as a cricket." Unfortunately, Cassidy died at the age of forty-six, four months after his election. There were those who now believed that a medical man was needed in the mayor's chair. In keeping, therefore, with the custom of alternating between English- and French-speaking magistrates, Aldis Bernard, the oldest practising dental surgeon in Canada was picked to complete Cassidy's term. Even though he had the city charter amended to allow Montreal to take responsibility for the health of its residents, Bernard was in ill health himself and chose not to run for election when his term ended.

In 1873 the Vienna financial market collapsed, the repercussions spreading to London and Paris. European investors stopped buying Canadian securities. The tough economic times led to a depression in Canada. John A. Macdonald's Conservatives, derailed by the Canadian Pacific Railway scandal when it was learned that his government was on the take from U.S. financial interests, were replaced in Ottawa by Alexander Mackenzie's Liberals.

The next year, when Hingston was elected to the governing board of the College of Medical Doctors of Quebec, Montreal's ruling elite finally chose a leader who could deal with the depression and the rising mortality rate that dogged the city. By then at least 900 people, two-thirds of them children under seven, had already died of smallpox in Montreal: 763 French Canadians, 81 Irish, and 55 Protestants.

A group of influential citizens headed by Senator Thomas Ryan, a crony of Sir Francis Hincks, prevailed on Hingston to stand as a mayoral candidate. In those days, the mayor of Montreal had no power other than suasion; the real authority behind the City Corporation lay with three commissioners. The title of mayor was little more than a badge of honour conferred by the "public bodies" who ran the town: oligarchs like Hincks; the industrialist Charles Séraphin Rodier, who owned more land in Montreal than anyone; Henry Hague Judah, a prominent Jewish lawyer; a former Montreal mayor, William Workman, who made his fortune in hardware and real estate, and who, incidentally, was in Ford's Theatre in Washington, D.C. the night Abraham Lincoln was shot, and Peter Redpath, the sugar baron. All endorsed Hingston's nomination on February 15, 1875. The following day Hingston went to the episcopal palace to sign the pledge that Bishop Bourget demanded from all local Catholics who sought public office: "I, William Hales Hingston, a candidate in the next election declare that I believe in the religious principles found in the Catholic program and that I plan to submit totally and unequivocally to the bishop of the diocese of Montreal on all religious or mixed questions."

The pledge, as Hingston was about to discover, was no mere formality. Bourget had invented a year-long festival in 1875 commemorating the 50th anniversary of the blessing of Montreal's first cathedral; street processions between the various Catholic churches in the city were planned almost every other week, and as mayor, Hingston would be expected to participate in a number of related events. Each procession began with Bourget's papal Zouaves, resplendent in their grey and gold uniforms, followed by acolytes, deacons, priests and monsignors, and by crowds of so many women that "dust from their skirts clouded the streets."

Running against Hingston was Jean-Louis Beaudry, a smooth-talking discount merchant who had made enough money to start his own bank, the Banque Jacques-Cartier. Beaudry had been mayor during the 1860s and was hoping for a political comeback but he had little clout with the city's French-speaking establishment. Four days before the election, Beaudry withdrew and threw his "cordial support" to Hingston.

Voters went to the polls through a snowstorm on March 1. It was no contest. When the votes were counted Hingston had won by a 4,335-vote majority; 658 voted for Beaudry. As soon as the results were known, a crowd of supporters carried the mayor's gas lanterns from the front door of his predecessor, Aldis Bernard, and planted them in front of Hingston's house on Phillips Square, a custom that lasted another 118 years until Jean Doré's election in 1986. The use of lanterns to identify the mayor's residence began in 1868 when a monogrammed lamp was installed outside Mayor William Workman's house.

Hingston had achieved victory, happily as he pointed out, "without having spent one moment of time or one shilling on a campaign to obtain a position which no one should seek, but which, coming as it did, no one was at liberty to decline."

The day after the election, *The Star* set out to have Hingston disqualified on a technicality. Hingston's name had not appeared on the list of eligible voters because, the newspaper claimed, he was in municipal tax arrears. It was all so much muckraking. Hingston had paid his taxes before the election. "Dr. Hingston is neither indebted to the city, nor is he party to or interested in any suit with the Corporation," *The Herald*, a rival paper, assured readers the next

Mayor Hingston on the cover of the Canadian Illustrated News, *1875*

day. "It appears the rumour originated in connection with a transfer of land to a second party some time ago, the sale of which was not carried out, and the assessments thereon, although duly paid, were not discharged in the doctor's name."

William Hales Hingston was sworn in as Montreal's sixteenth mayor at an annual salary of $4,000 on Monday, March 8, 1875. The new City Hall, which still stands, was under construction, so the ceremony took place in the "bare and cheerless" second-floor council chambers in the west wing of Bonsecours Market. Even with his impressive backing, Hingston knew he would need plenty of help in his crusade to improve public health. His inaugural speech was direct and forceful:

"If men and women in cities elsewhere die, in Montreal they are killed, slain, by indifference of city officials and public ignorance, and the subsequent wholesale slaughter of the innocent, to give it no milder term, is truly appalling."

The speech was a success; the *Montreal Witness* praised Hingston for his ability "to clothe the driest statistical material in poetic language."

The men on his council were, as Hingston himself put it, of "unusual intelligence, yet possessing some angularities of character and disposition." They included George (the Faithful Watchdog) Washington Stephens; James (the People's Jimmy) McShane; an outspoken French-Canadian nationalist and Superior Court judge, Louis-Onésime Loranger; the city's leading grocer, George Childs; Ferdinand David, a carriage maker; and a prominent lawyer, David Ross McCord. Counted among the lesser lights were William Clendenning, Richard Holland, Joseph Duhamel, Thomas Wilson, Joseph Crévier, Alexander McCambridge, Thomas Foster, Jacques Grenier, John McLaren, Joseph Brunet, Alfred Roy Jr., Amable Jodoin and Adolphe Dagenais.

Hingston proved to be the quintessential physician-politician: quick to diagnose and react. His first directive as mayor was to to restrict each councillor to ten minutes' worth of debate on any subject. He also insisted they be on time for council meetings.

With the arrival of the spring thaw, streets in the city degenerated into mud canals, and as *The Gazette* complained, "gangs of men have been busily engaged scraping the surface of the ice, gathering their deposits into heaps leaving them to be washed back again. It would be better if the manure heaps were carted away instead of being allowed to fester. In the warm weather, exhaling the odours which are to say the least unpleasant, if not directly conducive to disease and death." It was prophetic. By mid-March, the paper reported that a patient suspected of having smallpox was taken away from a house on Cemetery Street in an ambulance. "The van was surrounded by a number of children, who had been playing in the vicinity and were attracted by the old-fashioned appearance. The patient was led out carefully protected by a cloth covering and the team drove off. Perhaps the driver of the wagon or those in charge never thought of ordering the children away, but it should have been done."

Smallpox is a monstrous, incurable, contagious disease; the virus is part of the orthopox family which includes cowpox and camel pox, and in extreme cases the entire body – mouth, nose and throat – is covered with blisters that then break, leaving scarring lesions and leaking blood from every orifice. By mid-April, *The Star* noted that two new cases of smallpox had been admitted into the hospital, "making the total number now in the institution, fifteen, a large increase of late." The so-called hospital was nothing more than a stone farmhouse on Mount Royal known as Hall House, which stood on property that had been expropriated from Benjamin Hall for Mount Royal Park and had been converted into a temporary quarantine unit. It was totally inadequate.

The first death from the disease that year was reported on April 13 – the epidemic that was to claim at least another 2,000 lives had begun. To his dismay, Hingston discovered there were "no laws to be found in the books that could be enforced to carry out the most basic sanitary measures." Civic statutes dealing with public health were "unformed, unfinished and immature." The British Parliament had passed a vaccination act in 1867 which imposed penalties for those who failed to vaccinate their children and infants against smallpox. Without similar legislation the city could not conduct a proper vaccination program or oblige smallpox patients to be quarantined. He spoke of his frustration to a meeting of the Health Committee in April.

"I attended a case recently in Griffintown where there were four children. I urged the mother to give me the one child infected with the smallpox, but she refused and as a consequence the other three children were seized with the disease." Protestant and Catholic hospitals each operated their own ambulance systems and the duplication of services, which cost the city $2.50 a day to maintain separate carriages, made no sense to Hingston. He suggested ambulance service be made available to anyone, anytime "for whatever differences exist as to religion, there is no difference in the disease." He also proposed building a smallpox hospital.

The city's budget was presented on April 9; the municipal deficit that year was $258,000 yet Hingston managed to get council's approval to spend $50,000 on two units to house smallpox patients, one for Catholics, the other for Protestants. The Hôtel-Dieu agreed to use the money to build a hospital that would accommodate forty patients; the General Hospital turned down the money, saying "even if a building could be built for $25,000, its maintenance would be a continual drain." Even more significant, Hingston got approval to spend $269,000 to enclose the stagnant St.

Martin creek that ran through the centre of the city. Not to do so, he declared, would be suicide.

"Anyone can see that if he steps off a cliff, he will in all probability be killed, so you don't need to enforce a law to prevent him from doing so. But he does not see that if he and his family live and sleep in an atmosphere filled with swamp gas, or if they drink water from a dirty pool or river, destruction is as certain, although by a slower process."

There was little respite in the mayor's duties, although it wasn't all drudgery. In June Hingston marched in the annual Saint-Jean-Baptiste Parade, commemorating French Canada's patron saint. It was, he said, "an exquisite pleasure," and he looked forward to the day when the event would be so popular that those taking part would be counted, "not by the tens of thousands, but by the millions." The crowds that gathered for the outdoor celebrations undoubtedly contributed to the spread of disease and by July 23, the Board of Health reported twelve people that month had died from smallpox, another six from typhoid, five from diphtheria, and "a large number" from cholera.

"From these figures it will be seen that diseases arising from the lack of proper sanitation are not decreasing," the board reported. "Uncovered privy vaults are a direct cause of the excessive mortality."

Hingston's reaction was immediate. On Monday, July 12, a bylaw was introduced ordering 18,000 vaccination notices to be sent out. Under the provisions of the proposed act, all children would have to be vaccinated within four months of birth; pupils attending school must be vaccinated; inspectors were authorized to make house calls and remove anyone suspected of having the disease; anyone suspected of carrying the disease might be prevented from entering the city or be quarantined, and signs in French and English, with the word Smallpox, "shall remain posted and remain so posted on a residence while the person remains ill."

There was public resistance, especially from east-end residents in the primarily French-speaking neighbourhoods. Those opposed to vaccination had their reasons. Some doctors, and a few of Hingston's own councillors, notably Joseph Duhamel, were not convinced vaccination was effective. Duhamel argued that it wasn't Montreal residents who were infected, but "sick people brought into the city from the Eastern Townships." Doctor Joseph Émery-Coderre was of the opinion that the available data in support of vaccination was by no means conclusive, and that one of the side effects was syphilis in an age which had no effective cure. They began organizing public meetings to voice their opposition. Still others – a vocal, ignorant minority – believed vaccination was a plot hatched by the English designed to infect French Canadians. "It is very inopportune to demand such a measure at a time when our population is under the influence of strong prejudices involving vaccination," *La Minerve* informed its readers. "To make vaccination obligatory at present would be a thing impossible." Vaccinators who attempted to go door-to-door in French neighbourhoods were often "treated with rudeness, indeed with violence and two of them were pitched down stairs."

A parade marking the centennial of the birth of Irish nationalist Daniel O'Connell on August 6 attracted thousands of loyal Irish Catholics. It was a deliberately provocative, sectarian event designed to assert the presence of that community in the city. O'Connell was revered by Catholics as "Ireland's Liberator" and despised by Protestants. Hingston wasn't present; he had gone to Halifax to attend the Dominion Medical Convention. The deputy mayor, Joseph Duhamel, marched in his place. Hingston was still out of town on August 11 when council met to consider the vaccination bylaw. A huge throng opposed to the measure, driven by the spellbinding oratory of lawyer Henri Saint-Pierre, pressed along St. Paul Street. Passing through the massive doors of Bonsecours Market, several hundred made their way up the staircase into the council chambers which "were excessively hot, and savoured an odour far from agreeable." Shouting and jeering gave way to more forceful tactics. Rock-throwing demonstrators hurled stones through the council chamber windows. As "the storm without grew," Alderman Loranger moved that the vaccination bylaw be tabled for six weeks. "The vote was taken under very peculiar circumstances," *The Gazette* reported. "A volley of stones came crashing into the building and council adjourned in confusion. The aldermen were afraid to leave the building lest they should be stoned..." Two aldermen were, in fact, bloodied in the mêlée before the crowd continued its rampage, making its way up St. Catherine Street to the home of the city's health inspector, Doctor Alphonse-Barnabé Larocque. The English newspapers of the day were appalled by the events. "There will always be doctors with hobbies like Doctor Coderre, and lawyers hungry for notoriety like Mr. Saint-Pierre," *The Daily Witness* observed the day after. "The great evil is ignorance which makes a whole population the prey of people of that kind. Coderre, honest enough – hobbyists generally are honest – planted a prejudice in the minds of his people: how capable the people, who have for nights been harangued on the vaccination question, are of judging that question, the events of last night make evident. A few of the ringleaders may have had notions about their personal liberty, but the mass of people appeared to be there in prospect of a row."

News of the smallpox riots spread across the country. *The Sherbrooke Gazette* denounced opponents of vaccination as "ignorant and pigheaded."

"For some years," the paper declared, "the inhabitants of Montreal have been suffering from the ravages of Small Pox to a greater extent probably than any other city in the civilized world. The deaths have been chiefly among the French-Canadian half of its population who do not practice vaccination but from them it has constantly spread. The creation of a Small Pox hospital has been rendered abortive by the insensate clamour of sectarianism... Meanwhile, people are dying by the hundreds. A few medical men in the city who have been born a little too soon or a little too late have set up a crusade against vaccination and demagogues have taken to ride the whirlwind."

Hingston cut short his trip to Halifax to deal with the crisis and was back for a special council meeting on August 18, where he sought to defuse much of the anger. Police stood guard as a crowd of "dirty looking rascals, mainly boys 16-20" filled the visitors' gallery. Hingston didn't blame those parents who truly believed that vaccine would harm their children for the disgraceful riot, but chastised members of the legal and medical professions for misleading the public. Turning to the unruly crowd in the gallery he warned that if there were any further disruptions, they would be ejected. "The effect of his speech, delivered in French, was magical, and silence was instantaneous," minutes of the council meeting indicate.

In addition to the continuing smallpox crisis, which that week claimed still more victims (nineteen Catholics, one Protestant), Hingston was tossed yet another explosive issue to contend with. After four years, the Privy Council in London, Canada's highest appeal court at the time, finally rendered its verdict in the Guibord affair. The Council's decision reached Montreal on August 13. Guibord, it ruled, was entitled to a Christian burial with the church paying the cost. The diocese was ordered not only to give Guibord a religious funeral, but had also been judged liable for the $6,000 in legal fees that had mounted over the years. It was a victory for the Institut Canadien. Guibord's body could now to be taken from its temporary mausoleum in Mount Royal Cemetery and transported to Notre-Dame-des-Neiges Cemetery for internment. The court order sparked what amounted to a holy war in Montreal. Supporters of the Institut Canadien, and its Protestant allies, took delight in Bishop Bourget's humiliation. But despite the court order, Bourget remained defiant.

"The Irish intend to unite with the French and will gather en masse at the gates of the cemetery to deny entry of Joseph Guibord's body," Bourget warned Hingston. "Defying the church cannot be done without the most regrettable consequences," added the bishop's pawn, Benjamin Victor Rousselot, who as parish priest was directly responsible for the Catholic cemetery. Rousselot reminded the mayor that "when hot-headed people collide, you know what result must follow when the flammable meet."

On August 30, the church was served with a *mandamus*, requiring that Guibord's body be interred in the Catholic cemetery. All that now remained was how best to carry out the writ without provoking the citizenry. The death the following day of the city's sixty-four-year-old fire chief, Alexander Bertram, proved to be providential. Bertram had been head of the city's fire brigade for twenty-three years, so it was decided that a civic funeral, complete with a 100-man police honour guard would be held for Bertram on Tuesday, September 2. While public attention was focussed on Bertram's funeral procession, Guibord's corpse would be removed from its vault and quietly transported to the Catholic cemetery.

As a diversionary tactic, it didn't work. As Bertram's funeral cortege rolled through the streets towards Mount Royal Cemetery, a mob had already gathered at the cemetery as Guibord's body was loaded into a hearse. As the hearse pulled away, demonstrators lunged at the horses and tried to

Rioters prevent Guibord's coffin from entering Notre-Dame-des-Neiges Cemetery.

overturn it. The hearse sped through the streets at a quick trot, until it reached the gates of the Catholic cemetery. There, it was met by a huge crowd of perhaps 300 demonstrators shouting, "Down with Guibord, take your rotting shit elsewhere." Agitators slammed shut the cemetery gates; some in the crowd vowed to die before the coffin would be allowed to pass. Outnumbered and fearing for their safety, Guibord's supporters retreated and took the body back to Mount Royal.

"The state of things cannot last forever," thundered *The Star*, the city's liberal mouthpiece. "The ascent of the mob over authority has been so clearly established in Montreal that her best interests are suffering, her fair fame has been tarnished, and the evil disposed here have gained the upper hand of law and order." The French newspaper *Nouveau Monde* countered with the suggestion that any attempt to give Guibord a Catholic burial would drive the people to revolt.

At this stage of the Guibord controversy some suspected that because Hingston and almost all the city's police officers were Roman Catholics they were working in collusion with Bourget, and that is why the court order had not been carried out. The harshest criticism came from one of Hingston's own councillors, George Washington Stephens, who accused the mayor in a letter to *The Star* of "making a grave error." Because of Hingston's handling of the affair, Stephens wrote, Montreal was "under the disgrace of being ruled by no law."

On Sunday, September 12, Bishop Bourget issued a pastoral letter defending the disruption at the cemetery. At the same time, he declared that the law would be respected and Guibord buried in the Catholic cemetery. However, Guibord's grave would be forever profaned, "not only cut off from consecrated ground, but shall be for the future, accursed."

Although the Guibord affair was a concern, the public health of the city a continuing crisis, there was yet another overwhelming personal matter in Hingston's life that he had managed to keep from the public. The very Sunday that Bishop Bourget issued his interdiction in Montreal, the Roman Catholic Bishop of Toronto, John Joseph Lynch, read for the first time marriage banns between "William Hingston, Mayor of Montreal, and Margaret Macdonald, daughter of the lieutenant governor of Ontario."

No work is more important, no work more philanthropic, no work more benevolent than that of making the public aware of all matters relating to Public Health.

William Hales Hingston

CHAPTER SEVEN

"A FUNERAL AS CANADA HAS NEVER SEEN"

In the weeks to come, Hingston focussed relentlessly, not on the prepa-
rations for his wedding, but on the real possibility that the Guibord
affair would end in bloodshed. Anxiety that someone might attempt to
steal the body had always been just below the surface and Bishop Bourget's
declarations did nothing to temper the controversy, which had now gained
international attention. "Are we to understand that His Grace, in interdict-
ing this spot, putting upon it the curse of the Church, means also to curse
the resting place of Guibord's wife, of one who was faithful?" asked the *New
York Herald*. "What would Christ do?" a *Star* correspondent wanted to know.
"He would go at once and bury the man's bones. If the laws of the country
require this man to be buried in a certain place, it is the duty of all the priests
to bury Guibord and with him, their pride."

Hingston defended his reticence to become involved before a council
meeting on Tuesday, September 14, 1875. He felt, and rightly so, that
because both cemeteries were outside the city limits, the issue was beyond
his jurisdiction. In his view the vexed question of Guibord's burial was not a
city matter, but up to the courts and the diocese to resolve. Moving the body
required that it be taken through five neighbouring villages: Outremont, St.
Jean Baptiste, St. Louis, St. Antoine and Côte-des-Neiges.

"I am no more required to [bury Guibord] than any of the 200 magistrates in the district of Montreal," he said. "When I agreed to be mayor of
Montreal, I did not undertake to keep all the surrounding municipalities in
order." As soon as he heard a riot was threatened, Hingston rode out to the
cemetery as quickly as possible. "Bringing in the police to deal with the situation would only have been a provocation," he explained, pointing out that
officers were prohibited from carrying weapons outside the city limits.
"There was no disturbance when I got there, no blood was spilled. I preferred to face the crowd myself."

Margaret Macdonald Hingston

Four hours after the council meeting ended, Hingston caught the overnight train to Toronto for his wedding. The nuptials at St. James Cathedral took place on a rainsoaked Thursday, September 16. People stood outside the church in a downpour for an hour to catch a glimpse of the guests. These included the Liberal prime minister of Canada, Alexander MacKenzie and his wife, Ontario's Premier Oliver Mowat and the influential Senator George Brown, founder of *The Globe*. Margaret walked down a red carpet on the arm of her father, recently appointed Ontario's lieutenant governor. She carried a bridal wreath of orange blossoms and wore a simple white silk creation with a standing collar, satin front trimmed with Honiton lace and three flounces that had been designed in London by Queen Victoria's dressmaker. "A quantity of real and artificial flowers" decorated the altar and during the Mass the bride and groom knelt on prie-dieus draped with crimson velvet as Archbishop John Lynch blessed the union, calling it "a marriage of paradise" in which Upper and Lower Canada were joined. The reception was held at Government House which then stood where Roy Thomson Hall is today. The honeymoon was brief. They spent ten days in New York, but by Sunday, October 3, were back in Montreal. That morning husband and wife showed up for Mass at St. Patrick's where *The Star* took note that "the choir sang Mozart's Twelfth Mass, *Gloria in Excelsis*, as a compliment to our worthy mayor and his fair consort." As a salute to the couple, the organ recessional was Mendelssohn's Wedding March.

The next day, Hingston toured the contagious disease quarantine unit in Benjamin Hall House. While he was away, his council had decided Montreal could not afford a hospital designed specifically to house smallpox patients and had instead voted to build "a cheap class of small detached building, cheaply constructed, and well ventilated." That decision was unacceptable to Hingston, who was appalled at the conditions he found during his inspection of Hall House: thirty-two patients jammed into five small rooms with no bathrooms or water closets at all and only buckets for fecal matter, with "water for washing" collected from the roof.

"The mortality is high, not so much from the disease itself, but from the pneumonia which so often results from the want of sufficient breathing space," he told a meeting of the Health Committee. If the aldermen continued to ignore the situation he would, he said, "consider it my duty to at once take the necessary measures to make the present building more habitable."

Adding to the urgency, many Montrealers continued to ignore the smallpox threat that came from public gatherings. Street processions on two successive Sundays, September 26 and October 3, marked the fiftieth anniversary of the consecration of the city's first Roman Catholic Cathedral, St. James the Major, which had been destroyed in the fire of 1852. Tens of thousands paraded from Notre-Dame Church on Place d'Armes to St. Anne's Church in Griffintown, which undoubtedly spread the incidence of the disease. By the end of October, people were dying at the rate of thirty a week.

Doctor William Fuller, alarmed by the incursion of smallpox into the Point St. Charles district, accused city health officials of ambivalence. "I suppose you want to see a good blaze before you are convinced there is a fire... A medical gentleman elected for mayor on account of sanitary agitation, and a great deal of money expended with what result? The prospect of another epidemic!"

As the smallpox misery simmered, the Guibord affair continued to percolate. In mid-October, Bishop Bourget had issued a second pastoral letter that was read throughout the diocese. It reminded the faithful that the Privy Council in London had "no effect in the eyes of Catholic people... The church in its own affairs is independent, having reserved ground exclusively for the burial of its children, it has the right to refuse it to those whom it judges unworthy." There had been several efforts to steal Guibord's body, so, in order to make certain that once he was buried his grave would not be disturbed, the Institut ordered a special stone coffin to be custom-made: "Twelve feet long, four feet wide to receive the remains. The coffin will be covered with a stone slab riveted and bolted with six iron bars, and will require about ten horses to remove it."

Hingston met with Bourget, and also with the parish priest, Victor Rousselot. It was an amicable meeting, both men being "of a very high tone of mind." Bourget evidently reminded the mayor of his pledge to obey his bishop, and that as mayor his first duty as a Catholic was not to go out of his way to accommodate Guibord's burial. Hingston, who was too intelligent for the excess of fanaticism, replied that as a Catholic who had taken an oath to uphold the law, he owed, as mayor, his first allegiance to his office. Hingston tried to channel the bishop's thinking into compromise, moderation and conciliation. He asked Bourget to refrain from making any further public statements, assured him that the date and time of the transfer of the body would be shrouded in secrecy and asked the bishop to instruct his priests not to say another word from the pulpit about the matter. He also requested that the gates to Notre-Dame-des-Neiges Cemetery be removed from their hinges so that Guibord's body might pass through without interference at any time, with no advance notice.

On October 28, council met to consider what public security measures might be required. Convinced that a riot "beyond the power of civil authorities to suppress" was likely to occur whenever the burial took place, Sessions Court Judge Charles Coursol ordered four militia units under the command of Lt. Col. John Fletcher to be called out to keep the peace on the day of the funeral. Both Hingston and the chief of police had received anonymous death threats: "I will order you to be assassinate [sic]. So take care of you. Goodby until we meet in a crowd."

At the height of the Guibord crisis, Hingston was unanimously elected a director of the Montreal City & District Savings Bank. The bank had been another of Bishop Bourget's social initiatives. He opened it in 1846 because the commercial banks at the time couldn't be bothered handling small accounts of the poor, working-class, French-Catholic population. Bourget also wished to stem the flow of investment capital out of Quebec into the United States. William Workman, a Unitarian Irish immigrant who had made his fortune in hardware and real estate and whom Bourget converted to Catholicism, was the bank's first president. Other founding directors included Francis Hincks, Louis-Hippolyte Lafontaine and Louis-Joseph Papineau. On November 9, Hingston received an invitation "to attend a friendly gathering whenever you desire to honour the directors with your presence." There was no chance of meeting the board until after Guibord had been buried.

On Monday, November 14, Hingston briefed the prime minister, Alexander Mackenzie, who was in Montreal for a Liberal event at St. Lawrence Hall on what the plans were. The long-running drama reached its climax the next day. Just before dawn on Tuesday, Hingston, astride his fine horse, *Bibakiba*, rode through a sticky, damp snowfall to the Champs de Mars where 950 soldiers, each supplied with twenty rounds of ammunition, were marshalling. There he conferred with Lt. Col. Fletcher and argued the case for keeping the militia a fair distance behind Guibord's bier. Fletcher agreed that his men would not move until Hingston gave him the signal. With that, Hingston rode out to Mount Royal cemetery to supervise the removal of Guibord's body. There, he ordered the undertakers to abandon the idea of transporting the corpse in the cement coffin. It was so heavy, he pointed out, that moving it would only "add to the dangers of the occasion."

Only when the dark procession started making its way through the cold sleet and had already set out on its five-kilometre trek around the back of the mountain, did the soldiers, five kilometres away in the Champs de Mars, begin marching through the chalky snow up St. Lawrence Boulevard. They sang as they marched: *Mulligan Guards* and *Marching Along!* The street was lined with people who "either leisurely inspected the volunteers or followed them as far as Mile End." One eyewitness, the future Canadian senator Raoul Dandurand, who was fifteen at the time, in his memoirs remembered seeing "Dr. Hingston, the best equestrian of the time, mounted on a magnificent pure-bred stallion, lead the procession, wearing his official regalia, with his tricorn and a sword." Rumours circulated that "some boys were on their way up from Griffintown" to cause trouble and that a mob was coming from St. Jean-Baptiste Village. The funeral cortege made its way through the gates of Notre-Dame-des-Neiges, into the Catholic cemetery and up a muddy hill where it delivered Guibord unscathed to his family plot, which held his wife, Henriette Brown, dead two years earlier. Without incident, Guibord's coffin was lowered on top of hers. With that, Hingston rode to the crest of a nearby hill and signalled the militia, still a couple of kilometres away, to a halt. Guibord's grave was filled with scraps of iron and tin, and then sealed with Portland cement.

"Guibord is buried and all is quiet. No excitement in any direction," *The Daily Witness* recorded.

"Both Protestants and Catholics wisely stayed away. It was a funeral as Canada has never seen. The method of the whole thing was quiet and businesslike. Even the bands were silent in marching through the streets on the homeward march. So quiet was the occasion, that newspaper reporters who improve every opportunity seemed to become sleepy under its influence. It is evident that the clergy have kept their word with the mayor and have succeeded better than he expected... Now that this source of discord is in God's good providence, peacefully concluded, let all citizens vie with each other in doing what they can do to heal the breach."

Hingston, on the right, astride his horse Bibakiba, *presides over Guibord's burial*

It was clear to all that Hingston had masterminded the burial and in doing so had at last proven himself respectable, to be of intrinsic virtue and social value and acceptable to the Protestant community. The *Public Health Journal* cited Hingston for the "tact, prudence, wisdom and loyalty with which he averted a terrible calamity.

"No man was ever placed in a position of greater difficulty or danger, or was hampered by more legal and sectional difficulties, but our mayor carried out a measure in a way which left no sting in any breast; no exultation of triumph on the one side, no heart burning on the other."

Three days later Hingston received a letter from the governor-general congratulating him for his "exertions in preventing any breach of the peace and in securing a respectful observance of the law by the inhabitants of Montreal." Queen Victoria had herself taken an interest in the case and Dufferin expressed her "great satisfaction" with the way the Guibord affair had been resolved, and sent Hingston a personally autographed lithograph. "Perhaps you will inform the bishop of what Her Majesty has telegraphed," Dufferin wrote.

"I have had the satisfaction of telegraphing to the Queen how successful you have been in preserving the peace of your town and in preventing bloodshed. Her Majesty was extremely anxious on the subject as she justly felt that any riot or disturbance in so large and important a city as Montreal would bring discredit upon the Dominion at large.

"I am well aware that there were many circumstances connected with the burial of Monsieur Guibord, which were likely to cause irritation in the mind of the Catholic community and it is very much to their credit and to the credit of those who have influenced their conduct that they should not have been invoked into any unworthy and discreditable demonstration... I should be quite willing you should communicate my personal thanks and congratulations to the Bishop of Montreal and to those Curés to whose loyal advice and exhortations we have been undoubtedly in a great measure indebted for the peaceable issue of this event."

There was little time to savour the plaudits. With Christmas coming on, Hingston needed all the goodwill he could muster. The death toll from smallpox continued to rise. The English-speaking Protestant community remained ambivalent. To them the disease seemed incidental and not particularly threatening. The French population was apathetic and accepted death from smallpox with a resignation that Hingston found incomprehensible.

The ranks of the unemployed continued to soar as the depression wore on and unskilled workers, unable to find work in the country, migrated to Montreal. There was no welfare or public assistance for those who could not find jobs, and each day the administration was concerned about the ever growing threat of anarchy.

Hingston declared his intention to deal with the first problem on November 30, 1875, by asking the Quebec Legislature to amend the city charter to allow it to establish its own municipal Board of Health, "where a constant supply of vaccine lymph could be had by physicians and others requiring it, in such a way as is done in the Health Bureau in Downing Street, London, where a supply is furnished for the whole British Empire."

Then, one month after the Guibord controversy was resolved, Hingston was faced with another explosive crisis. On Wednesday, December 14, a small crowd of rootless unemployed led by two twenty-year-old labourers, Edmond Bernard and Marcel Edmond, marched up Beaver Hall Hill to demonstrate outside his house. Hingston wasn't at home. So the following day about 800 of the starving poor gathered and this time descended on City Hall. Along the way, some in the crowd snatched some loaves from a bread wagon "with which they amused themselves by playfully tossing at one another." When they arrived at Bonsecours Market, the crowd was ordered to disperse. They refused, and began chanting, "Work or Blood." Stones were thrown, windows at City Hall again broken, and the police chief, Fred Penton, was hit in the face. Penton was about to read the Riot Act, but Hingston quietly ignored him. "These people are not criminals, but working men who lack the means to gain their daily bread," Hingston said as he stepped out onto the balcony to speak to the crowd. If they agreed to disperse, he would, he promised, find work for them.

He was as good as his word. Telling his councillors "not to bring relief by distributing charity, but by giving work," he moved quickly on the issue. At an emergency meeting on December 17 he carefully proposed a program that he had hastily put together with the city clerk, Charles Glackemeyer, to provide immediate, short-term relief. "City Hall is marked by a bustle and activity that for many months has been a stranger to its corridors," *The Gazette* observed. There were limits to what could be done, but Hingston stretched them. Three councillors were dispatched to Ottawa to get federal support for municipal initiatives, including improvements to the Lachine Canal. Talk of building a second bridge to be called The Royal Albert across the St. Lawrence, "at a spot near St. Helen's Island," was quickly rejected as a pipe dream.

There were other possibilities. The city had already spent more than one million dollars since 1870 to expropriate Mount Royal, 430 acres in all, and, the internationally renowned lanscape architect, Frederick Law Olmsted, had been engaged to turn it into a park. Olmsted didn't especially want the commission; he was busy laying out the grounds of the United States Capitol in Washington, D.C. "It would be wasteful to try to make anything else than a mountain of it," he had advised the city when he first came to inspect the site in October. "Regard the work to be done on your behalf as primarily a work of art." Works of art tend to be expensive, and Hingston had already determined that the only solution to the unemployment crisis was a public-works program that would require increased taxation with the burden placed on the rich. Construction of a road west from Rachel into the Mountain preserve had started on November 10. The winter of 1875 was an unusually mild one, which allowed Hingston to ram through approval for a number of other projects, including the grading of Sherbrooke Street between Amherst and Papineau, the excavation of sewage drains on Atwater Avenue, and landfill projects in Point St. Charles and Griffintown. Council met in an emergency session on December 21 to consider increasing working men's salaries by two cents an hour, from seven to nine cents for a nine-hour day. Alderman McShane attempted to play politics with the issue by expressing the view that "when men are hired, no discrimination will be allowed in favour of French-speaking labourers to the detriment of old country men." Hingston cut him short. "When people are suffering from want, it is scarcely the time to introduce questions of this kind, as to whether a sufferer is French or Irish, Protestant or Catholic."

Incredibly, within one week Hingston, assisted by his city clerk Charles Glackemeyer, had found enough work for 1,300 men. The plight of the unemployed, coming as it did on the heels of the smallpox and Guibord riots, had not escaped international media attention. Newspapers in New York, Boston and Toronto had magnified the city's problems, referring to "rampant, unbridled violence" caused by the unemployed in the city. Hingston was clearly irritated by the coverage and, just before council adjourned for Christmas, addressed the issue.

"The people have assembled, it is true, and gathered in a crowd of several thousand. But they have behaved in a surprisingly orderly manner, and have not deserved the misrepresentation to which they have been subjected. I wish to state, Gentlemen, that by your action this afternoon, you have given work to 1,300 destitute men – men who have shown themselves worthy of being provided for by the calm spirit evinced under most trying circumstances. What would a mob of three or four thousand have done in the cities of Glasgow, New York or Liverpool? I hardly think they would have acted in a manner so orderly as our own suffering fellow citizens. I hope the city of Montreal will never again be placed in a condition to require like legislation."

There were of course ratepayers who had growing misgivings about the expenditures. Some, like *The Star*, thought building a park was an extravagance that the city could ill afford. "The city is in debt, and daily becoming deeper... fancy improvements belong to the future when the city

has a surplus," it complained. Others were in no mood to accept the responsibility for the welfare of impoverished, French-speaking Roman
Catholics. There were Protestants who sneered at the misery of the unemployed, who suggested that "The proper place to demand work or bread"
was not from the city, but "from the Gentlemen of St. Sulpice who had the
exclusive jurisdiction for the education and the support of poor indigent and
distressed people.

"These Gentlemen have squeezed millions out of the French Canadians,
and should now, in their distress, be helped, not out of the funds of the city,
but from those who are by law bound to support them."

I find the anti-vaccination views disseminated by a small but ceaselessly active section of medical and legal thought nothing more than deeply rooted prejudice against what the scientific world has generally sanctioned, and I find disease, disfigurement and death following in the wake of those ignorant teachings...

WILLIAM HALES HINGSTON

CHAPTER EIGHT

"Smallpox is as Common as Dirt"

B ells from every Roman Catholic church in the city pealed in joyous unison on New Year's Eve to mark the close of the 1875 diocesan jubilee. The chimes were a grating cacophony to one newcomer to the city, Leonard Gaetz. Gaetz was a handsome square-jawed, bull-necked preacher who arrived from the Maritimes during the height of the Guibord affair to become the pastor of Great St. James Methodist Church, which then stood on St. James Street where the Bank of Commerce is today. Ordained in 1860 when he was only nineteen, Gaetz was already one of the most influential Protestant clergymen in the country. He had such a knack for vivid expression that at twenty-six he was asked to deliver a major sermon in Halifax during ceremonies in 1867 marking confederation. He was so grandiloquent that *The Calgary Herald* once remarked "his speech was worthy of being engraved with a pen of iron onto plates of brass." Gaetz had spent several years in Pictou, then in Fredericton, N.B., before being appointed head of what was then the largest Methodist congregation in Canada.

Protestants ran Montreal, but the city was still very much a Roman Catholic town. Now, with Bishop Bourget on the defensive after the Guibord affair, Gaetz saw an opportunity to promote an Orange Parade on July 12. Elsewhere, Orangemen marched to commemorate the Battle of the Boyne, an historic encounter in 1690 in which an army of Protestants defeated England's last Roman Catholic king, James II. Not in Montreal. Even though the Loyal Orange Association of British North America boasted 200,000 members across the country, and 3,000 over the age of twenty-one in Quebec, there had never been an Orange parade in Montreal. In fact, in 1858, one Catholic ran a pitchfork through an Orangeman who dared jeer from the sidelines during the St. Patrick's Day parade.

Orangemen were as dogmatic as Roman Catholics and perhaps even more ruthless. Their parades elsewhere featured provocative tunes such as *"Kick The Pope," "Croppies [Catholics] Lie Down,"* and *"The Orange Lily, O."* Gaetz chided Montreal Orangemen for not being more assertive. He was not himself an Orangeman, but a sworn enemy of Ultramontanism which he described as "historically and experimentally a system of intolerance and aggression." Gaetz argued that if Catholics could take to the streets in seemingly endless religious processions, surely Orangemen were entitled to their day. Hingston, whose sisters were both married to Protestants, could hardly disagree. True to his beliefs, but sympathetic to others, Hingston sanctioned the holding of an Orange parade in July.

A few days later, Hingston took part in a costume ball at the Victoria Rink, tramped around the mountain on snowshoes and was present at the annual dinner of the Montreal Snowshoe Club in St. Lawrence Hall on February 12. Three days later, he was acclaimed to a second term as mayor. An indication of how highly Hingston was now regarded was that this time, Sir Francis Hincks personally endorsed his nomination papers.

Hingston had, as *The Star* observed, filled his office "with the fullest approbation of his fellow citizens without regard to creed or politics." Hingston didn't show up at City Hall on nomination day. The night before he had gone to a concert at the Theatre Royal given by the Prince of Wales' Rifles Band for his father-in-law, Ontario's lieutenant governor, who was in Montreal visiting Margaret. They sat in a private box to the right of the stage. "Owing to the unpleasant state of the weather, the attendance was not so large as might have been expected," noted *The Star*, "but those who were present passed a most enjoyable evening." Later that month, at the personal invitation of the Dufferins, Hingston and his family travelled to Ottawa to attend the most lavish full-dress ball ever staged at Rideau Hall on February 23. Only 300 invitations had been sent out and to be included on the guest list was a mark of high prestige. Margaret, wearing a "white satin puffed petticoat, green satin train, high waist of green satin, ruff edged with gold and green, satin hat and white plume," outranked her husband on the protocol list. She was escorted into the ballroom on the arm of the secretary of state, Richard Scott, behind the chief justice, the prime minister and the governor-general. Lord Dufferin whirled Margaret Hingston through the second waltz of the evening, Strauss' "Approach of Spring," and as they danced paid her compliments that made her blush.

"In the present tightness of things monetary," reported the *Canadian Illustrated News*, "the ball has been a godsend to the tradesmen innumerable." It was also a godsend to Hingston. It confirmed his social position as a trusted Catholic in a Protestant court. He was no longer as circumspect as he had been. His marriage and his political success, it seemed, had soothed his anxieties and tempered his hesitancies.

It was in an atmosphere of "unusual and unprecedented gaiety," that Hingston was sworn in for his second term as mayor on Monday, March 13, 1876 at City Hall in Bonsecours Market. His wife, "elegantly attired in a café au lait silk gown, black velvet jacket and straw hat," listened as her husband, decked out in the fur-lined scarlet robes of office and his massive gold chain, delivered a speech "in the purest of French." His second inaugural address to council pledged to accelerate the fight against smallpox. "Vaccination is a matter of opinion based on observation and scientific research, and everyone has a right to hold whatever opinion he may choose with reference to the practice," he said, "but there is no difference of opinion as to the communicability of smallpox.

"The man or woman who exposes his or her own child to the risk of infection does a wicked thing, but one for which the right of ownership may be set up as an excuse. But the man or woman who carelessly or negligently or wantonly exposes the life of another does that which approaches as nearly to murder as can be well conceived."

The following Friday, "wearing very conspicuous green colours for the occasion," and nursing a bad cold which "prevented him from inflicting a speech," Hingston took part in the thirty-ninth annual St. Patrick's Day parade.

Hingston's civic obligations had taken a toll on his professional duties at the Hôtel-Dieu, on his business interests, and on his private medical practice as well. He still saw patients, but only those within a limited circle. In May, for instance, Harriot Dufferin wrote to Hingston asking him to examine her sister, Gwendoline, who had recently married and was living in Montreal.

"Do you think there is any doubt that she is in the family way?" Lady Dufferin wrote. "She herself seems to disbelieve it, though I cannot discover any reason to suppose that she is not. [...] I hope that in all the commendations you give here, you will be very positive, for she knows nothing and is afraid of being a 'Coddle,' [nuisance] so the inquiries to her should be treated with great discretion. I am sure you will understand why I write to you upon this subject. My sister has no other in Montreal to whom she would speak upon this subject. I hope Mrs. Hingston is quite well. Pray remember me to her. I remain yours truly," Harriot Dufferin.

Mrs. Hingston was quite well, indeed. She, too, was expecting a baby.

Her pregnancy would be the least of the complex issues that Hingston was about to face.

Bishop Bourget sustained a further blow to his authority when Pope Pius IX rejected yet another of his appeals to the Vatican to establish an independent Roman Catholic university in Montreal. A Papal Bull, *Inter Varias Sollicitudines*, gave Université Laval exclusive jurisdiction over higher education and exhorted the province's bishops not to allow students "to run wild by allowing them to wander about Quebec," but to encourage them to enroll at Laval, which would "supervise their moral conduct and facilitate their advancement in the acquisition of knowledge." Quebec, it declared, should be regarded as "the metropolis of the Catholic religion in Canada, since it is the mother of sixty dioceses, and offers easy access to the people of all parts of Canada." The Papal Bull signalled trouble for the future of l'École de médecine et de chirurgie de Montréal and its affililation with Victoria University. Hingston, and the doctors who owned the school, braced themselves for the fight. They were not about to fall into line and obey the pope's marching orders or surrender their school without a struggle.

Outmanœuvred in Rome by the scholarly archbishop of Quebec, Elzéar Taschereau, disillusioned and in ill health, Bourget resigned as Bishop of Montreal on May 11, 1876. "He belonged to a school of thought so different from our own that we may not even claim to be impartial critics," *The Nation* remarked on his leaving. "He loved power and he exercised dogmatic control over his clergy and his people. Misjudging his own strength, he quarrelled with his own bishops who in turn denounced and destroyed him." Bourget was replaced by his portly and relatively less dogmatic protégé, forty-nine-year-old Édouard-Charles Fabre, whose family had been major players in the 1837 *Patriote* rebellion.

On May 24, Hingston prematurely dedicated Mount Royal Park as a "pleasure ground" for all Montrealers, especially for the enjoyment of those "labouring men, fatigued and worn with toil."

"Guard it with care that you may transmit it as a legacy to your issue. See that no one ruthlessly or wantonly or thoughtlessly mars its beauty. Every tree upon it enhances that beauty. Let not the knife nor the axe cut the names of the would be perpetrators."

His remarks were cut short by a Royal Salute from the cannons of the Montreal Field Battery. The park's landscape architect, Frederick Law Olmsted, was present at the dedication, but didn't say a word. Olmsted was conspicuous by his silence. Aghast to discover that construction crews had begun building roads through the park before he had a chance to finish his preliminary design, and that "the opportunity of making a suitable park has been lost forever," Olmstead was thinking of withdrawing from the project.

"The superintendent who was not under the orders of the engineer, and who varied at pleasure from his advice, was not during construction ever informed in any manner of the most essential instructions which I had prepared for the work," Olmsted later wrote to Hingston.

"Preliminary work done on the park," he complained was "radically different in character from that which I supplied you. The engineer employed to build the road never read my detailed instructions, never saw the drawings, and denied all responsibility for the plan which was followed," he added.

Olmsted would not sue the city for damages to his reputation, he told Hingston, because "it is impossible for you to make me adequate compensation." Miffed as he was, Olmsted returned to the drawing board, and came up with a revised plan, the first of several, in which he abandoned his original vision of a "a true park-like ground, broad, simple, quiet and of a rich Sylvan and pastoral character, facing a harmonious natural foreground to the view over the western valley." To help pay for the park, Olmstead had intended to include an exclusive residential district where the Royal Victoria Hospital stands today, but that scheme, like so much of his design, fell by the wayside.

Brazil's unassuming emperor, Dom Pedro II, paid a visit to Montreal on June 6, the first crowned head of state ever to do so, but Hingston couldn't spend much time at city hall with his distinguished guest. That day aldermen clashed over the location of a permanent smallpox hospital in a lengthy and complicated procedural wrangle that required Hingston to be present. The Parks Committee wanted the Hall House hospital removed from the new park. The Health Committee wanted it to remain open where it was for another year until the money to build a new one, and a suitable location for it, could be found. Everyone recognized the need for a new facility, but none of the aldermen wanted it in his ward. Île Ronde, in the middle of the St. Lawrence River was proposed as one site; Hingston's own land, the Price Farm on the Upper Lachine Road, was suggested as another. Even though there were more pressing items on the agenda, the quarrel between the two committees went on all afternoon with nothing being decided. It was not the first time municipal departments wasted time contradicting each other. Later that summer the Roads Committee would encourage animal waste to be deposited on certain streets while the Health Committee fought to have the practice stopped.

"It is indeed a nice state of affairs that the citizens should be taxed in one direction to maintain health officers, sanitary police and hospitals, while in another they are supporting a department which is deliberately sowing the seeds of disease and death," griped *The Montreal Evening Star*, "A more deplorable case of cross purposes was never cited."

After Édouard-Charles Fabre was installed as the new Roman Catholic Bishop of Montreal, Hingston held a reception at city hall in his honour and invited him to bless the new city hall, now nearing completion. The invitation didn't sit well with Leonard Gaetz, who complained that "City Hall is the property of this community, not the Roman Catholic church, and R.C. priests have no more right to the filling up of that chamber to be used in what some Protestants look upon as an idolatrous service."

It was in that charged atmosphere that about 300 people wearing orange sashes and many of them sporting orange lilies walked in Montreal's first Orange Day parade on July 12. They left from the Methodist church on St. James Street, headed east to west to the Orange Lodge on Victoria Square, then walked around the block to Nordheimer's Hall for dinner. One woman sporting an orange ribbon was assaulted by two other women who tore "fistfuls of hair and ribbon" from the victim and elsewhere, a gunshot was heard. Seven participants were arrested for being drunk. Other than those isolated instances, Montreal's first Orange parade went off without a hitch. Credit was given to Hingston. "It is with the utmost satisfaction we announce that the first open celebrations of the Battle of the Boyne which has been held here passed over without anything very serious or unpleasant to record," *The Star* opined. "It is owing in great measure to the good advice given by both the Roman Catholic clergy and influential laity that nothing of a lamentable nature took place."

Three days later Hingston was present at the Masonic Hall on Place d'Armes for the funeral of his predecessor, Aldis Bernard. The old dentist had died in California where he had retired for his health four months earlier. His death came two weeks after the massacre of General George Armstrong Custer and the entire U.S. Seventh Cavalry at the Little Big Horn, and there were fears in Montreal that Bernard's body might not make it back across the continent through Indian Territory safely. Then, on Sunday, July 30, Hingston sat on a chair in the sanctuary before the high altar in the church of St. James the Greater on St. Denis Street for a Mass celebrating the feast day of the patron saint of the diocese of Montreal. Bishop Bourget did not attend. He was according to news reports "in completely prostrated condition, so much so, there is not the least hope of recovery. His Grace is attended by Doctors Hingston and Trudel." Any obituaries would have to be premature. Bourget would recover and become more of a spiritual influence in his retirement than he had been while sitting on his throne.

As the depression deepened, hard times increased and city spending continued to rise. When the city's leap year budget had been introduced on February 29, it proposed tax hikes of between seven to ten per cent – $10 to $12 for every $1,000 of valuation. A Citizens' Taxpayers Association, made up of angry and rich property owners in St. Antoine Ward, was formed and petitioned Hingston to call a public meeting to explain the increases. The city's accumulated deficit had soared to more than $10-million in five years. In addition, rumours were circulating that some aldermen, "poor men, in bad times had become wealthy." The meeting was held at Mechanics' Hall on August 15. Sir Francis Hincks was at Hingston's side that Tuesday night to help calm alarmist voices. Hincks opened by pointing out that twenty-seven years earlier when he had been minister of finance of the United Canadas, "the whole debt of United Canada was less, less gentlemen, than the debt of Montreal at the present time." Hincks blamed the province for ignoring Montreal's financial predicament. His suggestion: "a full and searching inquiry, to trace out, to examine into the affairs of the Corporation."

During the ratepayers meeting Hingston listened to complaints about the cost overruns of the new city hall and the mountain park. The city's fire chief, Alfred Perry – the same Alfred Perry who twenty-nine years earlier allowed Parliament to burn – had evidently not tempered his bias against French-Canadians. He accused the head of the fire-department committee, Alderman Louis Onésime Loranger, of fraud.

Hingston was the last to speak. He angrily dismissed Perry's accusations. "During the eighteen months that I have been custodian of the honour of the corporation, I have never seen anything to lead me to suspect anything approaching that horrible word," Hingston said. "I will say, that the city like individuals, has been extravagant, and the city like citizens, now experience the inconvenience which follows upon extravagance. There is the whole matter. They thought hard times would never come, but hard times came."

The meeting ended appointing a committee to investigate civic spending. When it reported six weeks later, it recommended the mayor be given veto power over any council decision, and be made more accountable for civic spending. On October 27, the city ignored the recommendations and approved a loan worth 750,000 pounds to complete several public works including city hall and the mountain park.

With his term in office drawing to a close, Hingston began to devote every waking hour to combat smallpox with an evangelist's zeal. There had been an alarming increase in the number of incidents reported at the end of August: twenty-seven deaths from the disease were up nine over the previous week. There was, Hingston warned, now a danger of "an epidemic in every ward." *The Herald* roused public opinion in Hingston's support: "Small Pox has been a destructive visitor to our city; it has stalked here, there and everywhere. The seeds of the disease have been floating all around us, and

"Small Pox has been a destructive visitor to our city..."

the victims which it has carried off have not been insignificant," the newspaper observed. "The reason for this has been that many of our inhabitants not only object to vaccination but entertain the most dangerous notions on the subject of its contagious character ... it is no wonder that in certain quarters of Montreal, smallpox is as common as dirt."

Preoccupied as he was with health issues, Hingston enrolled his seventeen-year-old nephew, Edward Hingston-Smith, in medicine at McGill, paid his tuition, hired a second maid for his wife, now five months pregnant. Then in the first week of September he went with his old friend, Dr. James Grant from Ottawa, to Philadelphia for the U.S. Centennial Exhibition where he heard the telephone and saw the Remington typewriting machine demonstrated for the first time. In Philadelphia he also attended the International Medical Conference in the chapel of the University of Pennsylvania. Among the eminent delegates was the English surgeon Joseph Lister, who was experimenting with disinfectants such as carbolic acid and presented a paper on antiseptic preferences in the practice of surgery. At the meeting Hingston was recognized as one of "the greatest living American surgeons" and elected a conference vice-president.

Returning to Montreal, he introduced legislation to establish a Municipal Board of Health, the first of its kind in Canada. The bylaw was patterned on Britain's Vaccination Act, passed in 1867, which imposed severe penalties on those who failed to have their children and infants vaccinated. It empowered a select committee of nine aldermen and nine qualified citizens to bring about sweeping changes. It gave the city control over food inspection, sanitary inspection and general sanitation, including outhouses and lanes. Doctor Armand Larocque was appointed the first public health officer and twenty-four public vaccinators hired to work with him. Even more important, the law "rendered the city liable for the quality of animal lymph used for vaccination." Furthermore, anyone who interfered with the work of the public vaccinators was liable to a stiff $40 fine – more than one month in wages to the average citizen.

The Board of Health set up shop in what *The Herald* described as "a miserable shanty" on the northeast corner of Place Jacques Cartier. It was there on October 13 that Hingston assembled twenty-three of the city's doctors, a cross-section of "the oldest, ablest, and youngest men in the medical profession," and had them endorse a declaration agreeing "that the protective power of vaccine has been proved beyond all question." Among those who signed were Thomas Roddick, then professor of clinical surgery at the Montreal General Hospital, Robert Craik, a professor of chemistry at McGill University, and a brilliant newcomer to the profession in charge of the General Hospital's smallpox unit, William Osler. Then, armed with their support, Hingston launched the city's vaccination drive on Friday, October 20, with an unusually long speech before a meeting of the Health Committee. "The times are as pregnant with mischief as the air is with disease," he began an address that would methodically, step by step, reply to all of the objections raised against vaccination. Smallpox was so prevalent in the city, he said, it was "disturbing its tables of mortality, affecting its reputation and injuring its trade.

"There are those who believe small pox drops upon individuals as rain drops from heaven, touching this one, sparing that! It is communicable in every way," he observed, suggesting those opponents who rallied against vaccination, in fact contributed to the pandemic. "I find anti-vaccination views disseminated by a small but ceaselessly active section of medical and legal thought, I find a deeply rooted prejudice against what the scientific world has generally sanctioned, and I find disease, disfigurement and death following in the wake of those teachings," he exclaimed.

"Why does the disease visit Montreal so severely? We nurse it," he said, answering his own question. "In Quebec City, Three Rivers, and Toronto no one writes or rails against the principles of vaccination. That the converse is true in Montreal is evident from the circumstance of the mortality immensely greater among that nationality whose beautiful language has served as a vehicle for the dissemination of a most deadly error." During his presentation Hingston conceded that children in the past had been poisoned by a public vaccinator, "and that many parents would rather see their children die than allow them to be vaccinated."

Still, most French Canadians, he believed, "are not opposed to vaccination so much as they are to the quality of the vaccine used." Assuring them that the city would be liable for the quality of lymph used by its public vaccinators, he added that he had "no hesitation in saying that a vaccinator who knows his business would vaccinate a thousand children with fewer disagreements than a competent dentist would have in extracting the same number of teeth."

A print run of 20,000 copies of Hingston's *Remarks on Vaccination* was ordered in French and English and distributed throughout the city. The English-speaking media applauded Hingston's resolve. "For once council has got into a working condition. In the past, the contrary was too generally the case. Then, members did not look beyond the spending of as much of the revenue in their own wards as they could get. Quarrels between the chair and the aldermen were intense and frequent, committee meetings were held in secret... now, happily a radical change is becoming apparent," *The Herald* applauded. The *Canadian Illustrated News* portrayed Hingston on its front cover as St. George, a knight in full armour slaying a dragon labelled smallpox.

The cost of slaying the dragon turned out to be much more than

VOL. XIV.—No. 17.   MONTREAL, SATURDAY, NOVEMBER 4, 1876.   { SINGLE COPIES, TEN CENTS. \ $4 PER YEAR IN ADVANCE.

MONTREAL.—ST. GEORGE (MAYOR HINGSTON) AND THE DRAGON (SMALL POX.)

Hingston portrayed as St. George, the patron saint of England,
slaying the small pox dragon

the cash-strapped city had bargained for. One alderman, Jacques Grenier, griped that the vaccination program was being conducted "on too large a scale," and that the city couldn't afford it.

"If a child's life is worth $1,000 to the country, the money is well spent," Hingston countered.

Public vaccinators didn't have an easy task. Parents came up with excuses and refused to have their children vaccinated; some said their children were too sick, others told vaccinators they preferred to have their own family doctor do the job, then conveniently neglected to have it done. Complicating the problem, enabling legislation applied only to those families within Montreal's boundaries, leaving the surrounding communities free to ignore the rules. Attempts to get the Quebec government to introduce a province-wide, comprehensive vaccination program failed. "Whereas three bills were submitted to satisfy three orders of mind, one came out satisfying fully, I believe, no order of mind," Hingston complained.

Still, after only two months of public vaccination, Hingston was able to report that the mortality rate from smallpox had fallen from 5.2 per cent to 3.7 per cent for every 1,000 residents. It would take another three years before the disease almost disappeared from the city. According to the official estimates, 12,000 people were infected, and 4,911 people died during the 1870s' epidemic. Hingston was now so popular, he was called upon to remain in office for an unprecedented third term. He declined. There were more important obligations in his life. Margaret gave birth to their first son on January 15, 1877. The event was celebrated in council chambers with rounds of congratulatory applause. The baby was named for his father, William Hales. The family would call him Willie or Uncle Willie throughout his life.

Hingston's eldest child William, shown at age three, was born while Hingston was still mayor

Hingston left office on March 11. As he surrendered his ceremonial chain to Jean-Louis Beaudry – this time successful in his comeback bid – Hingston delivered a farewell address, satisfied with what he had accomplished: "A Board of Health has been organized, and order has come out of chaos." He left City Hall but didn't put civic business behind him. In recognition of his service, he was appointed vice-president of the Montreal Street Railway in 1877 and remained on the board for the next six years. He also agreed to sit as chairman of a committee looking into the city's inadequate system of waste disposal. In a report tabled six months later, he described Montreal as being "exceptionally unfortunate," because it was unable to properly dispose of "health destroying and death producing" waste material. He discovered that one hundred and sixty-eight streets had no sewers at all and the forty-two streets that did, lacked a standardized system of connecting drains with "pipes varied in size between one to three feet in diameter."

His report recommended setting up a Board of Sewage Commissioners to work with the Roads Committee to co-ordinate a system of waste disposal.

Within two years the mortality rate from smallpox fell to 1.8 per cent, the lowest it had been in ten years. "It is gratifying to state that entire families who were formerly hostile to vaccination in any form have been so thoroughly convinced of all absence of danger, they now bring out whole families to be vaccinated with the animal virus, and their friends do likewise," Hingston remarked. But, as he warned, "smallpox has its periods of dormancy and its periods of activity." If authorities weren't vigilant, he predicted, another epidemic could be expected within ten years.

What is the duty and office of a physician? To deal with abnormal functions and to change, if possible, or to remove unhealthy structures in the human body; to restore health to the sick and wounded in spirit...

WILLIAM HALES HINGSTON

CHAPTER NINE

A SCHOOL OF ONE'S OWN

It was the dawn of a new era in surgical technique. The anesthetic properties of cocaine in medical practice were introduced, brain tumours were removed successfully for the first time and appendectomies were starting to be performed. A cystoscope for examining the inside of the urinary bladder had been developed in Germany. Doctors were learning that diseased and damaged tissues could be repaired with a scalpel. In Montreal, William Osler, who had been moonlighting at the smallpox hospital, used the extra money he made to import twelve microscopes from Paris and offered the first courses of microscopy and histology in Canada.

Hingston was better trained than most, and his mind knew as much about surgery as the majority of his colleagues in Montreal. Even though he had acquired a reputation as a fearless doctor eager to take on the toughest operations, he continued to place more faith in clinical results rather than theory. When Thomas Roddick began using Lister's antiseptic carbolic spray at the Montreal General Hospital with outstanding results in 1877, Hingston remained a skeptic. Roddick used carbolic acid as an antiseptic to dress surgical wounds and that brought about fundamental change in surgical practice that Hingston was slow to embrace. "Surgeons nowadays are afraid of pure air," he railed. It was Hingston's assistant, Joseph-Antoine Stanislas Brunelle, who talked him into introducing carbolic spray at the Hôtel-Dieu, and he did so, but only in procedures "where there were unpleasant odours." In private, "where plenty of pure fresh air was to be obtained," he wouldn't consider using it. "One day Listerites will be as rare as white crows, if not like the Dodo, utterly extinct," he said.

Hingston was elected president of the Canadian Medical Association in September, 1877. In his inaugural speech to the association's annual meeting in Montreal on September 12, he strayed from his prepared text to denounce abortion as "a revolting , wicked and detestable crime which disturbs every system of moral and religious belief." As much as Hingston's remarks were rooted in Catholic doctrinal purity, Margaret was pregnant again and the speech was a highly subjective one that evidently reflected his view about the sanctity of life. The digression was prompted, he said, by the "astonishing frequency of abortion" he was discovering among "respectable and married women."

"Who amongst us has not been appealed to by married women in fashionable society to thwart the designs of providence in their regard?" he asked his fellow doctors. "And, who amongst us does not know the earnestness of that appeal where delicate health, narrow means and claims of society, the displeasure of a husband, are urged most tearfully in support of an undesired maternity? What young man amongst us has not been obliged to reject a bribe? What practitioner who has not found his advice 'not to kill' spurned by one who looked to him for help in ridding her of the fruit she was bearing?"

In Hingston's opinion, the fetus was not "a mere aggregation of fortuitous atoms, a plastic germ, a kind of colloid or protoplasm which developed into a human" but "a living creature suspended in the female womb."

"The fetus in utero has the same right to the enjoyment of life as the child after it is born. At the moment of conception there is physical life, more probably animated life, and many are of the opinion that the anima, or the soul, are united to the body at the very moment of conception. The fetus enjoys physical life of its own, and is intended by the laws of nature to enjoy animated life." Looking out over the crowd with the confidence of a man of deep conviction, he stated that even if a pregnancy endangered a mother's life, a doctor's first obligation was to save the life of the unborn child. "A woman assumes the risk of dying when she becomes pregnant... if a mother has the right to deprive the fetus of life, the fetus has the same right to deprive the mother of hers," he reasoned. "The great principle underlying this question is Thou Shalt Not Kill."

Apart from being a doctrinaire Catholic, his reasoning was typical of Victorian male society. Hingston shared the views of his masculine contemporaries: Women of the Victorian age were either fragile, ornamental and morally pure in need of protection, or harlots to be pitied, rehabilitated or disdained. An English physician, William Acton, had defined "the correct female," as one without any sexual urges. Acton was of the opinion that women who enjoyed intercourse were risking "growths of the womb" or "mental depression." As Hingston himself put it, "women, when they fall, fall from a higher plane and fall much further than men do. Men fall more quickly; not so far, but more quickly."

Now recognized as one of the country's most influential doctors,

Hingston was back doing what he liked best, practising medicine and perfecting his skills in the operating theatre. His name was still frequently in the papers, no longer as mayor but as a leading surgeon. His patients swore by him. One of them, Patrick Carlin, walked into *The Star's* newspaper offices to boast about "good treatment at the Hôtel-Dieu, and the successful performance of an operation by which his clubbed foot has been straightened and made useful.

"*He had sought for years to have this defect remedied,*" *The Star* reported, "but always in vain until Dr. Hingston performed an operation upon him in the presence of several eminent medical men, which has resulted in a complete cure. The poor man is exceedingly grateful and rejoiced at his good fortune."

Hingston corrected a number of such deformities "not without the apparent qualification of rashness," he tells us. In one lecture he explained how he "swept the knife across the sole of the foot, dividing tissue after tissue, until the bones were reached [...] the excessive arch was then in great measure but not completely remedied. The dressing consisted of vaseline for two days, or afterwards, carbolic lotion or red wash."

As he returned to his thriving medical practice, Hingston preferred treating French-Canadian patients rather than Anglo-Saxons. In his expert opinion French-Canadians didn't "suffer such acute pain under the knife as do other and more sanguineous persons. Many of them object to the use of chloroform and submit to painful operations without betraying the slightest emotion; the shock to the system is certainly less, and there being less tendency to severe inflammatory action, the healing process goes on with surprising rapidity." Hingston believed that intermarriage between French and aboriginals had created a new Canadian ethnicity which he claimed was a distinct, more robust and a healthier race than the Anglo-Saxons, who regarded aboriginals as socially inferior. "With the French it is not so; wherever the early missionaries went they taught their people not to dispossess the natives, but to marry among them, not to rob them of their property, but to have children and inherit it. The result is a mixture of French, Celtic, and Indian blood with many characteristics of the red man preserved but modified by repeated dilution with European race. The mixed race is a productive one."

*   *   *

On January 6, 1878, Hingston had misgivings as he arrived at the chapel of the Sulpicians' Grand Seminary on Sherbrooke Street for what he considered a troubling occasion. Eight mitred bishops, including George Conroy, the Pope's emissary to Canada, Bishops Fabre, Taschereau, and the bishops of Sherbrooke, Rimouski, Trois-Rivières, St-Hyacinthe and Ottawa, had gathered together prominent members of Quebec's Roman Catholic medical community to consecrate Université Laval's new campus in Montreal. Laval's charter as a "national university," with jurisdiction within the canonical boundaries of the Archdiocese of Quebec, had been confirmed by the pope in his 1876 Bull, *Inter Varias Sollicitudines*. Under the Pope's ruling, Laval was entitled to affiliate with any Catholic institution in Montreal, but couldn't open one on its own. Taschereau decided to establish Université Laval's medical faculty in Montreal, and wanted it to be at the Hôtel-Dieu Hospital. He hadn't bothered to ask anyone at the Hôtel-Dieu what they thought of his idea. He would be in control of the new faculty but the Diocese of Montreal was expected to pay the bills for running it. One of Taschereau's underlying motives was to keep Bourget and the Jesuits in check and to prevent the Jesuits from obtaining a University Charter for the classical college they had built, Collège St. Marie. Hingston had strong loyalties to Bourget and to the Hôtel-Dieu, and he quailed at the prospect of Laval's interference. Not only did it spell trouble for the future autonomy of l'École de médecine et de chirurgie and the doctors who owned the school, but it threatened the École's twelve-year arrangement with Victoria University. Even Montreal's bishop, Édouard-Charles Fabre, wanted the new campus under his jurisdiction, but obedient to his Quebec superior, wasn't inclined to press the issue. "Montreal accepts only with repugnance the yoke of its elder," Fabre said. "Laval's character is different, its activity is not directed to the same objectives." To staff its Montreal campus, Laval raided the École for a number of doctors, including two of Hingston's assistants, Jean-Philippe Rottot and Alfred-Toussaint Brosseau, a "brusque, overly self-confident" botany professor with a booming voice who had studied under Joseph Émery-Coderre. Laval offered Hingston a lucrative teaching position at the new school, but Victoria Universty had first claim on his attention. He was not prepared to entertain any offers from Laval and pledged his "loyalty above all to my venerable teacher, Doctor Munro."

Hingston and the other doctors braced themselves for the fight. Having twice been ignored by Université Laval, the Hôtel-Dieu and its École de médecine et de chirurgie had emerged as a leading academic teaching hospital and wasn't disposed to end its accreditation with Victoria University just to please an interloper. Its position was rooted in the conviction that if there were to be a French-speaking Roman Catholic university in Montreal, it shouldn't be Laval. What followed was a thirteen-year imbroglio which today might seem farcical if the ramifications had not been so tragic.

At the end of January 1878, Hector Peltier, the École's chief instructor, died and Hingston was in line to succeed him. Much to his disappointment, the Hôtel-Dieu's Superior, Mother Justine Bonneau, gave the position to his antagonist, Coderre, and also put Coderre in charge of the hospital's St. Patrick wing. A serene, radiant and shrewd woman with striking features, Bonneau was only thirty-four when she was elected Superior for the first time. Under the Hospitalière rules, Superiors could only serve two consecutive six-year terms and during the 1870s and 1880s, she and Marie Pagé alternated as head of the order. Ten years younger than Hingston, Bonneau like Sister Pagé, was from St. Philippe, south of Montreal. Bonneau was born into a poor family and when she was eight her father sent her to the United States where she was raised by a Protestant family. There she learned English but, according to one account of her life, felt miserable because she was not permitted to practise her religion. At sixteen, she returned to Quebec and tried to enter the Hospitalière convent, but wasn't accepted as a postulant until she was nineteen. Deeply spiritual and imbued with a profound social conscience, she was also a firm believer in the principle of hierarchical obedience. Bonneau was uncomfortable with Hingston's determination to remain as a teaching professor at Victoria University. Hingston was informed of Bonneau's decision to demote him in a letter from the school's secretary, Doctor Eugène-Hercule Trudel. "The Hôtel-Dieu still controls its medical services, that is why she has assigned Coderre to replace you in the care of the Irish," Trudel wrote. "She would be disappointed if you took this personally – in this circumstance she is simply exercising her proper authority. Her good feelings for you remain, and she has already approved of the diplomas you will be presenting to the University of Victoria's graduating class this year. She is still ready to offer you the surgical chair at the clinic if you fall into line with her views."

The demotion was more a blow to his pride than to his income. It was the beginning of an increasingly frustrating time as Hingston and his medical associates took steps to protect their enterprise. At the same time, Hingston also found his social role being gradually diminished.

Hingston's second son was born on April 5, 1878 and was baptized Donald Alexander at St. Patrick's Church, named for his maternal grandfather then in the fourth year of his five-year term as Ontario's lieutenant-governor. During her pregnancy Margaret had not abandoned any of her social duties. She busied herself as a volunteer with the Women's Historical Society and as a founding member of the Society of Decorative Art, was involved in the project to open Canada's first art gallery – directly across the street from her house on Phillips Square – which would eventually be inaugurated a year later on May 26, 1879.

As the best known director of the Montreal City & District Savings Bank, Hingston was called upon to deal with a financial crisis that swept through the city that summer. First the Consolidated Bank went out of business; then on August 7, the Exchange Bank folded seven years after it obtained its charter. The following morning, the Ville Marie Bank closed its doors, shaking investor confidence. A number of small depositors who had accounts with the Montreal City & District Savings Bank grew anxious. By Friday morning, August 8, crowds of depositors descended on the bank's handsome Italianate headquarters in St. James Street. Hingston arrived on the scene determined to stop the panic. As soon as the bank opened, he leapt onto the counter and told the customers that while they were welcome to withdraw all of their savings, they should think twice before doing so. "Your money might be stolen, you might be tempted to spend it. It is you timid people who will suffer, and the anxiety of the bank is for you. It has none for itself."

To demonstrate his unconcern, he instructed the bank's general manager, Henri-Jacques Barbeau, to open the vaults, which held $900,000 in cash, saying anyone who wanted their money was welcome to it. The bank, he said, "would be relieved if people withdrew their savings," because it would save having to pay interest on their accounts. The bank normally closed at 3 p.m., but Hingston said that it "would continue to pay out as long as anyone was at the counter, even should it extend after dark." Commented *The Star*: "This statement from a gentleman held in such high esteem by the general public had a reassuring affect on the multitude." To further demonstrate his confidence, Hingston deposited $500 into his account. That day five tellers paid out one-quarter of a million dollars, but because of Hingston's intervention, the run on the bank was short-lived. Most of the money was re-deposited the following week. The Montreal City & District Savings Bank was an efficient operation and never in any danger of failing. Its resources were deep, counting as it did the Grand Trunk Railway, St. Patrick's parish and John Molson Jr., the brewer, among its investors.

In September, Hingston was in London, Ontario for a meeting of the Canadian Medical Association, where he was elected a director of the CMA's education committee. The appointment gave him a platform to express his views about the high standards required in a doctor's education: "Physicians can no longer hope to retain their position in society without the perfection

The Montreal City & District Savings Bank on St. James Street

of their intellect which is the result of education; which is as Cardinal Newman says, 'the clear, calm, accurate vision and comprehension of all things, as far as the finite mind can embrace them, each in its place and with its characteristics upon it...' If the cultivation of the intellect was necessary when men were content to observe, and to base practice on observation, how much more necessary it is now, when the most acute and logical minds are sorely puzzled between what are claimed to be scientific truths and what are bold and reckless assumptions."

Sir John A. Macdonald and his Conservative government had been returned to office in October, 1878 just as the Dufferins left Canada for a new posting in St. Petersburg. Hingston and his wife bid their farewells at the Citizens Ball at the Windsor Hotel. From St. Petersburg the Dufferins went on to Constantinople, then to India as Viceroy and Vicereine, and later to Rome and Paris where Dufferin was British Ambassador. No matter where they went, the friendship between Harriot Dufferin and Margaret would endure – they exchanged letters for years afterwards. Of all their diplomatic postings, the Dufferins liked Canada best.

If Hingston had hoped to remain a vice-regal consulting physician to Dufferin's successor, the Marquis of Lorne, he was sorely disappointed. Lorne, as it turned out, was homosexual; his wife, Queen Victoria's daughter, Princess Louise, had no need of a colonial doctor. Within a year of her arrival in Canada the princess moved back to England, letting her husband remain a bachelor governor-general for most of his posting.

One year later on October 3, 1879 Université Laval opened its medical faculty in the Château Ramezay but managed to attract a mere thirty students. In the words of its rector, Abbé Thomas Etienne Hamel, "So far, the university exists only on paper, and as a threat." A good reputation was essential to the École's financial viability, and with such an extreme menace dangling before them, the doctors took steps to build on its solid foundation and upgraded its curriculum. The Hospitalières, too, improved conditions at the Hôtel-Dieu hospital replacing beds of straw with spring beds.

In May 1880, Hingston travelled to New York for a convention of the American Medical Association where doctors plunged into the debate on evolution and Darwin's *On the Origin of Species by Means of Natural Selection, or, The Preservation of Favoured Races in the Struggle for Life*, which tried to reconcile science with religion. Hingston was not impressed with the arguments he heard. "What branch of science do you wish to pin your faith to?" he would ask. "I am tired of the sciences which are as changeful as the figures in a kaleidoscope: nothing stable, nothing permanent, but bold and bald assertions."

Upon his return, he was elected president of Montreal's Medico-Chirurgical Society. In September he attended the Canadian Medical Association convention held in the House of Commons in Ottawa, presenting a paper on the surgical treatment of wounds in which he "advised absolute cleanliness of the wound, absolute cleanliness of the surgeons' hands and those of his assistant." He objected to the use of adhesive plaster or bandages, preferring to leave "the wound open to glaze." He also repeated his opposition to Lister's carbolic spray, claiming it was not especially useful as an antiseptic technique. Hingston again dismissed Listerism as a theory, "based on the microscope and the imagination." That germs exist, he agreed, "is beyond cavil. They may be found in earth, air and water, in tissues living and dead, but that they are noxious is very far from being proved."

Far more noxious to Hingston was Université Laval's ongoing struggle to succeed in Montreal. As the dispute wore on, the protagonists on either side grew edgier. Archbishop Elzéar Taschereau turned to a semantic argument. What Laval was attempting to establish, he said, was a medical faculty, not a school of medicine. He was prepared to let doctors teach at both the École and at Laval, but those who taught at Laval would have to follow a different curriculum, give longer courses, and conform to the rules set by Laval's rector. It was a schizophrenic notion; half the Hôtel-Dieu doctors would have ties to Victoria University at Cobourg, half to Université Laval.

Archbishop Elzéar Taschereau

"Some persons may be curious to know how the new movement of Laval is going to affect the French medical school affiliated to Victoria University. From all we can learn it is to be absorbed and swallowed up, although the victim has been undergoing a sort of lubricating process before it would go down," reported the *Canada Lancet*, an in-house medical journal. "At first, Laval was only inclined to break bones, and only take two or three of its professors from the French school into its Montreal succursale, taking it for granted that Victoria would consent to die without a murmur. But the remaining seven or eight members of the staff were not willing to be snuffed out so easily, and getting legal advice, they found they could retain their charter, and thus continue to maintain their school in spite of Laval. Consequently, Laval had to consent to swallow the whole staff of Victoria."

What Laval had done was unethical, but was it illegal? The École's doctors thought so. Doctor d'Odet d'Orsonnens, head of the Hôtel-Dieu's Medical School, had gone to Rome in 1880, stopping in England on the way back where he presented the school's case to the Lord Chancellor, Sir Farrer Herschell, an expert in colonial constitutional law. Known for his common sense, Herschell studied the matter and concluded that Laval's charter limited it as a strictly local university in Quebec City and therefore it had no authority to open faculties of law, medicine, theology or arts in any other city within the archdiocese. "For that reason," Herschell wrote, "faculties established by the Université Laval in Montreal or elsewhere other than at

Quebec cannot form any part of Université Laval... the university cannot establish itself in different places."

Taschereau ignored Herschell's opinion. Clearly committed to do battle against the Hôtel-Dieu and its school, the churchman enlisted the support of the Quebec government and had the university charter amended. It was easy enough to do. The premier of the province, Joseph-Adolphe Chapleau, was a law professor at Université Laval and in Taschereau's pocket. Chapleau's conservatives lacked a majority in the legislature and had already announced that any legislation it passed would be subservient to the church. Chapleau was a sickly man into the bargain, in no position to challenge the primate of Canada. Bishop Bourget, who could not resist playing a final role in the ecclesiastical melodrama, came out of retirement to attack the scheme. Taschereau's subsequent attempts to discredit him only added to Bourget's prestige in Montreal. In a timely editorial, *Le Monde*, the most consequential Catholic newspaper in the diocese, and Bourget's mouthpiece, reduced the argument to its essentials. "The only reason Laval wants a university in Montreal is that it needs the money from Catholics in this part of the province to survive. The truth is that Catholics in the diocese of Montreal are tithed twice as much to support their religious, educational and charitable institutions than are their counterparts in the Quebec diocese. It is not that they are not willing to make additional sacrifices, but if they do, they want to make sure that the standards of the university held here by Laval in trusteeship aren't second-rate."

Bourget's bravado was contagious. Montreal's mayor, Jean-Louis Beaudry, and one of the country's leading Roman Catholic senators, François-Xavier Trudel, took up the cause. Seven thousand Montrealers signed a petition objecting to Laval's presence in their city. Hingston made common cause with Doctor Coderre to draw up a petition against the amending legislation and together they managed to collect the names of 107 of the city's 120 Roman Catholic doctors. The Jesuits in Montreal also fought the bill. Nevertheless, the enabling legislation was rammed through the house just before midnight on June 13. But the matter was far from over. Still unable to secure hospital privileges at the Hôtel-Dieu, Université Laval took the next step to secure its beachhead in Montreal by opening its own teaching hospital in the old Donegani Hotel on Notre Dame Street. Set up with the help of the Sulpicians, the fifty-bed institution was called Hôpital Notre-Dame and placed under the direction of the Sisters of Charity, the Grey Nuns. Hingston was invited to run it, but predictably he refused. Instead, Alfred Toussaint Brosseau, the short-tempered, forty-three-year-old surgeon "who terrorized his assistants and frightened his patients," was put in charge at Notre-Dame.

* * *

On the morning of July 2, 1881, as U.S. President James A. Garfield was about to board a train in Washington, a religious fanatic named Charles Guiteau shot him twice. The first bullet grazed the president's arm, the second fractured his rib and lodged behind his abdominal cavity. At first it seemed that Garfield might survive, but by the end of July his condition deteriorated. Hingston's reputation as one of the continent's leading surgeons was such that the American Consul-General in Montreal, John Quincy Smith, a former Ohio congressman, recommended that Hingston be summoned as a consulting surgeon. If anyone could help save the president's life, Smith argued, Hingston was the man. There is no indication that either the White House or Hingston himself took the suggestion seriously, but the significant American community in Montreal did. Hingston made it clear that he couldn't go to the aid of the president. He wasn't licensed to practise in the United States and wouldn't offer any medical opinions concerning a patient he was unable to examine. Moreover, he wasn't prepared to travel to Washington. His wife, Margaret, was five months' pregnant. All he would suggest is that the carpets in the president's bedroom be removed – advice which was apparently taken. Garfield again rallied, and again it seemed he might live, but he suffered a relapse and on September 19, died.

* * *

In Montreal, the bitter differences between Laval and the Hôtel-Dieu persisted throughout the summer. Bishop Bourget sailed for Rome with a high-powered delegation from Montreal, including Mayor Beaudry, on August 6 and once again stated his case for an autonomous university in Montreal. But Taschereau had backstairs influence at the Vatican. Bourget was politely reminded that he was now retired and no longer had the authority to meddle in diocesan affairs. In his favour, however, Leo XIII reassured him that Rome would remain neutral and not take sides in the dispute.

That summer Hingston's nephew, Edward Hingston Smith, graduated from McGill University and obtained his medical licence. Perhaps unwilling to be caught between doctors with competing loyalties and reluctant to be ensnared in the politics between rival schools in Montreal, Smith moved to Fullerton, Nebraska, to start his practice. Early in August, Hingston was in Halifax where he delivered a paper on *Certain Features in Ovariotomy* at the Dominion Medical Association, then returned to spend the rest of the summer at Varennes with his family. On November 19, 1881, Margaret gave birth to their daughter Katherine Eleanor. The baby died four days later and was the first to be buried in the Hingston family plot in section S (Lot number 25) of Notre-Dame-des-Neiges Cemetery. Hingston appeared more distraught at the loss of the infant daughter than Margaret. Shortly afterwards, Margaret's father, Donald Alexander Macdonald, whose term as the Queen's representative in Ontario had ended in a scandal over his extravagant spending, moved to Montreal where he bought a house at 558 Sherbrooke Street W. to be near his daughter and grandchildren.

Macdonald's last year in office had been tainted when it was learned that he had spent $5,500 of taxpayer's money on an official trip to Winnipeg. The mission was denounced in the press as the "corkscrew brigade," because of the exorbitant amount of money that had been spent on wine during the trip.

Hingston was appointed chief of surgery at the Hôtel-Dieu in 1882 and at the same time became a full professor of clinical surgery at the École. To his dismay, he spent as much time squabbling with the Laval staff doctors as he did dealing with common concerns. The consternation was widespread. "The Montreal branch of the medical department of Victoria College has lately become amalgamated with Laval University – this robs Victoria University of half her glory, so far as the medical department is concerned," *The Canada Lancet* commented on the growing confusion. "The other half still exists in Ontario, viz. the Toronto School of Medicine. This school is advertised as the Medical Department of Victoria University... this position is now rather anomalous when it is remembered that the Faculty of this school is at particular pains to parade itself, among a certain class, as having specially close relations with Toronto University only." The École's founder, Pierre Munro, grew increasingly agitated as the professional wrangling increased. Certain that he was about to lose not only the École he founded, but become liable for the loan he and the other doctors had personally guaranteed to finance its new building, Munro fell into a deep fit of despair. He believed he was ruined. On Thursday evening, April 13, 1882, as Hingston was at home preparing to leave for the Governor-General's Ball at Queen's Hall, he learned that Munro had committed suicide – he had slit his throat with a rusty scalpel. At the coroner's inquest the next day, Hingston "bore witness to the deceased's high personal character."

Munro's death, he said, was the "tragic termination to a long and useful life, in a moment of mental disturbance, as the result of long and severe suffering, of one of the most distinguished anatomists Canada has ever produced."

As is the air, such is our health and temperament.

WILLIAM HALES HINGSTON

CHAPTER TEN

The Climate of Canada

The birth of another daughter on February 20, 1883, was one of the
few comforting episodes in what was otherwise a brutal period in
Hingston's life. Margaret presented him with a healthy six-pound,
six-ounce girl and they christened her Mary Aileen. At the time, Hingston
was under considerable pressure. He worried about his future, his straitened
finances and his ability to provide for his growing family. Then, on the same
day that Aileen was born, Archbishop Elzéar Taschereau, impatient at the
lack of progress on the Laval portfolio, came to Montreal for a meeting with
Bishop Édouard-Charles Fabre that went on for more than 15 hours. The
following day *The Gazette* reported that "his lordship has notified the
Montreal School of Medicine and Surgery that Rome having decided against
them, they can no longer be recognized. He has made a similar communication to the ladies of the Hôtel-Dieu. It is expected therefore that the medical staff of the institution will be entirely changed, and the hospital put in
the hands of Laval." Taschereau also warned that further attacks against
Université Laval and its campus in Montreal would no longer be tolerated.

Hingston was among a group of doctors who met with Bishop Fabre in
a last-ditch attempt to keep control of their school with access to facilities at
the Hôtel-Dieu. They might be prepared to break with Victoria University
if they could be assured that they could continue to run their own school and
and remain part of the hospital. Initially Fabre agreed to consider the proposal. Then one month later he changed his mind. "Upon further reflection,
the Pope not only wants us to stop attacking Laval, but to do everything to
accommodate it," Fabre wrote to d'Orsonnens. "It is a complex situation,
and consequently, I cannot assure the Hôtel-Dieu's future, even if it breaks
with Victoria. "

Then on June 25, Bishop Fabre hauled out the biggest spiritual weapon
in his arsenal, using the Eucharist as a political bludgeon. Fabre declared
that any doctor who continued to work for the University of Victoria, or any
parent who enrolled a son in its medical school, would henceforth be excom-

municated. "All questions concerning the management of schools and the appointment of teachers and professors belong to the church," he maintained. "Anyone who teaches without first obtaining the sanction of the church risks being found guilty of sacrilegious impiety."

What grounds were there, in fact, for withholding the sacraments? Had the bishop overreached himself? Hingston, who was now himself excommunicated, certainly thought so. "Surely the principle of teaching young men cannot be interfered with so long as the doctrines are Christian and proper," he countered. "In this country we have the right to teach our children and our young men as we think proper. I do not think the church, or even the Pope, has any right to interfere."

The nuns at the hospital found themselves in an uncomfortable squeeze as well; if the doctors were excommunicated and expelled from their École, the Hospitalières faced a substantial damage suit from the professors – the doctors who owned the school. If they were not expelled, the Hospitalières risked being driven out of their own institution and replaced by the Grey Nuns.

Everything, it seemed, was lost – the hospital, the school, even their souls. Hingston went to see his confessor, Patrick Dowd, the wily pastor of St. Patrick's. Dowd was a hard-nosed Irish priest who, in his twenty-two years at the church, had often managed to oppose his superiors without seeming insubordinate. He had crossed swords with his bishop on several thorny issues and each time had won. Dowd's most significant victory in 1872 had been to keep St. Patrick's as an English-speaking parish after Bishop Bourget tried to make it French-speaking. Dowd had connections of his own in Rome and suggested to Hingston that the doctors at the École send their own delegation to the Vatican to seek a dispensation – a delegation that represented doctors themselves and did not include Bourget or any of his cronies. Acting on Dowd's advice, Hingston brought other influential English-speaking friends to the table, and in the end, Doctor Louis-Edouard Desjardins was sent to Rome as the École's emissary. A cultivated man who collected Canadian folk songs and composed music, Desjardins had studied for the priesthood before taking up medicine in London and Paris. Upon his return he was the first Quebec doctor to specialize in ophthalmology. Desjardins obtained an audience with Giovanni Cardinal Simeoni, Prefect of the Propagation of the Faith. To everyone's astonishment, Desjardins succeeded where Bourget and the others had failed. On August 24, a telegram from the Holy See arrived in Montreal. "Excommunication suspended," Simeoni wired. "The school can continue this year."

The same day, Hingston, now no longer excommunicated, replaced Munro as Dean of Victoria College where he would remain for the next eight years. As a follow-up, Rome sent Dom Joseph-Gauthier-Henri Smeulders, a Cistercian monk, to find common ground among an unruly assembly of religious rivals. Smeulders would spend fourteen frustrating, futile months trying to find agreement among the parties.

Through all this, Université Laval continued to have trouble attracting students to its medical school. Small wonder. Students who enrolled were subject to strict disciplinary rules which prohibited them from going to the theatre or from attending political meetings. As *The Star* weighed in with its point of view: "The Russian government would hardly do more, and these students are not Russian, but French-Canadians. If Laval endeavours to drive young French Canada with such a tight rein, there can only be one result: it will drive all of their best men into the Protestant and non-Catholic universities."

Hingston continued to work behind the scenes, quietly and unobtrusively helping to devise a formula that would allow an independent French-language university to open in Montreal. The doctors' efforts suffered a major setback with the death on November 5 of Doctor Eugène-Hercule Trudel. Trudel had been the École's secretary since 1872 and at the forefront of the campaign against Université Laval. At his funeral it was said he was lucky to have died when he did; had he died three months earlier when he was excommunicated, Trudel's colleagues promised that the church would have witnessed another Guibord affair.

Doctor d'Odet d'Orsonnens was named Trudel's replacement as secretary and head of the École. Shortly afterwards, Dom Smeulders delivered his report and stated the obvious by declaring that Victoria University was not a Roman Catholic institution and therefore "all its rights and privileges" had to be guaranteed. At the same time he recommended that Université Laval become an independent institution in Montreal. The solution, "seems to be equally gratifying to the friends of both institutions, and all accept it as a victory," *The Star* noted. In order to help finance Université Laval's autonomy, Smeulders recommended that five cents of every twenty-five that the church collected for celebrating private masses go towards the expense of running Université Laval's Montreal campus. On Sunday, September 21, Bishop Fabre read the solution imposed by The Propagation of the Faith in Rome, declaring that this was the end of the dispute "and that in a spirit of faith and obedience, all parties must submit." Fabre further declared that anyone who didn't accept the decision and "publishes and disseminates critical writings opposed to the views of the Holy See," could not be excommunicated, but would nonetheless be committing a mortal sin. Ebullience at the Hôtel-Dieu over the decision was short-lived. Presumably Archbishop Taschereau was exempt from Fabre's penalties, for Taschereau was the first to denounce Smeulders for his "stupefyingly unacceptable interference." Taschereau again went off to Rome where he spent eight months disavowing the Smeulders solution.

Tired of the interminable wrangling, Victoria University simply withdrew its affiliation with the École, paving the way for Université Laval to move in. Laval offered a chair to Hingston but he and two of the École's doctors, Louis-Édouard Desjardins and L. G. Migneault, decided to remain with Victoria University. Hingston became Victoria's dean of medicine, distancing himself from the Hôtel-Dieu – his faith was the last remaining token of his association with the hospital. He stepped back into the English-speaking community where his religion was still a mark of his separateness. "My work now [at Hotel-Dieu] is almost exclusively surgical, I visit no place but the operating room, except when I have private patients," he confided to his friends. Most of his time was spent tending either to his business affairs at the bank, to his duties as vice-president of the City Passenger Railway or as a consulting surgeon. It is perhaps significant to note that when Doctor George Fenwick Campbell, who was in charge of surgical teaching at the rival Montreal General Hospital, was thrown from his carriage when his horse stumbled going up Beaver Hall Hill, it was Hingston who was first called to examine him. Hingston pronounced Campbell "considerably bruised, but no bones were broken." Another prominent doctor, Lapthorn Smith, remarked that "scarcely a train came into Montreal which did not bring a patient from some distant city to consult him, while he was frequently called to neighbouring and distant cities."

Hingston charged $1 for an office consultation, $2 if he had to make a house call on horseback. The fee for delivering a baby was $15, $20 if chloroform was administered. The amputation of a limb cost $10. A major operation could run as high as $100. Yet in those days before medicare, Hingston often waived his fees for patients who could not afford his services, and rarely pressed those who didn't pay their bills. "He felt that he literally owed himself to his patients, and that they always had first claim on him," his son, Willie, would later recall. "To him the practice of the healing art appeared not as a means of livelihood, but as a noble calling. The fees he charged were always ridiculously small. Yet he treated the unnumbered poor with the same kindly consideration as he did the richest."

At the end of August 1883, Hingston was in Kingston for the 17th annual meeting of the Canadian Medical Association, where he delivered a paper on *The Influence of the Climate of Canada on Health*. In September, the British Association for the Advancement of Medicine met in Montreal and Hingston was elected association vice-president. He delivered the same paper to the meeting of September 2, 1884. The lecture was so well received he turned it, and other related talks he had given to the Natural History Society over the years, into a book: *The Climate of Canada and its Relations to Life and Health*. For the most part it is an essay about eugenics – the study of the hereditary qualities of a race or breed, that combined meteorology, sociology and anthropology to show how different climates affect basic body metabolism, shape character traits, and to illustrate how humans adapt to forces of natural selection.

In large measure the work was influenced by Charles Smallwood, the McGill University meteorologist who had moved to Washington. Hingston said his only motive in doing the book was to make a contribution, "since very little had been written on the subject.

"Climate influences our minds and bodies, affects our stature, strength and complexion, causes and cures disease, prolongs or shortens life," he argued. The book was a natural history touching on patriotism, and reinforced Victorian prejudice as it explained the influence of God – "the great disposer of all things" – on the sciences.

Today, much of the text seems overwrought and the thesis naive and outdated. Some of it is downright racist: "The races of men show remarkable organic differences; the darker the skin, the less sensitive the individual." Some of the stereotypical notions are, from the vantage point of the twenty-first century, curiously quaint and amusing: "Ireland has contributed generosity, warmth of heart and virtue; Scotland, the solid elements of prudence, England the qualities of truth and honour." His description of First Nations' peoples are condescending if not offensive. "The Indian is capable of extraordinary abstinence from food, and as capable of extraordinary indulgence. He can sit down to a half-a-dozen feasts in succession... the boa-constrictor, before and after a feast is not unlike him."

Still, there are passages remarkable for their prescience. Hingston railed against the dangers of smoking and dismissed the nicotine habit as "hurtful and disgusting" long before anyone was aware of the health hazards of cigarettes and cigars. He advocated "simple and frugal habits in life" and warned against the dangers of alcohol, not because he was a teetotaller – he wasn't – but because the quality of liquor distilled in Canada was inferior to

that in Europe. "Every traveller who has considered the subject, agrees in
the necessity of of avoiding stimulating beverages," he wrote. "Stimulants
which in Great Britain might be taken with impunity and sometimes with
advantage, are here productive of mischief... the baneful effects of new products of distillation are greater than are those of older products. Softening
changes of age are required to develop the ethers and to destroy the fuel. In
Canada, hard drinkers soon pass away."

The book questions North American eating habits, pointing out that
Canadians eat "sumptuously and extravagantly, too much and too quickly."
He reserved special contempt for restaurant food. Food, he pointed out, has
two purposes – to nourish the body and to sustain its heat. "The modern
system of hotel living gives to gluttony a licence unrestrained by avarice –
the only instance where one does not pay for what he commands nor make
return for what he destroys. The digestive tube, presided over by a sense of
taste which is stimulated by the tricks and refinements of the gastronomic
art, commonly show signs of disturbance, and the pearl-like organs at its
superior extremity [the teeth], which by nature are harder, firmer, stronger
than any other tissue, and destined to last a lifetime, too early and too often
give evidence of decay." Hingston also recommends a rigorous fitness program: "When persons are in the process of acquiring wealth, they generally
take too much exercise; when wealth has been accumulated, they usually take
too little. The wealthier classes, and those who have become quickly rich,
would seem to have acquired a contempt for exercise. The men – yes! and
the women too."

The Climate of Canada also discredited the practice of clear-cutting bore-
al forests. Hingston wrote that "nothing seems to influence climate more
distinctly than the forests and herbage."

One persistent theme in Hingston's treatise is his admiration for French-
Canadians and for their survival, against all odds, as a distinct ethnic group.
In his opinion, French-Canadians were a "hardy, long-lived and most pro-
lific people.

"They brought with them to this country something more powerful than
name or wealth or chivalric grace: a courage to contest empire with nature,
and by her lord, the Red man: a sincerity of belief which promised them in
the end a victory; a perseverance; a vigour and an energy which knew no
interruption, no rest. The children of France in seeking these shores,
seemed to be little impelled by cupidity.

"There was nothing cruel in their advent. They devastated no region,
usurped no possession, but quietly and peaceably – olive branch in hand –

endeavoured to take root in the soil with the Red man, share in his occupation, his sports, his pastimes and sow, reap, build and ally himself in marriage."

Hingston also admired their commitment to large families which "surpasses immeasurably that of the British, they even equal the Irish in their fecundity," he wrote. "Wherever they go, they carry with them habits of cleanliness, order, diligence, prudence and politeness." He reserved his highest praise for French-Canadian women, whom he wrote, were "mild, modest and agreeable, with an intelligence generally superior to the men."

Canada's climate, he concluded, was conducive "to the highest development of a healthy, long-lived intelligent people. Statistics already prove the climate to be favourable to health and life; time will show it to be favourable to mental development – the *mens sana in corpore sano* – for it can hardly be doubted that here, not less than among the peoples of North American free states – and Canada is as free as the freest among them, all the conditions exist for the development of the highest point of culture and civilization attainable by man... I have no doubt that we will yet see worked out in this country, what has never happened in the Old World – the amalgamation of several distinct races." Hingston was proud of the country's growing ethnic diversity. Long before the notions of multiculturalism were advanced, he anticipated a new national character emerging from different nationalities which would "dovetail into each other, like the different colours and shades and gradations of colour blend on the artist's palette and form a new tint unlike any of the constituents."

The Climate of Canada sold more than 4,000 copies and was well received critically. Philéas Gagnon included it in the *Bibliographie Canadienne*, an 1895 inventory of major Canadian books, describing it as "a worthwhile endeavour, written in a patriotic vein, to prove that Canada is an exceptionally healthy country."

As a published author, Hingston and his wife were among the 200 guests who braved a blizzard that paralyzed the city on Ash Wednesday, February 18, 1885 given for the celebrated humourist, Mark Twain. Twain was in Montreal to read at Queen's Hall from his new book, *The Adventures of Huckleberry Finn*, only to arrive during the heaviest snowfall in 16 years. Among the city's leading citizens who showed up to welcome him were Sir Francis Hincks, coal magnate Alexander Tilloch Galt and a newcomer to Montreal, William Van Horne, who was then managing construction of the Canadian Pacific Railway through Manitoba. The society columns reported that all those present "appeared delighted to have had the chance at shaking hands with the literary man, who wore a grey tweed lounging jacket ...his good natured face bearing a constant smile while his twinkling eye seemed overbrimming with fun." The following Thursday, February 26, Hingston himself was on stage lecturing on "the exhilarating influence of a Canadian winter." *The Gazette* reported that his talk was " lengthy and highly interesting," and that his remarks were " frequently applauded."

*Hygiene and religion, properly understood should
harmonize in order to elevate all the faculties of man...
for the body it is health, for the mind, reason, and for
the soul, spirituality.....*

WILLIAM HINGSTON

CHAPTER ELEVEN

A Second Plague

Shortly before midnight on February 28, 1885, as a driving wind whipped Montreal into a sarcophagus of snow, Hingston was disturbed by a pounding at his door. It was Tom Rodger, chief medical officer of the Grand Trunk Railway, a 37-year-old Scots-born physician who'd been practising medicine for fifteen years in Point St. Charles. Earlier that evening he had been called to examine a conductor, George Longley, who had arrived on a train from Toronto coughing, complaining of chills and a high fever. Rodger suspected smallpox, so there he was in the middle of the night, asking Hingston to admit Longley to the Hôtel-Dieu Hospital.

Hingston hesitated. Normally, he would have examined the patient himself but Margaret, seven months' pregnant, was upstairs; so considering the blizzard and the late hour Hingston agreed.

Rodger had a reputation for being "a fair, straightminded, honourable doctor," but what he did not tell Hingston was that earlier he had been turned away from the Montreal General Hospital because the admitting doctor had also suspected smallpox and refused to accept Longley. "Rodger never gave me any reason to suspect that the express purpose of his midnight visit to me was to relieve the General Hospital even at that hour, of their undertaking to keep the case until Doctor Rodger could arrange to get it in elsewhere," Hingston later maintained. "When we considered that the sick man could not be left at the railroad depot to do incalculable mischief, nor could he be taken to a hotel or lodgings or to the police station, I gave an order for his admission to the Hôtel-Dieu, with the understanding that my medical friend, who asked for it, should convey him there and take charge of him." Hingston handed Rodger a *laisser-passer* which read "Please Admit Bearer – St. Augustin Ward – private, WHH," and on the other side, "Rev Hospitalier, Hôtel-Dieu." With that, Rodger drove off in his sleigh to the hospital where Longley was duly admitted.

Longley was diagnosed with varioloid, a mild form of smallpox, and he was sent home. One month later, however, on April 1, an orderly at Hôtel-

Dieu, Pélagie Robichaud, died of smallpox. Then Robichaud's sister, Marie, died, and sixteen other people in Montreal were diagnosed with the disease. On April 14, the Hôtel-Dieu made a catastrophic error and, as a precaution, emptied its wards of almost all of its patients. Smallpox was now loose in the streets.

Longley may not have been, as some historians have suggested, patient zero. Two weeks before he arrived in Montreal, the February 13th meeting of the Medico-Chirurgical Society was told of a major outbreak of the disease in Kingston, Ontario, where 27 had died. Even before that, rumours of smallpox in Montreal's St. Lawrence ward had been circulating. The doctors present were, however, far more preoccupied with a cholera outbreak in Paris. They had convened that evening to discuss measures that might prevent cholera from infecting Montreal. During the meeting Hingston complained that "it was a disgrace" that the province "had not a better health law" to prevent the spread of contagious disease.

A huge five-day winter carnival at the end of January had attracted 30,000 visitors to the torchlight parades, tobogganing and snowshoe races, and people came to see "the bombshells and rockets that filled the air with stars and brilliant rainfalls of light." They also came to see the huge ice palace built in front of the Windsor Hotel; the condora, a towering ice cairn on the Champs de Mars, and the magnificent ice-lion sculpture in Place d'Armes. The smallpox virus could have come from anywhere. Three days before Longley arrived, there were reports of smallpox in a house on Mayor Street and of people leaving the building before it could be quarantined.

Then, to complicate matters, Doctor William Elijah Bessey, who had replaced Larocque as the city's Public Health Officer in an acting capacity, began vaccinating with what seemed to be disastrous consequences. Zealots still opposed to vaccination received their best ammunition when it appeared that Bessey was using contaminated lymph, resulting in erysipelas, an inflammation that pits the skin with purple blisters. Bessey was no neophyte. The forty-two-year-old doctor had been practising medicine for twenty years, ever since he received his degree from McGill in 1862. Originally from Esquesing in Halton County, north of Oakville, Ontario, Bessey never bothered to learn French, and although a satisfactory practitioner, he took a chilling, bureaucratic approach to his job. Hingston was called in to evaluate Bessey's competence, and decided that number of cases of erysipelas had been exaggerated. Of the two thousand vaccinations Bessey had carried out in April, only six were suspect. As Hingston pointed out, a rash was a natural reaction to vaccination, and parents who didn't know that could easily mistake it for erysipelas. One of the problems, of course, was that many French-speaking parents were unable to make the distinction because Bessey couldn't speak their language. Hingston recommended caution. He suggested (1) vaccinating only a few persons at a time in the same building, (2) only vaccinating children in perfect health, (3) making no more than three fever marks [punctures in the skin], and (4) suspending vaccination for a few days until "the crude and unsettled conditions of the atmosphere" had improved.

That roused Montreal's formidable resident anti-vaccinationist, Doctor Joseph Émery-Coderre. Coderre was as outspoken as he had been ten years earlier and this time he had the support for his campaign of a fifty-two-year-old English-speaking doctor, Alexander Milton Ross. Ross was a colourful character who had been trained in New York as a hydrotherapist, which meant he believed in the healing power of fresh water. During the American Civil War, Ross had worked with the underground railway and helped slaves make their way to Canada. He was apparently well connected at the White House where he regularly informed President Lincoln about Confederate operatives working in Canada. Like Émery-Coderre, Ross preached that "majorities have no monopoly on the truth" and that smallpox was caused as the result of filth. Vaccination, Ross argued, was "a fetish" that contributed to "scrofula, syphilis, consumption and many other disgusting diseases." His solution: clean up the rot and decay with "their death dealing odours, drink cold, fresh water and breathe fresh air." Allied with Émery-Coderre, Ross claimed that vaccination was not only useless but when practised during an epidemic actually contributed to the spread of the disease.

On May 10, the Board of Health stopped vaccinations. Bessey resigned as acting medical health officer in protest, complaining that he wasn't being paid enough "for the great responsibility and amount of work entailed."

He withdrew only temporarily, hoping no doubt to be confirmed in the position. But Bessey's reputation, in the words of Alderman William Dicker Stroud, president of the Protestant Society for the Protection of Women and Children, was that of "a man who made lots of mistakes, and a man who made such mistakes was not fit for the position." Instead, city council gave the job to Louis Laberge, a thirty-four-year-old fluently bilingual graduate of Victoria University. Laberge had practised in New England for several years. Bessey left Montreal for Grand Rapids, Michigan, where he eventually opened a practice. His departure went almost unnoticed.

That spring, Montreal's residents were much more unhinged by fighting in the North West. On March 26, Métis leader Louis Riel had started an open rebellion at Duck Lake, killing twelve Royal North West Mounted Police and wounding eleven. On April 2 there was a massacre at Frog Lake in which nine people, including two priests and the Indian agent, died. As *The Gazette* put it, Montreal "has two wars on its hands, one against the rebels in the North West, and the other against the filth of her streets, and of the two, the latter is by far the the most to be dreaded."

The Riel Rebellion opened religious and linguistic wounds in Quebec that had been festering for more than a decade. Depending on your point of view, Riel was either a mystic or a madman. He had been legitimately elected as a Member of Parliament three times, but not allowed to take his seat in the House of Commons. In the eyes of Catholic Quebec, he was a defender of French-Canadian culture in the west; in the North West, he was regarded as the founding father of the Métis nation; in Protestant Ontario Riel was a terrorist, the first Canadian separatist. Hingston had encountered Riel briefly at the Hôtel-Dieu in 1874, and perhaps met him again in 1876 when Riel was under Doctor Henry Howard's care at the Longue Pointe Asylum. Hingston's impressions of Riel have been lost, but he would likely have concurred with his old friend Howard, who thought Riel had "the appearance of a gentleman, frank and honourable." With Riel's defeat at Batoche and his surrender on May 15, anti-French sentiment in Montreal became intertwined with the scourge of smallpox.

*   *   *

Bishop Ignace Bourget died on June 8. The funeral in Montreal for the city's greatest promoter of Roman Catholicism attracted the largest crowds ever to witness such an event. Hingston was present for the Requiem in Notre Dame Church on June 12. Whatever their differences, Hingston judged Bourget "a saintly man" and would entertain no hint that the bishop's concept of Roman Catholicism could ever be questioned. In fact, when Hingston learned how Bourget knelt in prayer, on his knees with arms outstretched in supplication for an hour at a time, he initiated the same posture. Hingston's faith was anchored in Bourget's ultramontanism, but tempered by the social vision of Henry Edward Manning, an Anglican priest who left the Church of England to become a Roman Catholic cardinal in 1875, and by another English convert, John Henry Newman, who had been named a cardinal in 1879.

Bishop Bourget's body was conveyed through the streets and placed in a vault in his still unfinished cathedral. Hingston took part in the extended funeral services; his wife did not. She was in Varennes during that grim, stifling period, where on June 17, she gave birth to a son, named Reginald Basil.

On July 20, the streets of Montreal were again packed "by a dense crowd of singing, perspiring humanity," as thousands turned out to welcome the returning "travel-stained and sun-tanned" troops who had suppressed the North West rebellion.

By mid-August, Hingston began to feel the heat of the dying summer; the smallpox death toll had climbed to 120. He had been monitoring the situation and although concerned, he was not unduly alarmed. The epidemic was largely contained in St. Mary's Ward and was, he thought, still manageable. He agreed with a

Sir Francis Hincks

Gazette editorial which claimed there was "No alarm felt in any quarter, and no cause for such."

That all changed on August 18 when Sir Francis Hincks died of smallpox. His body was carted off to Mount Royal cemetery in the middle of the night where, without ceremony, it was ignominiously buried. His death gave smallpox a public face. It was no longer a French-Canadian Catholic disease. Overnight, Montreal became a city shunned and feared, blackballed and blacklisted, forced to adjust to the infamy of living with an epidemic which, in reality, was no worse than the one encountered ten years earlier. By the end of August, 239 deaths had been reported. To put matters in perspective, the rate of infection was roughly the same as it had been in 1875. Unlike 1875, however, it wasn't as widespread throughout the city. In addition, editorial opinion in the English-language newspapers this time turned almost hysterical, aimed in part at browbeating French-Canadians. All through August and September, *The Star* flogged the story and *The Herald* further inflamed French public opinion, suggesting that Hincks would still be alive if he had not employed diseased French-Canadian servants.

The Herald printed a letter blaming the "French part of the community," for the epidemic, chiding "the priestly class [R.C.] [who] make a harvest through the number of burials, for each one means five dollars." "French operatives, they are dirty, they do not vaccinate... let English capitalists, manufacturers, and employers drop off all the French help, have only English speaking people who are vaccinated, and who are not afraid to use soap and water, and it will soon be seen how it will stir up action."

On September 4, the governors of the Quebec College of Physicians and Surgeons arrived at Hingston's house to draft recommendations for dealing with the health crisis. His first priority was to avoid panic: "With a little delay, a little calmness and wisdom from men who in ordinary times are remarkable for these qualities, the disease, which I should say is not as great as is imagined by people at a distance, will be stamped out from our midst. I am afraid that a large section of the people have lost their heads and are at present acting in a manner which in a couple of weeks from hence they will not consider wise or prudent." He chaired another public meeting at Nordheimer's Hall, organized by the College of Physicians and Surgeons, in which the doctors reaffirmed their faith in vaccination, and he continued to work energetically but cautiously to deal with the epidemic. His earlier treatise, *Remarks on Vaccination*, was reprinted on September 16 – which incidentally was his tenth wedding anniversary – with the names of 30 more doctors added to the original list he had collected in 1876. Among the names was a new disciple, James Guérin, a witty young doctor who "had a happy faculty of making friends in every walk of life." Guérin joined the staff of the Hôtel-Dieu where he quickly "made a very satisfactory start, adopting the most modern style of teaching and of experiments."

Hingston's pamphlet was once again distributed throughout the city. He was determined to subdue the hysteria. "Small pox has its periods of dormancy and its periods of activity, at one moment overspreading a district, and at another disappearing," he wrote. "It is fatal in direct ratio to its epidemic character – cases occurring here and there in spots, are not so fatal."

On September 26, an order-in-council establishing a Central Board of Health for the province was passed. Hingston was named to run it. The Board had sweeping arbitrary powers and, as chairman, Hingston said he would use them "to put an end to this epidemic and relieve the anxiety in the public mind." Vaccination was made compulsory, and adjoining municipalities were ordered to provide hospital accommodation for their own smallpox victims. Hingston ordered the Provincial Board to open an emergency smallpox hospital in the Manitoba pavilion at the city's Exhibition Grounds at the corner of Park Avenue and Mount Royal Boulevard. A health court was also set up with the authority to forcibly remove smallpox patients from their houses and take them to hospital. Under the provisions of the act, those who died from smallpox during the day had to be buried within six hours, and those who died at night had to be buried within 12 hours.

Riled by the forced measures, public reaction in French-speaking neighbourhoods was predictable. On Monday, September 28, a mob of what *The Gazette* described as "the blindly fanatical and stupidly ignorant," took to the streets in a four-hour rampage, breaking windows at the house of the municipal health officer, shooting at City Hall, trashing the Medical Health Office on Place Jacques Cartier, then moving on to Victoria Square where it broke every window in *The Herald* building. When the chief of police, Hercule Paradis, attempted to intervene, he was attacked by thugs and beaten. Street mobs, convinced that vaccination was nothing more than a scheme to enrich doctors by collecting fees to treat the disease, continued the vandalism intermittently until the end of October. *The Herald* stood firm in its views. "In whatever light the question is viewed, it is seen that while the law is the same for English and French alike, and while it will be enforced on all citizens alike, it will prove particularly beneficial to the French Canadians of our city among whom the death rate is so appalling... *The Herald*, in urging compulsory vaccination cannot therefore be said to be acting adversely to French Canadian interests."

In Montreal's English-speaking neighbourhoods, smallpox both was and was not a menace. As Michael Bliss writes in *Plague*, his book about the crisis, "It was not killing many of the English and you could live through the whole epidemic without seeing a case [just as you could live in the city without speaking a word of French], but the plague's damage was both material and moral."

The city's material reputation was further sabotaged on November 4 when police were called out to quell a riot in Rolland Lane where residents had to be forcibly removed to the smallpox hospital and then again on November 16 when twenty thousand citizens packed the Champs de Mars to protest against the execution of Louis Riel in Regina. The city's moral reputation was displayed in the newspapers which each day reported the proceedings of the smallpox court. A fair impression of the situation can be gleaned by looking through its records:

"Napoléon Goulet, 1234 Notre Dame St. had his sentence remitted as he was very poor, and his children had all died;

"Patrice Tremblay pleaded guilty to refusing his wife and children to go to hospital, but promised amendment and so had his sentence suspended to give him an opportunity of complying with the law.

The Rolland Lane riot

"Isaac Dupuis, 945 Ontario Street was fined $2 for refusing to allow his house to be disinfected…"

Doctor Émery-Coderre stepped up his opposition in November, responding to Hingston's pamphlet with one of his own: *Anti-vaccinateur Canadien-Français*. Then *Harper's Weekly*, a mass circulation magazine published in New York, picked up on the controversy. "There has been nothing in connection with the ravages of the smallpox in Montreal more pitiful or deplorable than the ignorance of its French residents of that city concerning the true character of that awful disease, and the exhibition on their part, of blind unreasoned prejudice against those means of preventing and exterminating the disease which are furnished by science through vaccination and isolation," *Harper's Weekly* informed readers on both sides of the border. "Since the beginning of the epidemic the authorities have been hampered and baffled in their attempts to stop its ravages by an organized resistance from the French Canadians." By the time the Harper's article appeared, the epidemic was essentially over, "all of the west and a third of the east of the city cleaned up."

Hingston, who was now virtually in control of the provincial Health Department, travelled to Washington, D.C. as head of a Canadian delegation sent to persuade U.S. authorities to modify quarantine regulations and lift the travel restrictions which for three months had disrupted cross-border trade, leaving Montreal isolated. He was back in time to celebrate Christmas with his family, and on January 7, 1886, attended a Bishop's University reunion banquet at the Windsor Hotel.

Four days later Hingston was astonished to open his newspaper and read that Doctor Thomas Rodger had named him a scapegoat for the smallpox epidemic. Rodger told a board of health inquiry that it was Hingston who had initially misdiagnosed Longley as suffering from chicken pox. The way Rodger told the story, he didn't inform the nursing sisters at the Hôtel-Dieu that Longley had smallpox because he was under the impression that "Doctor Hingston, in his letter, had given all necessary instructions, and in fact my professional relations with the patient ceased from the time he became a patient in the Hôtel-Dieu." Rodger said the few visits he subsequently paid to the patient were "for the purposes of making officially known to the railway authorities of the progress of the disease.

"I saw Doctor Hingston, and when we had left the ward, he remarked to me that this was a case of varicella [chicken pox]. I answered, 'No Doctor Hingston, it is not chicken pox, this case is one of smallpox and I beg you not to make a mistake'."

Hingston "emphatically and categorically," denied having such a conversation with Rodger. In a lengthy letter published in most Montreal newspapers on January 12, 1886, Hingston challenged Rodger's version of events:

"Words so unbecoming could not have possibly been used [by Rodger] especially to one his superior in years, and perhaps his equal in position," Hingston wrote. "I must do Doctor Rodger, in spite of himself, the justice to say that he could not, [and he did not] at any time within my hearing, make such a remark."

Hingston offered a detailed account of Longley's arrival at the Hôtel-Dieu pointing out that the nursing sister who filled out the admitting register named the disease varioloid (smallpox), not varicella (chicken pox). According to Hingston, Longley was quarantined in a room in the north wing of the hospital, "well suited to complete isolation," and that "no one in immediate attendance of the patient contracted the disease. Doctor Rodger affirms that when we visited the Hôtel-Dieu I declared his patient to be suffering from chicken pox. His affirmation is that though it was so plainly a case of small pox that he recognized it as such at once upon his first contact with it; it was so unmistakably small pox as to be recognizable on sight by the House surgeon of the General Hospital – a young practitioner, of I

think, two or three years standing, and who, as there had been no small pox
in the city since his professional experience began, might not have seen a
case of small pox in his life. Though the case was so plain to them, I with the
great advantage of knowing in advance the diagnosis of Doctor Rodger, I
who had first refused the case because it was small pox, formally declared
that it was not small pox at all, but chicken pox?! I am at a loss to understand
this statement.

"I have only to add, that I hope the alternative will never again be presented to a physician practising in a large city of 180,000 inhabitants, of
opening the doors of an institution in whose welfare he is deeply interested,
to a patient suffering from so foul a disease as smallpox or of leaving the
unhappy subject of it to perish on the streets at midnight during an almost
arctic winter."

*Medicine is a noble profession and its members have,
in every age, been amongst the most cultivated. When
their social influence is used commonly for the good, it
is beyond the power of man to measure their worth....*

WILLIAM HINGSTON

CHAPTER TWELVE

Deus Ex Machina

If the Laval episode was theatre in Hingston's life, its resolution had a *deus ex machina* ending. In this case it was not the gods who contrived the *dénouement*, but the Holy See. For almost 20 years the Vatican had spent an inordinate amount of time dealing with Quebec. Since 1862, no fewer than three, and sometimes as many as five, cardinals found themselves dealing with the university question. Cardinal Lodovicio Jacobini spent so much time on Quebec's interminable political, liturgical and theological disputes he often described himself as "the Canadian Cardinal."

The Prefect of the Propagation of the Faith, Cardinal Giovanni Siméoni addressed the problem with a *Star* reporter who had been visiting Rome. "We admire Canadians for their piety and for their devotion to the Holy Father, but you folks in Quebec are the greatest people for squabbling we have ever encountered," an exasperated Siméoni was quoted as saying. "You give us more trouble than any of the faithful in any other part of the world. No sooner have we succeeded in settling and disposing of some question that has been agitating you in Montreal or in some other part of the province, and we are just engaged in congratulating ourselves on the successful result of our labours which have apparently satisfied both parties, than the next mail brings us word that the whole question has been reopened and we are again asked to interfere. There is no denying it. You cause me lots of trouble."

Jacobini, who was Secretary of State of the Roman Curia, was heard to say after ten gruelling sessions with the Quebec delegation that he had experienced "hell on this earth."

Heeding his cardinals, Pope Leo XIII did the only sensible thing he could. In 1886 he elevated Alexandre Elzéar Taschereau, making him a prince of the universal church by naming him Canada's first cardinal. The Pope was also fond of Bishop Fabre. He often referred to him as "kindness himself." Not wishing to disappoint Fabre, Taschereau's Quebec diocese was subdivided and Fabre was anointed an Archbishop and given the Island of

Montreal as his archdiocese. This of course put Fabre in charge of the administration of Catholic universities in his own diocese. As he saw it, the issue had come down to a simple choice: a new Catholic university in Montreal or a branch of the existing Catholic university in Quebec City. This initiated a new round of domestic arguments between Taschereau and Fabre on the division of church assets, financing of the new diocese, and of compensation for Laval's trouble. Then the Jesuits raised substantive issues of their own. Expelled from Canada by the British who seized all of their property after the conquest in 1759, the Jesuits were reinstated in 1814. They too demanded compensation for the substantial loss of their buildings and properties. Université Laval thought it should have the Jesuit estates; English-speaking Protestants opposed giving the Jesuits anything at all. Once again, things stalled.

On May 18, 1887 it was agreed that the Montreal campus of Université de Laval would become semi-autonomous. The Archbishop of Montreal would appoint the rector but the board of governors responsible for running the campus would be made up of two Montrealers, the Archbishop and the Superior of the Sulpicians and the rector and the vice-rector of Université Laval from Quebec City. The conflict with Laval appeared to be nearing an end. After all the bitter wrangling Hingston was undoubtedly sated with church politics and administrative rows. But separating two interdependent institutions presented him with new challenges. The École had 225 students, 106 of whom were enrolled at Université Laval's medical faculty. Petty jealousies remained. He would have to work to unite a badly divided community. Still, the conflict did not slow Hingston's pace or diminish the scale of his surgical work. An eminent French gynecologist, Georges Apostoli who visited Montreal in 1887 and toured the

William Hingston and his fellow professors at l'École de médecine et chirurgie at the Hôtel-Dieu

Hôtel-Dieu, was so impressed with Hingston, he remarked, "If you didn't know his background, you would mistake him for an aristocrat, he is such a refined person." Another doctor, Donald Rowat, then studying at McGill University, remarked that Hingston's "personality and appearance were such that no student could allow him to pass by without inquiring who he was."

Hingston expressed himself with great clarity and precision in the classroom. He was, according to Rowat, "lucid, forceful and always interesting, giving advice that went beyond the subject at hand." Hingston's basic message never varied: that good doctors could not be taught, but had to learn over time. The essence of his approach was distilled in a valedictory address he delivered to one graduating class. "You have studied in your textbooks typical cases, and you have had the benefit of listening to physicians and surgeons of long experience," he said. "But you cannot acquire experience second-hand; you must acquire your own. No case, you will find, is in every point a typical case. Diseases do not run the course that the textbook indicates. There are very many factors that influence the ailment and consequently the treatment you must give. Note these things in your memory. Study your cases, and you will enrich your mind with that knowledge which experience alone can bring."

Professional and social responsibilities continued to weigh heavily on Hingston. He took on charitable works, becoming a director of St. Patrick's Orphanage Asylum, and rose through the ranks of the Knights of Columbus, the pre-eminent Catholic fraternal order. He helped organize the Golden Jubilee dinner honouring his parish priest, Father Dowd, and his former school-teacher at Collège de Montréal, Father Marcel Toupin, that was held on May 19, 1887. During the banquet Hingston saluted Toupin as a "quiet, gentle, modest retiring priest," who had partially sacrificed his "own beautiful French language," to work in English at St. Patrick's. Dowd he described as "a father to the orphan, a staff to the aged, and a powerful support to Christian education." The respect was mutual. Later that month Father Dowd wrote to Prime Minister John A. Macdonald recommending Hingston for a knighthood. In his letter Dowd demanded to know why the Irish Catholics of the Dominion hadn't been given their fair share of imperial honours.

"I would ask no exceptional or partial favours. I would beg nothing. But if our claim be equal if not superior to that of others, why should it not be acknowledged," the old priest wanted to know. "I only ask for even-handed impartial justice and I am sure it will not be denied by the present government in the distribution of jubilee honours. After this rather combative preface, I will now state my case: ... If honour and merit are to go together, why has not Dr. Hingston of Montreal ... [received a knighthood?] I do not hesitate to say that honours conferred by the profession, professional labours done, and positions of honour and of confidence in the profession held by him in the past, or actually in his possession, place him clearly at the head of the medical profession in Canada... Dr. Hingston's social position is so well known. I may add that God has blessed him with means to support any dignity he may receive. Try your best to aid in procuring a well earned honour for a good man. He does not look for it, but if honoured, he will accept, not so much on his own account, as because he thinks the Irish Catholics of the Dominion are entitled to ... an imperial title."

In June, the problem of compensating the Jesuits and Laval was resolved. The Jesuits would get $400,000; Université Laval was awarded $40,000 compensation for its troubles and withdrew from Montreal. In July, the government at last adopted the legislative machinery required to govern public health on a province-wide basis. Hingston could take pride in the fact that for the most part, the bill was patterned on the municipal legislation he had drawn up thirteen years earlier to deal with the smallpox crisis in Montreal. It standardized rules for the prevention of contagious disease throughout Quebec and for the first time allowed for the study of vital statistics in the province. Hingston was in Washington, D.C. in September for the Ninth International Medical Congress, a gathering of 3,000 physicians and surgeons from around the world. He came away from the meeting convinced, with some justification, that the state of medical education and its practice in Canada was superior to the American experience. He was back from the United States for the birth of his fourth son on December 4, 1888. The boy was baptised Edmund Harold Ramsay, named for his godfather, one of Hingston's closest friends, the Reverend David Shaw Ramsay, who was the parish priest in South Shields, England.

On December 17, Kingston sat down to "an elegant dinner in the Mess Room of the St. Lawrence Hall Hotel" for the annual University of Bishop's College Medical Students Dinner, where, according to the Canada Medical Record, "he received an exceedingly warm reception which he duly acknowledged, and alluded to his student days, and the primitive character of their entertainments."

*   *   *

In February 1889, the pope issued another Bull – *Jamdudum* – which ceded control of Université Laval to the Archdiocese of Montreal. A new constitution was written preserving the École's charter, and its privileges, allowing its doctors to become professors of the Faculty of Medicine of the Université Laval à Montréal. The campus was autonomous in every respect except that Université Laval in Quebec City still conferred degrees on graduates. Six out of the schools nine professors accepted the arrangement.

Doctor Joseph Émery-Coderre died in September and was mourned as "one of those old landmarks, those milestones along the highway of Montreal's past." As long as Émery-Coderre had been alive, there had been no prospect of any accommodation with Université Laval. Hingston succeded him as administrative secretary. To accept the appointment, he resigned as dean of Victoria University. He immediately named a committee to extricate the École from Victoria, and at the same time permit the École de Médecine to absorb the medical school Laval had opened in Montreal. While Hingston was prepared to be "affable and tolerant," in his approach to healing the rift, other members of his committee were not. The two warring camps were not easily appeased. Laval refused to allow the doctors to describe themselves as Laval professors, and unwilling to forgive Doctor Trefflé-Rottot for betraying their cause. As secretary of the École, Hingston found himself being pulled in opposite directions. He was also living in two different worlds: professionally working daily in French; socially, conversing in English. He had, however, cemented his reputation as one of the city's leading surgeons and, in keeping with his new station, moved to a new address.

The Phillips Square neighbourhood where he had lived for almost thirty years was changing. According to the *Canada Medical Record* the area "which was for many years first the fashionable residence quarter of rich merchants, then became the stronghold of the principal doctors, then was gradually abandoned to the dentists, is now being filled with shops."

Hingston sold his house for a handsome profit to James and Colin Morgan who built "the finest building in America devoted to the retail business" on the site. For many years it housed Morgan's, an upscale department store which today is The Bay. By the fall of 1889, Hingston and his family had moved into Montreal's Square Mile, a wealthy Protestant enclave where social boundaries were strictly enforced. Because Hingston was a doctor, a banker and a former mayor of the city, he occupied a privileged place. His limestone mansion in the Second Empire style, with its mansard roof and high front stoop, stood at an address then numbered 882 Sherbrooke Street West, on the southwest corner of Sherbrooke and Metcalfe Streets. It was directly opposite the Prince of Wales Terrace, a handsome row of apartments modelled after the Nash Terrace in London and built to house the

Hingston's house at 1000 Sherbrooke St. W.

Prince's entourage during the 1860 royal visit. Hingston's next-door neighbour was his old friend, George Drummond. In fact, Drummond had built his imposing mansion on property that Hingston had sold him. Hingston's house was modest by Square Mile standards. For one thing, it doubled as his office. To the right of the frosted glass front doors was a suite of examining rooms; to the left, beyond a reception hall, were the family's living quarters. Off the central corridor were a parlour, drawing room and a formal dining room. In keeping with upper-class social custom at the time, Hingston and his wife occupied individual bedrooms on the second floor separated by a morning room used by Margaret as an office. On the same floor were bedrooms for the two boys, William now 11 and Donald 10; a bedroom for six-year-old Aileen, and a nursery for Basil, who was three, and the baby, Harold. There were three other guest bedrooms and a bathroom. The servants' quarters were on the fourth floor under the mansard roof. The kitchen and storage rooms were at street level; a set of stairs to the second floor led to the main entrance. Although he could afford to splurge on appointments, Hingston was careful with money. The house was plainly furnished by gilded age standards and, compared to some of its neighbours, almost shabby. The walls were whitewashed, rather than painted. The

Basil Hingston, aged five

Hingstons believed that society was losing its moral compass in pursuit of wealth. They ran their household according to the philosophy that "those who rise to be princes merely by fortune have little trouble rising, but very much in maintaining their position.

"We have to have another standard of excellence other than money. A man's life cannot be gauged by the abundance of things he possesses," Hingston wrote.

Hingston's only costly indulgence was his thoroughbreds. He owned two horses and he and his wife were part of the smart set that frequented the Bel-Air Jockey and Montreal Hunt Clubs. The track was where he relaxed. "He scarcely took a holiday, devoting himself to his profession every moment of his time," his son, William Jr., recalled. "He felt that his patients had first claim on him, and no other activity must ever be allowed to interfere with his first duty."

On Sundays in the summer, Hingston would attend the first Mass at St. Patrick's, then catch the river steamer to Varennes, in time for breakfast with the family crowded together. He would romp with the children, stay for tea at four o'clock, then be back in Montreal by five. "Even this slight relaxation he would deny himself if one of his patients needed his care," his loyal son, William, added.

The final gasp in the fight with Laval came in October when the École's medical students organized a protest banquet attended by a number of doctors, in which they loudly rejected any integration of Université Laval's students or professors. Hingston was among the signatories of a petition to the Holy See asking the Pope to pressure Quebec premier, Honoré Mercier "to bring this important matter to a happy issue," by bringing in the required civil legislation that would "unite both faculties into one body as a powerful means of pacifying the universities and of promoting the cause of science." The Holy See complied, telegraphing the premier and telling him that by doing so he "will render a service to your fellow citizens, and you will also be agreeable to us." The legislation was introduced on November 19, and adopted on November 29. It allowed the École to retain its corporate affairs and to enlarge its staff by hiring all the doctors who taught at the Laval branch, build new laboratories and improve clinical facilities at the Hôtel-Dieu.

"We now have before us two great institutions, one in Quebec, the other in Montreal," a determined Premier Honoré Mercier told the legislature. "Both have turned out distinguished men. They fought each other in Montreal, and their quarrel lasted all these years. Today that quarrel is over."

It took another two years before the formal entente designating the École as the sole faculty of medicine for French-speaking Catholics in Montreal was signed on October 5, 1891. It would not be until 1919, however, that the combined facilities would become known as Université de Montréal, today the largest of the city's four universities.

Man is vain and craves for distinction of some sort.
He carries with him a desire not to be lost...

WILLIAM HALES HINGSTON

CHAPTER THIRTEEN
WELL EARNED HONOURS

The scalpel, forceps and saw are the surgeon's instruments, but for the tools to be used effectively in Hingston's time, speed, dexterity and confidence were of the essence. Surgery suited Hingston's temperament, as each operation presented a different challenge allowing him to act, intervene and control. Medical historian Pierre Meunier described Hingston's expertise in removing a nose and throat polyp, a condition then known as Frog-face, as "pure art." It is a rare condition in which a solid, fibroid tumour grows in the pharynx, invades the throat, then continues to grow outside the nose. Hingston had removed the tumours by "cutting across the bridge of the nose, right down his lip, using a saw, a strong knife and scissors." Folding the nose onto the cheek, he exposed the growth and

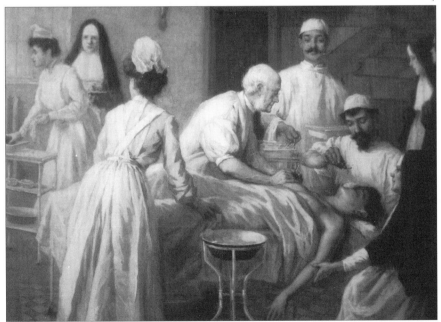

Hingston operates without antiseptic gloves in this portrait by Joseph-Charles Franchère. The original painting hangs in the Hôtel-Dieu hospital museum.

took it out. Because Hingston was guided by his extraordinary understand-ing of human anatomy and a remarkable sense of touch, Meunieur suggests "it would be impossible to imagine this kind of skill today." Hingston was also acclaimed for his successful treatment of a twenty-one-day-old baby girl born with a perforated anus. The infant's fecal matter was moving through her vagina. Hingston inserted a catheter into the vagina, through the perfo-rated wall between the vagina and the rectum. He then made the necessary layered incisions where the anus opening should have been until he reached the catheter. Inserting a flexible medical probe into the opening, when he withdrew it, fecal matter followed its natural channel. "During the short period the child was in my care," Hingston wrote, "most of the fecal matter flowed through the newly opened anus, and less through the vagina. My hope was that the perforation would eventually close."

As an experienced gynecologist, he was also a specialist in vaginal sur-gery, correcting birth defects and creating vaginas by cutting through the peritoneum, the transparent membrane lining the abdominal cavity where the vaginal opening should be. "Using a metal probe, fingers and the back of the knife, a relatively deep pocket can be made," he wrote in a paper on the procedure. To keep the passage from closing he recommended using "a sponge soaked in acacia oil." Hingston advised caution in the use of the blade. "When I first performed this operation, I used the knife almost exclu-sively, and there was a lot of haemorrhaging. It is essential [of course] to find the right passage. I know one esteemed though rather impatient surgeon who cut on the outer wall of the vagina, near the rectum. I'm treating an-other patient now who was the victim of an even more disturbing mistake: her vaginal passage was cut all but almost into the bladder!"

Among other notable operations of which he was able to boast was the removal of an enlarged thirteen-pound spleen, a difficult procedure and "one that he did not think he would care to repeat." Because of his dexerity in the operating room, Victoria University recognized him with an hon-ourary Doctor of Laws degree in 1891.

*   *   *

Montreal celebrated the 250th anniversary of its founding in 1892, and as a members of the Antiquarian and Numismatic Society, established to preserve local history, Hingston and his wife were present in Place d'Armes on May 16 that year for the laying of the cornerstone of the monument to Montreal's founder, Chomedey de Maisonneuve. The Maisonneuve statue itself would not be unveiled for another three years but Hingston was im-pressed enough with its sculptor Louis Philippe Hébert to engage Hébert to design the massive tombstone for the Hingston family plot in Notre-Dame-des-Neiges cemetery.

Aileen made her first communion at St. Patrick's on May 21, 1892, an event that for years afterwards was viewed in a sentimental light. Willie was Margaret's favourite son, Donald, every inch his father's boy, but Aileen was their daughter. They doted on her. As a parent, Hingston was strict but engaged with the his two oldest boys. The only time any of his children could recall their father losing his temper and resorting to corporal punishment was when young William and Donald, feeling privileged because Hingston was vice-president of the Montreal Street Railway, decided to sneak aboard one of the tram cars and ride for free. He strapped both of them. Hingston was emotionally distant from the youngest sons, Basil and Harold. They, for the most part, were raised by nannies. As Aileen grew older, she took her younger brothers in hand.

All families have their eccentricities, and Hingston's was no exception. None of the children were allowed to wear shoes in the house. Hingston thought carpets were unhealthy and didn't want the hardwood floors in the house scuffed. Every evening after dinner, the entire household, including the servants, recited the rosary on its knees in the parlour. The routine was relaxed when the family stayed at Varennes, where "saying the beads" was optional. When their father was present, the children rarely ducked out. All of the children were given riding instructions and when he was in his 60's, Hingston taught Basil and Harold to swim in the river at Varennes.

At the end of June, 1892 he and Margaret took Willie with them and sailed for England aboard the Allan Steamship Liner *Parisian* so Hingston could attend a meeting of the British Medical Association at Nottingham. There he gave a talk about the benefits of alternative medicine, raising eyebrows when he suggested that European surgeons might learn a little from the primitive methods of North American aboriginals.

"Take for instance the treatment of the newborn infant. The yielding abdominal walls are never compressed by an unyielding bandage, and the young bird in its nest is not more comfortable than the Indian babe," he said. "If in the depths of a forest an Indian breaks a leg or an arm, splints of the softest material are at once

Basil Hingston as a teenager

improvised – straight branches are cut, these are lined with down-like moss, or scrapings or shavings of wood; or with fine twigs interlaid with leaves of the evergreen, cedar or hemlock; if in winter, the whole is surrounded with with strips of willow or osier or young birch. To carry a patient, a stretcher is made of young saplings. ...No London carriage maker ever constructed a spring which could better accomplish the purpose."

During his speech Hingston also warned young doctors against the trend to become specialists before they had spent at least ten years in general practice. Specialization, he said, could only be achieved at the expense of something more important. "No separate department of surgery when isolated from its surroundings for the purpose of enquiry can, of itself, become an art. I cannot emphasise this too strongly. When in our profession, men of energy devote themselves to any branch of knowledge and apply their minds thereto with continued attention, they cease to realize that beyond and around them there are other branches of our art which cannot be divorced from each other without mutual injury. Nowadays, it is difficult for men even of superior intellect and of liberal knowledge to avoid being drifted away into one or other of the narrow rivulets leading from or flowing out of the general mainstream of surgery, and becoming so absorbed in the pursuit of partial truth as not to perceive that it is wanting in many parts; that it is incomplete, unfinished, and defective and can only obtain wholeness when facts are arranged and phenomena, however distinct they may appear to be, are brought under a common law... each part, each division, each subdivision, each specialty, is as the separate relieving, supporting each other." Commenting on Hingston's remarks, *The British Medical Journal* acknowledged that he had been worth hearing because he had "performed many operations on the brain and on the spleen, and has done good work in every department of surgery."

After the convention the Hingstons spent two days visiting their old friends the Dufferins, then toured the continent. They spent two weeks on a buying spree in Paris collecting reproduction Empire furniture for their new house. They visited Dresden where the cameo portraits used on the cover of this book were painted. They then went to Rome for an audience with the Pope during which Hingston was given the Cross *pro Ecclesia et Pontifice*, a significant award created by Leo XIII as a mark of honour for distinguished lay service to the church. Perhaps no one was as impressed with the ceremony than was Hingston's fifteen-year-old son, Willie, who gamely announced that one day he, too, would be pope.

Shortly after they returned to Canada in November, John Sparrow

Thompson was sworn in as the county's first Roman Catholic prime minister. He was forty-seven when he took the oath of office – one of Canada's youngest prime ministers. Astute, experienced and energetic, Thompson had been regarded as Sir John A. Macdonald's heir apparent. But when Macdonald died in 1891, the Ontario wing of the Conservative party balked at giving the job to a Catholic, and instead Sir John Abbott was sworn in as a caretaker. Abbott was dying when he took the job and within eighteen months he turned the government over to Thompson. Understandably, the new prime minister found himself besieged with requests from Catholics who expected him to start rewarding his co-religionists. Montreal's leading leather-goods manufacturer and a major Conservative party fundraiser, Michael Cromwell Mullarky, was one of the first to demand a knighthood for Hingston.

"He is a perfect gentleman in every sense of the word...," Mullarky wrote to Thompson. "There were a few hot-headed Irishmen who found fault with him because he called out the whole police force to protect the Orangemen on the 12th of July. I mention the facts in order that it may strengthen your hands to confer a title on the man who deserves it."

Hingston was, of course, much more than a doctor and surgeon, his energies dispersed over a large number of different interests. As the historian Robert Rumilly described him, "apart from his medical advice, his patients and colleagues placed their trust and confided in him for family counselling, valued his political and financial advice, and admired his common sense, seeking him out in difficult times." He was in demand as a speaker, and usually accepted engagements whenever he was invited. In September 1893, Hingston presented a paper on the history of surgery in Canada to a meeting of the Canadian Medical Association in Kingston, Ontario. "Surgery," Hingston pointed out, "preceded medicine in this country. The Governor of Nouvelle-France was always asking for surgeons to be sent out. The people did not need physicians."

The *Canada Medical Record's* account of the meeting noted that "Dr. Hingston described the marvellous advances of surgery during the past forty years, but was sorry that in some cases this divine art had degenerated to a commercial question, owing to the greed for gold which has extended to some of the members of the profession. He especially cauterized the practice of those one-ideaed gynaecologists who referred all female disorders to the uterus and instituted a daily tinkering process as a means of obtaining money."

Prime Minister Thompson did not forget what he had been told about

Hingston when he went to London to be sworn in as a member of the Privy Council by Queen Victoria. During his meeting with the Queen at Windsor on December 12, 1894 in which he discussed state business, he recommended Her Majesty include Hingston on her honours list the following May. The Queen, who knew of Hingston by reputation, agreed. Later that day as he was lunching with the Queen, Thompson had a heart attack and died. He was succeeded in office by Mackenzie Bowell, a vacillating right-wing political warhorse, an Orangeman who had risen through the ranks from his local lodge in Belleville, Ontario, to become Grand Master of Upper Canada, and finally Grand Master of British North America. Neither Hingston nor Bowell knew it at the time, but they would soon find themselves allied as strange political bedfellows.

On May 24, 1895 William Hingston was given an Imperial title and made a Knight Bachelor of the realm in recognition of his contributions to medicine. "This action of the British and Canadian Governments has given the greatest possible satisfaction not only to the profession of Montreal, but the whole of Canada, and indeed wherever Sir William Hingston's noble and gentle qualities are known," commented *The Canada Medical Record*. "The honour, coming from our beloved sovereign, not only honours the individual but the whole noble profession to which he belongs. Let this honour, which has come to our profession be an incentive to the rank and file of us to elevate and uphold its nobility by burying the few petty jealousies and differences which may exist among us."

Sir William Hingston
as painted by Charles Delfosse

The same year he was knighted, Sir William became a consultant at The Samaritan Hospital for Women which had opened as a non-sectarian hospital on Dorchester Street near Mackay Street, and was modeled after the New York State Women's Hospital. It was an ideal environment and Hingston was well qualified to advance the procedures and treatments.

Women felt secure in his hands, and with good reason. He was known to have challenged convention by opposing hysterectomies and the surgical removal of ovaries, which he claimed were then "being performed at epidemic rates."

"Many seem to see it as a panacea for real and imagined problems. Even in Montreal medical circles, some doctors take pleasure in showing off ovaries that they keep in their vest pockets," he said. "When will this epidemic stop?"

His views on breast surgery had also changed with time. "I've become much more conservative," he allowed, "but also more daring. I now operate on cases which before I never would have risked." Diagnosing breast diseases, he confessed, "often cause me great anxiety, and in spite of more than 30 years' experience I sometimes have the greatest difficulty in trying to determine what's wrong. Even the best doctors can complete their diagnosis, operate only to find that their diagnosis is wrong." Hingston believed in early detection, operating early and in being ruthless in the removal of tissue that is in contact with the diseased area. "Don't just remove the breast, remove the skin covering; go deep inside and work it out," he would tell his students. "But protect the nerves, veins and arteries." Nothing about the female anatomy was foreign to him. At one meeting of the Medico-Chirurgical Society Hingston showed up with a five-inch candle which he had removed from the bladder of a woman who, he reported, "had been using it for purposes of sensual gratification."

"On the last occasion, which to her, would be a memorable one, it slipped from her finger and was seen no more," *The Canada Medical Record* wrote at length about the incident. "After successively examining the vagina, the rectum and the bladder, Dr. Hingston located the foreign body completely within the latter organ. [The patient only knew it had gone 'somewhere down there.'] He removed portions of it with bullet forceps, but owing to the softness of the wax, those portions were inconsiderable. He therefore ordered the patient to hospital, where after chloroform had been administered, he succeeded in removing the whole of the candle, the longest piece measuring five-and-a-half inches in length. The most interesting feature of the case was, Dr. Hingston remarked, the facility with which he could manipulate his finger and an instrument upon it, through the urethra. "There was very little suffering experienced afterwards from the operation."

Hingston and his wife were present on October 8, 1895 as the former premier, Joseph-Adolphe Chapleau, now Quebec's lieutenant governor, inaugurated Université Laval's new building on St. Denis Street, "not only

as a school of science, but at the same time, a school of belief." The building still stands as the Athanase-David Pavilion, the administrative centre for
Université du Québec à Montréal. "After years of troubles, complete har-
mony appears to be restored, and it was a magnificent spectacle when 2,000
people assembled in the spacious hall to celebrate the completion of the fine
new building which is a delight to the friends of Catholic higher education,"
The Gazette reported the following morning. In truth, the new university
could not afford modern medical equipment and its medical faculty had fall-
en about ten years behind McGill University and its new hospital, the Royal
Victoria, which opened in 1893.

On November, 5, 1895 Hingston was honoured at the testimonal dinner
at the Windsor Hotel described in the prologue of this book celebrating his
knighthood. Taking note of the occasion, *The Canada Medical Record* observed that "The large and representative character of the gathering, as well
as the speeches of the various speakers, showed how fully all were in accord
with the recognition by the Queen of the merits, professional and otherwise,
of the guest of the evening, and that the distinguished honour conferred on
Doctor Hingston was regarded also as an honour conferred on the entire
profession in this province."

Two days after the banquet Prime Minister MacKenzie Bowell came to
Montreal to recruit Hingston as a Conservative candidate in the Montreal
Centre by-election that had been called for December 27. Bowell was the
fourth Conservative prime minister in three years and was faced with having
to call a general election. Although Bowell didn't trust Catholics, he found
himself having to defend French-speaking Roman Catholics deprived of
their rights in Manitoba. If he wished to remain in office, he needed a cred-
ible English-speaking Roman Catholic candidate from Quebec who would
support him.

Volumes have been written about the Manitoba School Question. In a
nutshell, it was a test of provincial rights. Created as a bilingual province in
1870, Manitoba now wanted to abandon its French-language minority by
shutting down Catholic schools. The Privy Council declared the move un-
consitutional and ordered the province to give Catholic schools a share of its
grant money for educational purposes. Manitoba refused, prompting the
federal government to step in. That opened the thorny issue of federal intrusion into education, until then – and still – a provincial responsibility. It was
a hot potato that no one wished to touch, let alone digest. Manitoba tossed
the issue to Ottawa; Ottawa bounced it to London, and now London had
ruled. If Bowell introduced remedial legislation to appease French-Canada,

he was damned in Orange Ontario and the West; if he didn't, he was condemned in Catholic Quebec.

The government was in disarray. Several of Bowell's Quebec ministers had already resigned from cabinet over his mismanagment of the portfolio. Then John Joseph Curran, who had represented Montreal Centre for fourteen years, was named to the bench, leaving yet another parliamentary seat vacant. With a general election looming, Bowell was desperate. He needed a prominent Quebec Roman Catholic to fill the vacancy. He needed Hingston. Hingston had never been a man to shrink from a challenge, and he didn't now. He agreed to run, but on his own terms. "At this hour to say no would be to show the white feather," Hingston said. "I beg to assure you, this is a quality with which I am not familiar."

Bowell needed a champion; what he got in Hingston was a mere standard bearer. It is a matter of conjecture just how conservative in party politics Hingston really was. He had always been closer to the reformers in his thinking, and if had he not been a Catholic, would probably have been a Liberal.

"[Hingston] does not believe the race belongs to the swift. He has stipulated the expenses of the campaign shall be met by others , that he shall not be expected to canvas, and that he be called an independent," *The Moncton Transcript* advised its readers. "Hingston, evidently, like a typical Tory, prefers the people at a distance."

Running against him, the Liberals fielded James (the People's Jimmy) McShane, who sat on the city council when Hingston was mayor, and who was himself elected mayor of Montreal in 1891. In office, McShane turned a blind eye to corruption at City Hall and was defeated in 1893. He was a sore loser who refused to accept the verdict and took the chain of office with him. It took a court order to force him to hand it over to his successor, Alphonse Desjardins. Ever the blowhard, McShane sidestepped the religious and linguistic issues and insisted on turning the by-election campaign into a class contest. Who, he asked, could better represent the interests of the "the honest workingmen from Griffintown" – a petty aristocrat like Hingston or a common man such as himself – "The People's Jimmy?"

Hingston, for his part, invoked "a spirit of patriotism, not partyism," and asked constituents to "think not of what is in the best interests of the party, but think of what is in the best interests of the country."

Just as the campaign got underway the president of the Montreal City & District Savings Bank, hardware tycoon Senator Edward Murphy, died of a heart attack on the street outside St. Patrick's Church on December 5, 1895.

YE TRUE KNIGHT TO YE RESCUE

An editorial cartoon incorrectly depicts Hingston's victory over his opponent
James McShane in their 1896 by-election contest

The board of directors named Hingston the bank's twelfth president, which, depending on how you looked at it, enhanced or diminished his prestige in the contest. Prominent Conservative ministers campaigned vigorously on his behalf. The minister of public works, Joseph-Aldéric Ouimet, the party's French-Canadian lieutenant, spoke at a rally on December 18; Sir Charles Tupper, a father of Canadian Confederation and now Her Majesty's High Commissioner to the United Kingdom, had returned from London as the prospective saviour of the Conservative party. Tupper spoke at a public meeting in St. Lawrence Hall the day after Christmas and the evening before the vote. Hingston remained at home with his family for the holiday. He had made it clear he would run, but not campaign. He could not, and would not, he said, "stand at the street corner buttonholing people for their votes."

It would, he explained, be unethical and dishonourable for him to solicit votes from people who knew his name but liked neither him nor his politics. Still, bookies offered 2-1 odds in Hingston's favour.

On the day of the by-election, December 27, Prime Minister Bowell observed his seventy-second birthday. There was little to celebrate.

Hingston lost.

What was remarkable was not Hingston's was defeat, but that he had done so well, losing by only 326 votes. McShane's victory would be short-lived; he was a Member of Parliament for less than six months, losing to the city's chief Crown prosecutor, Michael Joseph Francis Quinn, in the general election called on June 23, 1896.

In the long run, Hingston fared much better. Four days after losing the by-election, he was appointed to the Senate, filling the seat left vacant when Edward Murphy died.

"The appointment of William Hales Hingston was a barefaced proceeding," complained *The Globe*. "It would seem that he was bribed to take the field with the promise of a senatorship."

Hingston took his seat in the Upper Chamber on January 7, 1896, and from his secure vantage point watched Bowell's administration implode in spectacular fashion. The same day seven more ministers resigned; Sir Charles Tupper was sworn in as prime minister and faced the impossible task of breathing life into a comatose government. Hingston rose in the Senate for the first time on January 16 on a question of privilege in order to complain about what *The Globe* had written about him.

"There is not one word of truth in [*The Globe's*] statement. At no time during the contest previously or subsequently until Dec. 31, did I directly or indirectly approach any member of the government with reference to a seat in this house. It is true that on Dec. 31, a telegram from the head of the government offering me a seat in this chamber was received by me, and that same evening or the next morning, I sent a telegram accepting. That is the beginning and the end of it."

Hingston's denial was, to say the least, disingenuous. By the time Bowell approached Hingston, it was common gossip that the candidate would be rewarded. Bowell had been warned that unless he landed Hingston he would lose other ministers. Finance Minister George Foster said that in the weeks leading up to the by-election, the prime minister "peddled cabinet positions all about Quebec – everyone seeing what he was doing – getting a refusal each time, & so lowering the credit of his cabinet stock." Even Hingston's son, Willie, didn't believe his father, and added his own spin to the story.

"What really brought about my father's defeat was the rumour that if he won a seat in the Commons he would be denied a seat in the Senate, which was his proper place. So in voting against him, they really were voting for his elevation to the Senate."

In June, Sir Wilfrid Laurier and his Liberals, on a campaign to take "the sunny way" out of the Manitoba crisis, were swept into office. The new government worked out a compromise with Manitoba's premier, Thomas Greenway, to allow French-language instruction only if "ten of the pupils in any school speak the French language" and only for the last half hour of each school day. A Roman Catholic teacher could not be hired to teach unless a minimum of forty Catholic children were enrolled in a urban school or ten in a rural school. The Liberals saw it as a reasonable and satisfactory compromise. Hingston didn't. In the Speech from the Throne on April 1 the government congratulated itself on the settlement of the Manitoba School question. Hingston rose to reply.

"A settlement is supposed to mean something final," Hingston complained. "Yet by members of the government we are told it is not final."

"You might as well put a worm on a hook and ask is it satisfied because it ceases to wriggle," Hingston quipped as he defended the need for a religious framework to education. "Where no religion prevails in school, something more negative is sure to enter," he said. Laurier's compromise, he objected, threatened to deprive Manitoba's children of "the knowledge of Divine things."

"When the parent desires that knowledge to be imparted it is an injustice, and to whom? It is an injustice to God; it is an injustice to parents, and it is an injustice to the children and it is an injustice to the civil societies."

If he had to choose between mathematics and classical education or religion, for his own children, Hingston declared, "I would say, if choose I must, then classics and mathematics would disappear."

"Religion must be in the heart; it must be taught. It is the sacred right and duty of parents to bring up their children. You have not the advantage that I have of being in a French-Canadian community where the Bon Dieu is everywhere. Everything in the house of the French Canadian is intended to remind them of God and everything in their teachings and books is of the wisdom and mercy and unbounded love of God."

Quebec, he said, offered the model for the solution in Manitoba. "Leave Catholics to their instruction, and Protestants to theirs, with a supervising board overriding both." In Quebec, he said, the board interferes only when invited and he could remember it having been "maybe once in twenty years." His maiden speech in the Senate was the most substanial he made in his eleven years as a senator. In fact, his career as a senator was rather undistinguished. He saw his role as being "a moral conscience", contributing "to the dignity and usefulness of the Upper House." Hingston was an orator, not a debater, and spoke only when questions that directly affected his constituency, such as redistribution, health or banking bills were being discussed. He was often sarcastic. When, for example, Senator Lieut.-Colonel Charles Arkel Boulton, commander of Boulton's Scouts during the 1885 Rebellion, endorsed free trade with the United States, and suggested that import tariffs hurt the Canadian economy, Hingston replied that Boulton was "so severely logical I found it difficult to follow his argument – one in particular. The more we export and the less we import the worse for the country. I was under the impression that the more our exports exceed our imports, the greater the wealth of the country. In other words, the more we earn and the less we spend, the richer we become. Whenever I have leisure, I shall be glad to sit at the feet of my honourable friend and learn those lessons in political economy, which at present [as the president of a bank] are new to me."

Hingston's father-in-law, Donald Macdonald, died at his house in Montreal on June 10, 1896. The funeral was held in Alexandria, Ontario. The local paper reported "upwards of two thousand people were present, showing the high esteem in which the deceased gentleman was held, "but that "owing to the forty hours devotion being in progress in St. Einnan's Cathedral, the services were short. Among those present were noticed Sir William Hingston and his four sons." Curiously, Margaret isn't mentioned as being at her father's funeral.

At the end of August, Hingston spoke to a meeting of the Canadian Medical Association meeting at the Hôtel-Dieu. It was a rambling talk which reviewed changes in surgical thought and treatment he had witnessed in the past 36 years. The full text of his remarks would today only be of interest to an academic, but the speech served to show both how attuned and how out of touch he had become to the advances in medicine, how far he had drifted from the mainstream. He talked about the advances in brain surgery, how he could now trephine, or cut into the skull for epilepsy, paralysis, depressed bones and tumours "using a large circular saw for the purpose... the success which followed sometimes quite beyond my expectations." He talked about a new disease called appendicitis that had surfaced – he didn't think it advisable to operate, but when an abcess formed, he opened it but "did not deem it advisable to grope in all directions." He warned against the indiscriminate removal of the spleen, suggesting young doctors had become impatient, eager to cut patients open because they could not diagnose "in the twinkling of an eye, the nature of the malady that an older, more experienced doctor might diagnose, or they themselves, with experience. The knife should never be used to unravel the enigma, however puzzling," he said. It was his treatment of wounds that showed how dated he had become. He still took exception to the use of Lister's carbolic spray and "had stopped its use," reported *The Montreal Medical Journal*: "his experience of it was not satisfactory." In fact, before each operation he still recommended a 20-minute scrubdown with green soap using four separate basins of water.

The British Medical Association held its 65th annual meeting in North America for the first time in Montreal in September, 1897, the year of Queen Victoria's Jubilee. It was a huge gathering of more than one thousand doctors from the United Kingdom, the United States and Canada, the first international convention on so large a scale in Montreal. The most prominent delegate was Joseph Lister, elevated that year to the peerage and now known as Baron Lister of Lyme Regis. Prime Minister Wilfrid Laurier arrived the night before to open the meeting in spectacular fashion, sailing back from the Jubilee celebrations in England. Hingston was sidelined during the convention, serving as one of eleven vice-presidents. He was was still respected as a family doctor but no longer a luminary in the medical world. Presiding over the convention was Thomas George Roddick, the Clinical Professor of Surgery at McGill, who had promoted the use of Lister's techniques. The keynote speaker was William Osler, the brilliant surgeon at Johns Hopkins University in Baltimore who was bringing new scientific methods into general practice. It was Trefflé-Rottot, not Hingston, who welcomed the guests to the session at Université Laval and a French doctor from Paris who delivered the major French-language paper on Louis Pasteur.

The rebuff must have been painful to Hingston, who watched from the wings as Lister was given an honorary degree. Had Hingston looked through his windows he would have seen the night-time reception on the campus across the street where "thousands and thousands of incandescent lights trembled amidst the foliage of the trees and outlined the grounds, while festoons of Chinese lanterns lined the avenue." Hingston's satisfaction was to be found elsewhere, in the newspapers, between the lines of the extensive convention coverage. For that week, as doctors from around the world began arriving in Montreal, there was another outbreak of smallpox in the city. This time, however, the threat of a deadly epidemic was contained quickly as "the crush to get vaccinated continued in all quarters of the city unabated." Even if it wasn't publicly acknowledged, that was Hingston's most noteworthy achievement. "The latest reports prove decisively that the disease has been fought to a most satisfactory conclusion," reported the *Montreal Medical Journal*.

Another run on the Montreal City & District Savings Bank in October had Hingston making headlines again. He was called upon to defuse the panic which this time had been started when a depositor saw a story in a French-language newspaper read about the failure of La Banque D'Espagne (The Bank of Spain) and mistakenly belived it was La Banque D'Épargne (The Montreal City & District Savings Bank) that had gone under.

Hingston was undoubtedly a civic icon, and like icons, people revere them even if they are a bit old-fashioned. Wherever he and Lady Hingston went, their movement was dutifully recorded in the society columns. On Friday, January 8, 1898 for example, you would have found Lady Hingston at a reception for two hundred women given by Archbishop Bruchési in his palace. "As each lady was announced, she was received by his Grace with high bred courtesy and a few kindly words, and after kissing the episcopal ring, passed on."

Ten days later, buglers announced the arrival of Sir William and Lady Hingston and their nineteen-year-old son, Donald, as they stepped from their carriage at the Windsor Hotel to attend Governor-General Aberdeen's Historical Fancy Dress Ball. The affair was being held to raise money to convert Château Ramezay into a museum, and few social events in the city's history have been as opulent. *The Herald* billed the soirée as "a resurrection and idyllic re-incarnation of the stately and stirring [French] period. For one brief night, the phantom glory of New France blazed forth again." Hingston, who could be playful when he wanted to be, chose a costume that historically justified his role as the owner of Le Moyne's property at Varennes. He came as Charles Le Moyne, dressed to the nines in an eighteenth century black velvet surcoat richly trimmed with silver braid, knee britches, stockings and powdered period wig, and according to one observer, "filled the role with courtly grace." Margaret came as the First Baroness of Longueuil in "white satin petticoat covered with chantilly lace flounces and paniers of black satin lined with mauve brocade." Donald was disguised as Paul Le Moyne de Maricourt, the fourth of Le Moyne's twelve remarkable sons, the one member of the family who historically had great influence among the Iroquois.

Sir William continued to accumulate honours. On June 22, 1898, the

Dressed for Governor-General Aberdeen's Historical Fancy Dress Ball,
Sir William as Charles Le Moyne

*Dressed for Governor-General Aberdeen's Historical Fancy Dress Ball,
Lady Hingston as the First Baroness of Longueuil*

Dressed for Governor-General Aberdeen's Historical Fancy Dress Ball,
Donald Hingston, at 19, as Paul Le Moyne de Maricourt

University of Ottawa gave him an honorary degree. The exercises were opened by a selection of the Cecilian Society and a cantata by the students and the Academic Hall "was crowded to the doors." Addressing the graduating class in what the *Ottawa Journal* called "a neat speech," Hingston talked about the advantages of a higher education, and "exhorted the boys to be true to themselves, and their efforts must meet with success."

Hingston was undoubtedly gratified that summer when his namesake, William, who as a youngster had demonstrated piety unusual for a boy his age decided to become a priest. He was accepted into the Society of Jesus at Sault-au-Récollet in the summer of 1898 and spent his first year studying classics at Florissant, near St. Louis, Missouri.

Donald was studying medicine at Université Laval. Basil was in his second year of humanities at Loyola of Montreal, a member of the college's first student class. Among his junior classmates was Georges Philias Vanier, the future governor-general of Canada. Handsome and spoiled, Basil was "a very clever, popular boy of unusual charm," who excelled in athletics and, according to one report card, also "excelled in studies if and whenever he chose to apply himself."

Aileen went off to London to attend Roehampton School. Only nine-year-old Harold was still at home.

Hingston turned seventy in 1899. He was still vigorous, tall, fit and erect if a somewhat overbearing figure. That same year six of Montreal's richest men opened the Mount Royal Club in the former residence of Canada's third prime minister, Sir John Abbott. The club was intended as an exclusive sanctum for the city's commercial barons, but membership was also based on "what a person stood for, what he had achieved, and what he had contributed to the country." Hingston was one of just three Roman Catholics invited to join – the other two being Lord Shaughnessy, an American-born railway baron who had built the Canadian Pacific Railway into one of the world's leading multinational corporations, and Senator Louis Forget, a stockbroker who was one of the ten richest French-Canadians in the country and one of the club's charter members.

At the end of October, Canada sent the first of 8,300 troops to help the British fight the Boers in South Africa. It was Canada's first foray into a foreign war and stirred latent French-Canadian nationalist feelings in Quebec where public opinion was against support for a British colonial adventure. The war gave rise to a number of patriotic endeavours in the English-speaking community. Margaret Folson Murray, wife of a McGill philosophy professor, went to England shortly after the war was declared and where she met a number women who were "stirred by the Boer War and anxious to be of service." Murray approached Lady Hingston and asked her to become a founding member of a women's patriotic group, the Imperial Order of the Daughters of the Empire. At a meeting in the Windsor Hotel on February 13, 1900, the organization at Lady Hingston's suggestion, adopted as its motto, "One Flag, One Throne, One Empire." The IODE's initial objective was to assist returning Boer War veterans and their families, and to provide perpetual care for war graves in South Africa. In September, Sir William was appointed to the board of governors of the Victorian Order of Nurses and in October, Lady Hingston travelled to London with Harold and Aileen to visit the women's branch of the National Service Department. They stayed at St. Ermins Hotel on Caxton Street in Westminister, where Harold dutifully scrawled a note to his brother Donald about a family excursion to France. "In Paris, Aileen and I and another lady went up on Iphul [sic] tower. We went up on the top. It was very windy and very cold, so we settled to go down. PS: It was very stormy and 2 men were washed against the railings. Another broke his glasses." Harold also wrote his father about a tour through Parliament and the Tower of London where he "saw where the prisoners carved their names and where all of Henry VIII's wives had been killed." At Westminister he saw James Simpson's statue, "the man who invented chloroform. Aileen says you knew him. Good bye, your devoted son, Harold."

While his family was in Europe, Sir William had come down with a severe attack of influenza which left him weakened and bedridden for more than a month. He was, however, well enough to attend an event in his honour at Collège St. Marie on December 4, 1900 where students serenaded him with a charming song composed for the occasion that left him in better spirits: *Le Docteur Idéal*.

C'est pour l'art qu'il travaille
Et pour l'humanité;
Aux pauvres sur la paille,
Il fait la charité. Il est plein de science –
Plusieurs fois diplomé
En Angleterre, en France,
Et partout estimé.
Existe-t-il sur terre ce docteur idéal?
Vraiment ... la belle affaire. Il est à Montréal."

Old age in Canada is green, an active vigorous old age

William Hales Hingston

CHAPTER FOURTEEN
Vigorous Old Age

Hingston never thought of retiring. Even as he grew older, he refused to alter his daily routine. Except for the days he was in Ottawa, each morning found him erect in his pew midway up the right aisle at St. Patrick's where he took communion at Mass at a time when frequent communion was rare even among devout Catholics. After church he walked to his office at the bank in Old Montreal, then ate lunch at the Mount Royal Club before spending the afternoon seeing patients or teaching. He easily straddled the divide between French and English in the city. At Varennes, especially, he was part of the French-Canadian community; in Montreal, his English-speaking associates gave him the position he craved.

Queen Victoria died in January 1901; her reign had lasted sixty-three years and no one was indifferent to news of her death. Hingston called her "the greatest monarch probably that ever occupied a throne." In September, when Victoria's grandson and his wife, the Duke and Duchess of Cornwall and York, arrived in Montreal on September 18 the Hingstons were in the receiving line, but they chose not to follow the royal couple to engagements in Ottawa, choosing instead to remain in Montreal for the opening of the social season by attending the Montreal Hunt's breakfast three days later.

Donald obtained his medical degree from Laval in June and began his internship at the Hôtel-Dieu working with Sir William. Donald was twenty-three, the same age at which his father had obtained his own degree. Now there were two Doctor Hingstons in the family, but critical differences between father and son soon emerged. It is doubtful Donald ever told Sir William to his face, but he thought his father was a much better executive and financier than he was a surgeon.

Sir William observed his fiftieth anniversary as a doctor on January 8th, 1902. To mark the occasion the parishioners of St. Patrick's presented him with a portrait painted by J. Colin Forbes. The canvas depicts Hingston with his pince-nez casually hanging around his neck. It reveals an aging man with an air of pointed reserve, someone you would instinctively respect. *The Star* reported that the presentation was "rendered more momentous by the fact that everyone concedes to Sir William a first place in the ranks of the profession he has so long and faithfully adorned." Hingston didn't much admire the likeness. The artist, he said, "didn't leave out one vertical line." He thought Forbes had made him look too old and had the painting relegated to an upstairs landing. Hingston was beginning to feel his age, but still in fine form. "Old age in Canada is green, an active vigorous old age," he enthused. "When the tree falls, as in time it must, it falls like a mature ash, which with all its tender foliage meets the ground."

Many of Hingston's friends and contemporaries were also beginning to fall. Word came from England in February 1902 that Lord Dufferin had died. In August, Hingston's trusted assistant, Doctor Joseph-Antoine Stanislas Brunelle, died of a heart attack while on holiday in Mountain View, New York. He was only fifty. Then, the next day, Henri-Jacques Barbeau, the shrewd financier who had been manager of the Montreal City & District Savings Bank, dropped dead. He was sixty-nine. Hingston was a pallbearer at both funerals. For the first time in his life he felt incapacitated, but his sense of loss had more to do with his grieving than with any doubt that he could carry on without them. That summer Sir William was named to the Ottawa Improvement Commission, a forerunner of the National Capital Commission. It was a patronage appointment, and he rarely attended meetings.

Sir William Hingston
as painted by J. Colin Forbes

Aileen returned from Paris in the autumn of 1902. She had grown into an elegant, graceful young woman with a dreamy gaze and a vivid imagination, "When her face was in repose," one contemporary wrote, "a certain wistfulness of expression was never absent." Aileen made her social debut by being presented to the fourth Earl and Countess of Minto. She was now a mature, ethical being who helped her mother stage a successful charity ball for the Montreal Maternity Hospital on

Wednesday February 11, 1903, where she appeared in a "pale green crêpe de Chine gown," among "a crowd too great for absolute comfort." She found a job as a secretary at the Hospital for Incurables in Notre-Dame-de-Grace. Her first short stories, *Père Jean*, *When it Came* and *A Christmas Story* were published that spring – slight, serene tales that showed literary promise. She also served as her father's filial consort, traveling with him to the opening of Parliament on March 11, 1903, meeting eminent people and tending to his Senate correspondence. During that session, Parliament passed a Private Member's Bill banning cigarette smoking in Canada. Under pressure from the tobacco lobby, the bill was later

Aileen Hingston as a debutante

withdrawn on a technicality. Hingston had been prepared to steer it through the Senate for approval. Cigarettes, in his view were, "to youth generally hurtful, sometimes disastrous, never beneficial." Asked in what way and on what organs, he replied, "The digestive, nervous and circulatory, chiefly."

Donald, who had spent a year in England studying at many of the same clinics as his father, wrote his exams and became a member of the Royal College of Surgeons in Edinburgh in 1903. He sailed home in May aboard the *Umbria*, the last of the Cunard steamships to be equipped with auxiliary sails.

During the spring legislative session of 1904, Hingston introduced amendments to a controversial piece of legislation that would have given the minister of the militia arbitrary powers to hire and fire officers. In speaking against the legislation, Hingston said "it would be a great misfortune to give to any individual, on becoming minister of the militia, fresh from a contested election with all the warmth and excitement it engenders, the power of dismissing without cause, a man who might have worn his majesty's uniform for many years. I think it would be most unfair." Hingston's amendments to the Bill were defeated, but shortly afterwards the government reconsidered, and they were implemented. Writing to Hingston, the Secretary of State said his suggestion "was so just and so fair, I decided it should be accepted.

The deputy-minister strenuously opposed the proposal, considering that in military matters arbitrary powers should be retained. I dissented from that doctrine, and subsequently saw [the minister of the militia] Frederick Borden, and told him that your amendment should be made in the direction you proposed. It was removed from the bill."

In May, Hingston took Aileen, Basil and Harold to the Louisiana Purchase Exposition in St. Louis, Missouri – more commonly known as the St. Louis World's Fair – where they spent most of their time wandering through the twelve exhibition palaces. Hingston was particularly taken with the Palace of Electricity, where x-rays were being demonstrated. In October, he and Lady Hingston went to Rome with Aileen for an audience with the new Pope, Pius X. Aileen was impressed by the peasant pope's warmth and gutsy humanity. The Pope presented Hingston with the black plumed hat and breast star of a Knight Commander of St. Gregory the Great, a meritorious service award created in 1831 by Pope Gregory XVI. They sailed home on the Allan Liner, *Bavarian*.

Science had begun to outstrip applied medicine, and each day Donald was making Hingston painfully aware that he had not kept abreast of the phenomenal evolutionary changes in medicine. Hingston admitted as much to a reporter who interviewed him upon his return from Europe. "Surgery is making such rapid progress that it is very difficult to assimilate the knowledge that is being acquired as the result of special work in the various spheres in which men are actively engaged pushing investigations," he told *The Herald*. "There is always much to learn."

Then, changing the subject, he said he preferred to talk about the deplorable state of Montreal's streets. "I saw nowhere in Great Britain or on the continent roads in so bad a condition as they are in Montreal," he griped, "The roads in Europe, generally speaking, are as smooth as a billiard table. I marveled at their perfection."

As time went on, Hingston spent less time at the hospital. He is remembered as a prim, amiable old gent, who went out of his way to be sociable to young doctors. Emmett Mullally was surprised to discover that when he arrived from Prince Edward Island to open a practice in Montreal, Hingston was the first to call on him. "He was a gentleman with a generous sense of public service," Mullaly recalled.

Hingston confided in his eldest son, William, who was often called upon to relay to the rest of the family what Sir William was thinking. He sometimes worried that his children, especially Donald and Basil, were being seduced by the easy life. Whenever a dispute among siblings arose, William was usually called to mediate. In the autumn of 1904 Donald went back to Europe to study on a fellowship, and on the basis of the bills he was sending home, Hingston became alarmed that his son was becoming financially irresponsible.

In one letter to Donald, Lady Hingston suggested he find cheaper living accommodation in Paris. "Perhaps No 8 rue Clement Marot might be a good place. Your father was staggered when he got a notice of another 65 pounds. I suppose you can scarcely realize how the money goes but notice came about three weeks ago for 30 pounds and a few days afterwards for 60 pounds. Then the 65. Of course, your letter explains that the last is your provision for Paris. I imagine you to be as careful as you can – traveling is of course expensive. Your father keeps up with his work pretty well and looks vigorous."

Sir William does look vigorous in the striking 1905 portrait of him painted by Joseph-Charles Franchère, which today hangs in the Hôtel-Dieu Hospital museum. Surgical gloves had still not been introduced, and in the painting Hingston is seen operating in ordinary shirt and cuffs with his bare hands. Hingston at seventy, his son Donald said, not altogether approvingly, would still perform surgery without his eye glasses. "There was no stiffness, no self-consciousness in his manner, but complete simplicity," William would write. "He was a man whose very appearance inevitably attracted attention... even those who almost any day could see him on the street would turn to watch as he walked by, and at medical conventions he became at once the centre of attraction."

Hingston was in Ottawa whenever the Senate was in session, and took a particular interest in conjugal law. In those days, the Senate held divorce hearings to decide whether marriages should be dissolved. Hingston was no prude, but he was regarded by his fellow senators as a puritanical moralist. One particularly sordid divorce case involved a Francis Shaw suing his wife, Hariette Baker. Several different men were named as correspondents. It seems Mrs. Shaw pleasured more than one of her lovers at the same time. During the hearing in May 1906, Hingston proposed an amendment that would have allowed Shaw to re-marry, but not her. Hingston argued that "an obstinately vicious woman" shouldn't be free to marry again and "blast the happiness of an honest man. To whitewash women of that kind and to let them go forth into the community to become wives of honest men should be prevented," Hingston reasoned.

Senator Michael Sullivan, a medical doctor from Kingston, and like Hingston, a Roman Catholic wasn't as reactionary. "The duty of a Roman

Catholic is to refrain from putting his oar in this business at all. Leave it to the wicked Protestants," Sullivan countered. "We should not meddle with the matter in any way. If other people choose to commit sin, let them do it. We cannot restrain them." The Senate agreed with Sullivan, and Hingston's motion was defeated.

In 1906 Hingston was elected president of the Montreal Parks and Playgrounds Association, then in August the Doctors Hingston, father and son, went to Paris for the International Surgical Congress. Much to his delight, Sir William was unexpectedly elected president of the convention, an honour he had never imagined. After the meeting Donald continued to Switzerland and Hingston returned to London where, pleased but exhausted, he checked into the Alexandra Hotel on Hyde Park Corner. He had a painful stye and was homesick. As in almost every letter of his that survives, he was fretting about finances. Typical is the one he wrote to Lady Hingston from London.

> "The Congress International was in every respect a success. I was overwhelmed by the attention I received. Paris is very expensive. My bill is a curiosity. I am back in London where things are NOT cheap, but a porter has looked after my letters, and luggage and it would not be fair to go elsewhere. I wish I were on the banks of the St. Lawrence where I could be earning something now and spending less."

Sir William and his family at Varennes. Standing left to right: Donald, Basil, William and Aileen. Seated with Sir William are Harold and Lady Hingston

La vie est brève
un peu d'espoir
un peu de rire
et puis, bonsoir.

SIR WILLIAM HALES HINGSTON,
WRITTEN ON SENATE STATIONERY,
JANUARY 1907

CHAPTER FIFTEEN

"He Loved a Good Horse"

The third session of the Tenth Canadian Parliament resumed sitting on November 22, 1906, and although Hingston was present throughout he took no part in any of the debates. The Senate recessed for Christmas and he went home for the holiday, making an appearance at the courthouse with Lady Hingston for the Council of the Montreal Bar's annual levee on January 7. Two days later he was back in the Crimson Chamber when the sitting reconvened. He attended a dinner at the Canadian Club in Ottawa on January 20 to hear U.S. President Theodore Roosevelt's Secretary of State, Elihu Root. On Thursday, February 7, 1907, the day before Parliament adjourned, he caught the train back to Montreal and to a house full of relatives visiting from Winnipeg and New York. On February 17, the first Sunday of Lent, he went to Mass at St. James (Mary Queen of the World) Cathedral with his houseguests, Arthur and Elizabeth Bennington. That evening Hingston dined with the Benningtons at the Windsor Hotel without much of an appetite. Next morning he met his son William at the Jesuit College for breakfast, then presided over a 10 a.m. board meeting at the City & District Savings Bank, where it was noted that the bank's profits had increased 35 per cent during his tenure as president. He went on to the Mount Royal Club for lunch where he ordered the fruit plate, but "only picked at it around the edges." Complaining of indigestion he excused himself and walked to the Smoking Room. There, in front of the magnificent black onyx fireplace with its bronze spiral columns wound with garlands and embedded with ram heads, Hingston dozed off in a comfortable chair. A club servant discovered him a few minutes later in a trance "as though from the effects of a strong drug." Donald was called from the Hôtel-Dieu to attend his father, but by the time he arrived, Hingston was unconscious. He was carried from the club and down the street to his house, where William arrived to give his father Extreme Unction, the last rites of the Roman Catholic church. Shortly after nine the following morning,

February 19, William Hales Hingston died in his bed of ptomaine poisoning.

A COURTLY GENTLEMAN IS DEAD, announced *The Montreal Standard*. in bold capital letters. "It will be as a noble-hearted, pure, lofty gentleman that he will most lastingly and gratefully be remembered." SIR WILLIAM DIED AS HE WISHED: IN HARNESS TO THE VERY LAST reported *The Herald*. MORTE PRESQUE SUBITE, Cause des regrets universels," was the headline in *La Presse*. Toronto's *Saturday Night* magazine took note of his death: "Courtly, handsome and of keen intelligence and of wide culture, Sir William was a personality which all admired and many loved ... like every true son of Erin, and all round men, he loved a good horse and a clean, keen race."

Flags on Parliament Hill and at Montreal City Hall were lowered to half-staff in his memory. Archbishop Paul Bruchési sang the Requiem funeral mass at St. Patrick's Church on February 21, the day after Aileen's twenty-fourth birthday. The interior of St. Patrick's was hung with black and gold mourning banners. The funeral was unusual for the time because there were no flowers on the altar, no wreaths, no floral tributes of any kind. There were 3,000 mourners inside the church and as many as 30,000 lined the streets as the horse-drawn hearse carrying Hingston's inexpensive black cloth coffin passed by. Only a small engraved brass plaque identified the remains in the casket as those of: William Hales Hingston, 1829-1907.

"It always, as a doctor, shocked him that death should be made an occasion for display," William told news reporters afterwards. "My father loved flowers but believed they had no place beside a corpse." Hingston was buried in the family plot in Section S of Notre-Dame-des-Neiges Cemetery beneath a massive tombstone designed by the eminent Quebec sculptor, Philippe Hébert. A single word carved into the stone sums up Hingston's life-long conviction: *Credo*. I believe. Commemorative memorial medals in gold, silver and bronze designed by Hébert were issued.

*   *   *

Six months later, the same crowd of mourners returned to St. Patrick's for another Hingston family funeral. In June, Aileen, still grieving for her father, had gone to Pointe-au-Pic in the Charlevoix region to research a short story she was writing entitled *Le Croche*. Canada's foremost graphic artist, Henri Julien, the art director of the *Montreal Star*, had agreed to illustrate the book. Social custom required that she wear nothing but black for a year after her father's death and in a letter home she complained how stuffy she felt walking around a summer resort in mourning clothes. "We are the

very first of the summery colony
and if this sort of weather continues there are not likely to be
many more," she wrote to Lady
Hingston, "It is is very cold,
windy and rainy however we are
all splendidly prepared for it and
at present wearing my woollen
jersey and glad to have it. We
went for a long walk this morning and it was glorious. Such air!
I only wish you could take a little
of it, mommy dear." The weather improved, and the vacation
turned out to be idyllic – "a perfect blue sky and hot sun," with
"glorious walks" and rides in a
caleche drawn by "a perfect
beauty of a horse, which is the
envy of everyone around here."

Lady Hingston and her daughter, Aileen

In her last letter, Aileen asked her mother to send her $10 so she could
buy some "charming portières suitable for the sitting room at Varennes for
$5 a pair. I should like to bring them, and also a little table to match." Aileen
returned to Varennes from her holiday at the end of July where she joined
Lady Hingston. There, on a placid, warm Sunday afternoon, August 4, she
went sailing on the St. Lawrence with her thirty-two-year-old cousin,
Shirley Davidson, the grandson of Sir Peers Davidson, Quebec's chief justice. Young Davidson was an exceptional swimmer and all-round athlete, a
popular man about town who had been a member of the 1895 Stanley Cup-
winning Montreal Amateur Athletic Association hockey team.

They never returned.

Their skiff, with its sails set and both paddles in place, was found empty
later that Sunday off Deslauriers Island. Donald offered a $200 reward for
the recovery of the bodies. Five days later they were located ten kilometres
downstream. "My sister Aileen was accidentally drowned about 11 o'clock
on Sunday morning," Harold wrote of the loss. "I think my sister who was
steering the skiff must have lost her balance and fallen overboard and
Davidson left the boat and went to her rescue. The skiff drifted ashore with
the sail tied and completely dry."

The family was haunted by gossip of a double suicide. Stories circulated that Lady Hingston had refused Aileen and Shirley to marry because Davidson was an Anglican. The family certainly discussed the rumours. A notation on a scrap of paper found among Harold Hingston's possessions states "there was chat that Aileen and Davidson had a suicide pact." Other speculation had it that Davidson suffered a heart attack while manning the oars, fell overboard, and that Aileen drowned trying to save him.

The bodies were brought back to Montreal by steamer on August 9. Hundreds of curiosity-seekers gathered at the wharf as the sealed coffins were placed in a hearse and conveyed to the Hingston house on Sherbrooke Street.

Aileen's funeral was held at St. Patrick's on Saturday, August 10; Archbishop Bruchési blessed her casket as it was taken from the church to be buried beside her father. Davidson's funeral was held later the same day at St. George's Anglican Church.

In the weeks following the funerals, Lady Hingston's second son, Donald, added to her distress. He had fallen in love with Lillian Peterson, the delicate twenty-five-year-old daughter of the chief engineer for the Canadian Pacific Railway. Lady Hingston was less than thrilled by her son's romantic prospects. Lillian was an Anglican. Bruchési had banned mixed marriages in the archdiocese, but Donald was determined. To Lady Hingston's embarrassment, her son's engagement was the talk of the town.

Dr Donald Hingston to Brave Wrath of Archbishop Bruchési to Wed ran one headline in *The Gazette*'s society pages. Willie came to his brother's rescue. He persuaded Lillian to become a Roman Catholic and instructed her in the faith. On March 5, 1908, Donald and Lillian were married at St. Peter's Roman Catholic Church in Goderich, Ont. It was a small wedding; Basil and Harold were the groomsmen. "Owing to fact that the families of both bride and groom are in mourning, the event was a quiet one," noted *The Goderich Signal*. "Dr. and Mrs. Hingston left in the afternoon for their honeymoon trip which will include a three weeks' visit to Bermuda before returning to Montreal to reside. During her brief residence in this town, Miss Peterson won the hearty esteem of the townspeople, and her departure is deeply regretted in the circle in which she moved."

The couple returned to Montreal, moving in with Lady Hingston, who never warmed to her daughter-in-law. Donald and Lillian would have five daughters, Osla Margaret, Mary Elizabeth, Katherine Isabel, Andrea Aileen, and Cynthia Anne. Lillian was a talented artist who took up painting as an ideal way, she said, "to forget all your troubles." She specialized in floral portraits and her work was exhibited regularly at the Royal Canadian Academy.

Lady Hingston, who would have agreed with Chesterton's view that what was needed was not a church that moved with the world, but a church that moved the world, plunged into her volunteer work. She was actively involved in the planning of the First International Eucharistic Congress to be held in North America. More than 200,000 people, including foreign cardinals, bishops and priests took part in the gathering which opened in September 1910. Then she became involved with the Canadian Eucharistic Congress, held in Montreal a few years later. Among her other causes were the Catholic Literature League, the Catholic Theatre Guild, and the Catholic Womens' League of Canada. She was especially proud of Willie, who was nearing the end of his studies for the priesthood. His letters to his mother show he had no misgivings about his choice of vocation, but in one postcard sent after he had gone off on a religious retreat, he reported that he was "unfatigued and full of good resolutions" but allowed that "the taking of vows is easier than the keeping."

On May 29, 1911, all the family gathered in the Montreal suburb of Notre-Dame-de-Grace for the dedication of an avenue in Hingston's memory when Balmoral Street was duly rechristened Hingston Avenue. The Université de Montréal also honoured Hingston by establishing a medical scholarship in his name.

Two months later, on July 30, Willie was ordained a Jesuit priest at the Church of the Immaculate Conception and celebrated his first High Mass at St. Patrick's Church on August 6. He then left Montreal that autumn to complete his studies at St. Mary's Hall in Canterbury. From the moment he was ordained, it was obvious that Willie would be a good Jesuit and a fine priest.

Harold, now in early twenties, had become an accomplished sportsman and a popular man about town. By 1912 he had become president of the boxing and wrestling club at the Montreal Amateur Athletic Association.

At the end of May, 1913, Lady Hingston and the entire family sailed to England for Basil's wedding to Berthe Larocque on June 10 at Westminister Cathedral. William married them. As it turned out, it would be the only marriage that any of her sons made of which Lady Hingston approved. Basil's wife came from a pedigreed French-Canadian family whose ancestors included Abraham Martin, the farmer who owned the Plains of Abraham in Quebec City before it became a battlefield. Her grandfather, François-Antoine Chartier Larocque, was one of the founders of the City & District Savings Bank, and her maternal grandfather, Jean-Louis Beaudry, succeeded

Sir William's youngest son, Harold Hingston

Sir William as mayor of Montreal in 1877. Berthe's sister married the French consul in Montreal and was living in France as Baroness Stanislas d'Halewyn.

Basil and Berthe spent a two-month honeymoon in Switzerland. The rest of the family returned to Montreal on the *Laurentic* early in July. That fall Willie joined the staff at Loyola College teaching classics and philosophy, then, on January 31, 1914 in keeping with his vow of poverty, transferred the $50,000 share of his father's estate to his mother.

The Hingston's youngest son, Harold, would prove to be yet another trial for Lady Hingston. He, too, was determined to marry a Protestant, an irreverent, delicious American-borne socialite, Elizabeth (Libby) Leighton Brown. She was the effervescent daughter of Fayette Brown, a leading American athlete – who had set the U.S. record for the 100-yard dash when he was a student at Yale. Brown had moved his family to Montreal to run an insurance company.

Unlike his brother, Donald, Harold did not expect Libby to convert to Catholicism and was determined to marry her, no matter what his mother said. A formal wedding at St. Patrick's was out of the question, so Lady Hingston prevailed upon Archbishop Bruchési to grant the couple a dispensation to wed. The ceremony was private, taking place in the bishop's palace at nine o'clock in the morning on the hottest day of the year – July 31, 1915. "The bride wore a travelling suit of khaki cloth, with hat to match," read a brief item in *The Star*'s social notes, "The bridegroom was in military uniform."

By then, the Great War had begun. Lord Thomas Shaughnessy, the president of the Canadian Pacific Railway, had helped finance and raise a regiment called The Irish Rangers. Donald was the among the first to enlist on April 5, 1915, serving with the Medical Corps. While overseas, he designed a metal splint for shoulder injuries that is still used.

Harold enlisted in the Irish Canadian Rangers one month before his wedding and arrived at the front in March 1916. In the meantime, his wife Libby – pregnant with their first son – moved to London to be near her husband. It was there that she gave birth to their two children, Harold William (Pat), in May 1916 and Fayette Williams Brown George, known all his life as Billy, two years later. In his letters home to his mother, Harold revealed that as an officer, he was more concerned for his men than he was about himself. "Last night was awful, sleet all night so I slept on some straw on the floor and froze," he told his mother. "What do you think happened this afternoon? One

Dr. Donald Hingston in World War I

of my platoon developed measles and I had to send him to the hospital! However, they are not going to quarantine us thank goodness. We have not had our rations today. They have gone astray and so my men had practically no supper. I am waiting for word to leave but it may not come in which case we will have to stay here again tonight. I will bury myself in straw! I will get plenty to eat but it is hard on the men... I don't need anything. I bought a fleecelined waterproof trench coat in London which is fine so I keep fine and dry."

In April 1916, Harold wrote to his mother: "Here we are out of the trenches and we are not sorry, they are the worst trenches imaginable, all slime and muck and the smell is pretty bad..."

"I had a lot of fun with my guns. I think I accounted for a few Germans, as we saw about 12 of them in the open and of course that is 'meat' for a machine gun. I was sorry to leave my old platoon – they were a fairly tough bunch, and you grow very attached to them. We had quite a few casualties, but luckily, very few killed, and practically all the wounded were very slightly wounded. You see, if a man gets a scratch, he is put down on the official list as wounded."

Harold would not be so lucky. During the second Battle of Ypres in June,

Basil Hingston
"Tell all at home that I die happy"

shrapnel tore open his right forearm and he was sent to Endsleigh Palace Hospital in England to recuperate. He never completely recovered. "Struck off strength" in August 1917, he came home from the war shell-shocked, his marriage in ruins, and drinking heavily.

Willie signed up on December 12, 1916, and became military chaplain, first with the Rangers and then with the 66th Battery Field Artillery at Passchendaele.

Basil had hoped to avoid enlisting. He was now a father with two infant children, a two-year-old daughter, Aileen, and an infant son, also named Basil. He was working as a stockbroker in Montreal. But in August 1917, bowing to peer pressure, he joined the 244th Battalion Canadian Expeditionary Force. Just before noon on August 8, 1918, during the Battle of Amiens he led an advance of the 24th Battalion, Victoria Rifles through a wood near the French village of Guillaucourt. A German sniper shot him through the chest. "Tell all at home that I die happy," were Basil's last words, according to Military Chaplain Major J. A. Fortier, who wrote to Lady Hingston from the battlefield. "We came to him some five minutes after he had been struck by a bullet some few inches below the heart. As he saw me, his beautiful smile convinced me that he feared not death, and never have I been more conscious of a priest's power at such a moment. Basil did not suffer and the sacrifice of his life he offered most heroically. I shall say a Mass for the repose of his soul at the first opportunity. The great battle is still going on, still raging on, rather, and the possibility of saying Mass will not come until our Division is withdrawn for a rest."

Basil is buried in the Military Cemetery of Villers-Bretonneux in the French village of Fouilly. In Montreal his name inscribed on the Great War's honour roll in St. Patrick's Basilica.

Use the goods which God has entrusted to us to do something great for God and for our own souls...

LADY MARGARET MACDONALD HINGSTON

CHAPTER SIXTEEN

MOTHER AND SONS

At the time of his death, Sir William Hingston left the bulk of his estate to Lady Hingston. His lawyer, Gérard Jobin, acted as executor providing $200,000 in trust which yielded $18,000 a year – the equivalent of $400,000 at the start of the 21st century. The house and office at 1000 Sherbrooke Street were left jointly to his wife and to Donald. The property at Varennes was given to Aileen, Basil and Harold. With the deaths of Aileen and Basil, it became Harold's exclusively. Each of the five Hingston children inherited $50,000 when they came of age. Smaller amounts went to St. Patrick's, Loyola and other charities. Rumours circulated that Hingston had owned an island in the St. Lawrence that was seized after his death for non-payment of taxes but if he did, no evidence any longer exists.

With Sir William gone, public attention progressively shifted to his sons. Like many children of powerful men, Hingston's were awed by their father, and felt second-rate in comparison, but were determined both to honour his memory and at the same time, make their own contributions to the community. Medicine and education emerged as their priorities. As early as 1908 Donald had invited a number of his "Catholic confrères" to his house "to explore the possibility of building The Sir William Hingston Memorial Hospital for English-speaking Catholics." He and Helen Morrissey, an English-speaking nursing sister at the Hôtel-Dieu felt the time had come to open a facility for the city's growing English-speaking Catholic population. Both believed that no matter how good the treatment at Hôtel-Dieu, the psychological well-being of English-speaking patients was being compromised in an exclusively French-language institution.

Coincidentally, Loyola College was in financial difficulty after only twelve years of operation. Until it was put on a sound financial footing, any suggestion of a hospital among the English-speaking Catholics of Montreal was premature. Then with the outbreak of the Great War in 1914 everything was put on hold. During the war, Lady Hingston looked after the Knights of Columbus Kiosk in Phillips Square for returning soldiers and sailors and collected money for the Catholic Women's League in London. In March 1918 she was one of the organizing delegates to the Conference of Women on War Activities in Ottawa, the first national convention of women in Canada. Her contribution would be rewarded by the Imperial Order of the Daughters of the Empire which established the Margaret Hingston Chapter in her honour.

With the war coming to an end, Donald returned from overseas to teach embryology at Université Laval à Montréal. Father William Hingston also came back to Canada that spring and was at Guelph, Ontario, on June 8, 1918, when a small military unit raided the Jesuit novitiate there looking for men who might have entered the priesthood to dodge Canada's conscription laws. Hingston, a man of regal bearing, in full dress uniform, confronted the startled unit commander who was dressed in mufti. He demanded to see the warrant for the intrusion. Father Hingston later testified at the Royal Commission of Inquiry looking into the incident. The Jesuits were exonerated of all charges.

Harold Hingston came home that same June, an emotional orphan. His marriage to Libby turned out to be an unhappy match, she left him and took their two sons to Edinburgh. The other anchors in his life, his siblings, Aileen and Basil, were both dead. Shattered and still drinking, he lived for awhile out of a large linen closet on the third floor of his mother's house. It would take him ten years to come to terms with his losses.

Father Hingston was appointed Rector of Loyola College in Montreal on July 2. The school was on the verge of bankruptcy when he took over, in such dire straits that it couldn't afford a flag pole. 1917 had been the worst year in the institution's history. Perhaps naively, Willie expected that with his family connections it would be easy to raise $300,000 to keep the college going "and of this $50,000 or more could be procured outside Montreal."

In a letter enlisting the support of Quebec's lieutenant governor, Charles Fitzpatrick, Hingston described his vision for the school and the fundraising campaign as a "wonderful opportunity for big men to do something for a big church." He was depending on Ontario Senator Michael O'Brien, a railway contractor and president of the Great Lakes Dredging Company, to give $100,000 "in seed money." Admitting that "the sum suggested is large, the donation would be a princely one like those made every day to Protestant institutions," he pressed on: "We have the sons of some of the wealthiest catholics in Canada, several of whom could without difficulty give us $100,000 apiece," he wrote, outlining why he believed the objective could be reached: "Our record in the War has done credit to the Catholics. Our hockey team is the most popular in Montreal, Catholics are proud of our beautiful buildings on campus, the largest in Canada. We have no competitors. There is a great future for the college. Montreal is the largest centre of English-speaking Catholics in Canada. It is also the wealthiest... my appointment as rector is a popular one."

Father Hingston had also hoped to enlist as a patron the city's richest and most prominent Roman Catholic, Lord Shaughnessy. A cold and exacting businessman, good at sizing up financial situations, Shaughnessy didn't give Father Hingston much encouragement.

"The time is inopportune for such a money canvas, and any effort

Rev. William Hingston, S.J.,
Rector, Loyola College

in that direction would only be very disappointing in its results," he wrote in reply to Hingston. "People's thoughts and activities are united on the war."

The autumn of 1918 was marked by the end of hostilities abroad and by the influenza epidemic that closed schools, theatres and churches in the city. Lady Hingston rang up the cathedral office and every morning while the epidemic lasted, a priest was sent to her house to celebrate Mass in the family parlour.

She was present with her sons at Loyola College on St. Patrick's Day, 1919 when a flagpole made of Douglas fir was dedicated in memory of the thirty-six Loyola boys, including Basil Hingston, who had been killed in the Great War. The dedication marked, in Father Hingston's opinion, a symbolic turning point in Loyola's fortunes. "The old boys were coming home from the front, and Loyola did not have a stick to hang a flag from. Money on campus was that scarce," he said. " The B.C. fir, in money was only worth $300, but as a symbol it proved to be the rallying point for Loyola's faithful friends and supporters."

One month later, on April 22, Father Hingston launched the fundraising drive to save the college. His mother wrote a cheque for the "seed money" he needed to kick start the campaign. Lady Hingston gave $50,000, which was Aileen's share of her father's estate. Then, over tea Lady Hingston persuaded one of her wealthy neighbours, Margaret McNally, to match the contribution. McNally's son, Francis Smith was a Loyola graduate and, like Lady Hingston's son, was a Jesuit. Not to be outdone, McNally contributed $52,000. Lord Shaughnessy eventually came through, but only with $5,000. In the end the campaign raised $303,721.22, and Shaughnessy congratulated Father Hingston, pointing out that while he was pleased the campaign was so successful, "a substantial portion of the amount is made up by the very liberal contributions of your own family."

As rector at Loyola, Father Hingston revised the institution's academic structure, separating the college from the high school. He improved the curriculum to ensure that Loyola graduates would qualify for admission to all universities.

Indefatigable as ever, Lady Hingston continued with her charitable work. She was on the executive of the Red Cross and the Canadian Patriotic Fund. She served as president of the Ladies Auxiliary of the Knights of Columbus. She was the first president of the Montreal's Parks and Playgrounds Association, a member of the executive of the Canadian Handicrafts Guild, the Mental Hygiene Committee, the Girl Guides Council, the Victorian Order of Nurses, and vice-president of the Needlework Guild of Canada. She was also a member of the L'Institut des Écoles Ménagères, which trained French-speaking women to work as domestics in the city and on the council of the Victorian Order of Nurses. She attended the 6:30 Mass at the

Lady Hingston, sitting third from left, and friends

Cathedral every morning without fail, returning from church with breakfast pastries for the rest of the family by 8 a.m. As the St. Patrick's parish bulletin observed, "She had other daily devotions to which she was rigidly faithful, and she often said, that if it weren't for the strength which came to her from the practice of these, she would be quite unable to keep the world with its fascination of trifles far away enough to enable her to cultivate a mood of piety."

When Baron Shaughnessy died in 1923, Donald Hingston revived his plan for a hospital when he was able to acquire Shaughnessy's mansion on Dorchester Boulevard "on convenient terms, as a temporary home," for a medical insititution. The house, which today is the Canadian Centre for Architecture, was renovated to accommodate twenty patients, and it opened on August 24, 1924, as St. Mary's Memorial Hospital. Donald left the Hôtel-Dieu to become St. Mary's chief surgeon. Lady Hingston became the first president of the hospital's ladies' auxiliary and a room reserved for indigent patients was named in her honour.

Donald had always longed for a son, but after his fifth daughter, Cynthia Anne, was born his life became the hospital. He divided his time between the hospital and the Mount Royal Club, where he served on three committees – wines and cigars, billiards and cards, and general administration. St. Mary's was his life's work, his obsession. "Like his father, Donald Hingston was a man of strong opinions, likes and dislikes," recalled a friend and colleague. "He didn't take criticism well, and accepted opposition reluctantly. He liked driving, although he didn't drive well. He was absent-minded. As a surgeon he was fast and a good technician, and was devastatingly critical of affectation and pomposity." Donald spoke French with a pronounced English accent, and like his father, Sir William, Donald was a good teacher, "never too busy to talk to interns and residents. He was patient and considerate when teaching at the operating table, but as is true of most surgeons, was an indifferent assistant. He had the uncanny sense that comes with experience of knowing exactly when to get out of the belly. He was always available to any and all members of his staff to consult, help, or do cases beyond their ability. He was kind but rather aloof with patients, nevertheless well liked by them, and enjoyed their complete confidence."

Hingston empathised with what Sir William had gone through at the Hôtel-Dieu, and from the start was determined St. Mary's would operate as a lay hospital without interference from the church or any of its religious orders. Initially the Grey Nuns were contracted to provide nursing services. Within a year, the sisters thought they should move in and have a say in how the hospital was run. A jurisdictional conflict arose. Rather than allow the Grey Nuns to hijack his hospital, Hingston and the board closed it in October 1929. It took another five years of negotiating but St. Mary's re-opened on March 20, 1934, after two supportive Roman Catholic priests, Luke Callaghan and Michael P. Dawson, convinced the archbishop of the wisdom of allowing the institution to be run by a lay board of directors. "In one of the darkest moments, when our little group had been abandoned by its influential friends, Father Dawson and Canon Callaghan came to our help. In my opinion they saved St. Mary's," Donald Hingston confided to friends.

Now with a hospital that might serve as the nucleus of a medical faculty for an English-speaking Catholic university in Montreal, Donald's brother, Willie, had visions of Loyola getting its university charter. Father Hingston would not be as successful with his dream. Archbishop Paul Bruchési wanted Loyola to affiliate with Université Laval à Montréal, which in 1919 became Université de Montréal. Hingston had gone to Rome in 1923 to plead his case for an English-speaking Roman Catholic university in Montreal, but was unable to sway the Prefect of the Congregation of Seminaries and Universities, Cardinal Gaetano Bisleti, and therefore reluctantly withdrew his proposal.

Shortly afterwards, Father Hingston was reassigned to Winnipeg as assistant pastor at St. Ignatius parish. When he left Montreal, the Catholic Social Service Guild passed a resolution expressing "profound regret at the loss of his unfailing kindness and practical wisdom" and at the same time congratulated Winnipeg in securing "so zealous a leader and so devoted a priest." The following year St. Francis Xavier University in Antigonish gave him an honorary degree. In 1927 Father Hingston became editor of *The Canadian Messenger of the Sacred Heart*. On May 17, 1928, he was appointed provincial – or head – of the Jesuits in the Province of Upper Canada. Three years later, he received permission from Rome to open a Jesuit School in Vancouver, but heeding appeals from the Archbishop of Winnipeg, he instead went there to open St. Paul's College and High School in that city. His most significant contribution, however, was to take over Regiopolis College in Kingston. The College had been granted a Royal University Charter in 1837, which had been dormant since 1869. Hingston determined that the charter was still valid, and for the next five years worked to persuade the authorities to turn Regiopolis into a national university modelled on the Catholic University of America in Washington, D.C., but the Great Depression intervened, and the plan was abandoned. He did, however, acquire the College of Christ the King in downtown Toronto in 1930 and it became the Jesuit seminary known today as Regis College.

Father Hingston was ahead of his time in encouraging a lay ministry. He believed that the Jesuits' priority was to teach, and that their duties as parish priests should be subordinate to their role as teachers. To this end he turned the Jesuit Church of Our Lady in Guelph over to the diocese. The church was one of the first built by the Jesuits in English-speaking Canada, and architecturally, one of the most beautiful in the country. Father Hingston's decision angered not only the parishioners but many of his fellow Jesuits.

Father Hingston's term as provincial ended in the autumn of 1934 and he moved west, working as a teacher in Vancouver, Port Arthur, Pendleton, Oregon and Campion College, the Jesuit school in Regina, Saskatchewan. He returned to Montreal to care for his mother when she fell ill in 1936. Imperious to the end, she became even more resolute in her faith, upbraiding her grand-daughters for having been seduced by an increasingly secular world. Lady Hingston died in her bed, surrounded by her three sons on November 7, 1936 at the age of 87.

"The door of her heart, like the door of her old-fashioned residence stood wide open to all who had any legitimate claim to her assistance. She possessed a supreme gift of personal sympathy for the poor and the unfortunate," Doctor James Walsh wrote in a Catholic community newspaper, *The Eikon.* "Many a discharged prisoner, many an incompetent worker or wayward girl came to Lady Hingston for advice and guidance. Her influence in securing for many of them a fresh start in life often seemed liked miracles to those who witnessed them."

*   *   *

The Second World War broke out in September, 1939 and once again another generation of Hingstons answered the call to duty. Harold, now a recovering alcoholic, had stopped drinking and had become a successful stockbroker. He saw both his sons, Billy and Pat, enlist in the Royal Canadian Air Force. Billy joined up out of "a reasoned sense of patriotism." He had been a popular man about the McGill University campus, where he produced the Red & White Revue. He was described as a man who had everything: "good health, good spirits, good looks, a fine education, a thorough knowledge of French, a better than average mind, ambition, and an artistic and sensitive nature." He was serving with the 429 Overseas Squadron when he was reported missing in action on December 3, 1943, a few weeks after getting his wings. A letter home informed Harold that his

SIR WILLIAM HINGSTON

son and his crew had been "engaged in an operational flight over Leipzig," and that "there is every chance that they are prisoners of war, or with luck among friends who are helping them evade capture." News of his death was confirmed in January 1944. He is buried in the Commonwealth War Dead Cemetery in Berlin.

Basil's namesake also enlisted. He was married and living in Victoria before the war, working for the Royal Trust Company. A captain in the Royal Canadian Infantry Corps, Basil was on loan to the British army and was serving with the South Staffordshire Airborne Battallion when he was killed in a plane crash in Germany on September 19, 1944. No one knows exactly what happened – German resistance, bad weather and problems with supplies and reinforcements in the three months following the invasion of Normandy had led to heavy Allied losses. Basil is buried in the Arnhem Oosterbeek War Cemetery.

During the 1940s a different war was being waged on the home front, this one against a religious cult known as the Jehovah's Witnesses. The Witnesses were perceived as an aggressive group that distributed literature that went beyond the accepted bounds of the freedom of religious expression, defamed Christians in general and Roman Catholics in particular, and made a nuisance of themselves on street corners, harrassing and haranguing passersby.

As their numbers grew, Quebec's premier, Maurice Duplessis declared "war without mercy" on the Witnesses. Father Hingston's contribution to the cause was to write a fifty-page pamphlet *Jehovah's Witnesses Exposed*, which sold for a dime. Basically it relied on court documents to expose Charles T. Russell, the founder of the religion, as a charlatan, adulterer and convicted fraud artist. "Prophesying on one's own account has ever proved to be a lucrative avocation since there appears to be no end to prospective dupes," he wrote, "Always there have been prophets aplenty who have announced themselves as being commissioned by God to foretell the Second Coming of Christ. But their predictions have never been authorized by God and have always ended up being discredited."

It sold more than 800,000 copies. Incredibly, 10,000 copies were found in the basement of the Portuguese Embassy in Ottawa in 1973.

The Montreal City & District Savings Bank celebrated its centennial in 1946. Donald Hingston, who had been named a director in 1912, vice-president in 1931 and president in 1942. After the war Hingston was one of the first to recognize the potential of of turning it into the "consumers bank," and helping returning servicemen by specialising in home mortgages and

Centenary of the Montreal City & District Savings Bank, 1846-1946, Mount Royal Club, May 27th, 1946. BACK: *J.A. Towner, Hon. G. Bissonnette, L. Sutherland, J.O. Lupien, Cbs. Moncel, B.C. Gardner, de Gaspé Beaubien, S.R. Noble, G.F. Benson, A. Perreault, J.A. Bertrand, W.A. Wilkins, C.F. Elderkin.* MIDDLE: *Hon. L.M. Gouin, Jean Lallemand, L.G. Lacoste, J.O. Asselin, M. Trudeau, Hon. H. Groulx, Walter Molson, P. de R. Ouimet, J.T. Hackett, J. Muir, C. St. Pierre, G.C. Marler, C.A. Roy, G. Belleau, H.R. Drummond, E. Hurtubise.* FRONT: *F. Cyril James, Beaudry Leman, Guy Vanier, Hon. E. Bertrand, Donald A. Hingston, C. Houde, G.W. Spinney, John Bassett, T. Taggart Smyth, E. Montpetit.*

small business loans. When the bank observed its centennial in 1946, it had $109,452,000 in deposits. Hingston was able to report increased profits as the result of an expansive postwar economic boom. He opened three new branches and expanded the operations of several others. At the same time, he urged the bank to pursue not only profit, but "the lofty motives of charity and humanity," to help those in Europe and at home who had suffered as the result of war.

Donald Hingston became ill in 1949 and was quickly incapacitated. In a poignant note to his daughters written on his deathbed, he acknowledged his failings as a father and encouraged them to care for their mother after he was gone.

"As a woman ages, she may become unstable or querulous, or difficult. Return to her a portion of the great love she always gave you," he wrote. "Wrap your love thickly and warmly about her... those who have passed life on have a duty to their offspring... Life is given us by our parents. We are weak at first, then grown strong, and in time we pass that life on to others. Those who have passed life on have a duty to their offsprings. I feel that duty was thoroughly performed to you by your mother and in a lesser way, by me. Bring up your children to a goodly heritage, the principles and practices of the Catholic faith, the practices of strict truth, of honesty and faithfulness. The moment has come at last to say that word and it causes me agony: Farewell, my dearest girls, and thanks."

Donald Hingston died "helpless and in silence," at his home on November 18, 1950. His brother, William, sang the requiem Mass at the Church of the Ascension in Westmount. Interns from St. Mary's Hospital acted as ushers and nuns from both the Hôtel-Dieu and St. Mary's Hospitals joined more than a thousand mourners to pack the church. *The Gazette* eulogized Donald Hingston as a "man who made light of favours when he did them and seemed to be receiving when he was conferring." The Mount Royal Club closed the bridge room for the day in his memory. Shortly after Donald's death, his-son in law, E. Donald Gray-Donald, who married Osla Hingston in 1932, took over as president of the City & District Savings Bank and remained at the helm until he retired in 1976, at the bank's 130th annual board meeting.

In 1956, Father Hingston observed his 60th anniversary as a Jesuit with a diamond jubilee reception at Loyola College in Montreal. Six years later, when he was eighty-five years old he turned the sod on December 8 for a new men's residence on campus named Hingston Hall in his honour. He suffered a number of recurring heart attacks and on

November 30 1964, died in Toronto, "A man of fine mind, deep faith and good heart."

Harold Hingston died in Montreal six weeks later, on January 9, 1965. Although Harold had long abandoned religion and had consulted mediums and dabbled with spiritualists in an attempt to talk to his dead son, his "saintly martyred" brother and his drowned sister, he was buried from St. Patrick's Church in a private family funeral.

The death of the last of Sir William Hingston children was not the end of the family's record of public service. On Sunday May 13, 1973, the William Hingston High School was inaugurated in Montreal at 415 St. Roch Street. Two years later, his great-grandson, Brian O'Neill Gallery, was elected to Westmount city council, then served as mayor of the city from 1983 to 1987. Like Sir William, Gallery was prominent in federal Progressive Conservative party politics as chairman of the 500 Club, a group of influential party supporters during Brian Mulroney's government, and he sat as vice-chairman on the board of directors of Canadian National Railways, and was a director of the Export Development Corporation.

A great-granddaughter, Harriet Hingston Stairs, was a vice-president of the Bank of Montreal and another great-granddaughter, Katherine Gray-Donald, is Director of the School of Dietetics and Human Nutrition at McGill University and Cornelia Hingston Molson Vaughan was the first president of the Canadian Foundation for AIDS Research.

The last of Sir William Hingston's grandaughters, Andrea Dolan McNally, died on September 26, 2003. It is strange to think that Sir William Hales Hingston, born in 1829, just fifteen years after the war of 1812 ended and seven years before the Rebellion of 1837, having grandchildren who survived into the 21st century. The house at Varennes, where Andrea played as a child was sold in 1934 to James Douglas, an Arizona copper magnate who apparently refused to live in the United States so long as Franklin Delano Roosevelt was president. During the eight years Douglas had it, it was allowed to deteriorate. In 1940 Ian Ogilvie, a journalist, and his partner, Robert Humphrey, an architect, bought it, and spent ten years restoring the estate. During the 1960s it was turned into a bed-and-breakfast, and in the 70s, sold to the petrochemical company that now owns the seigniory.

Hingston would perhaps be happy to know that the fieldstone house is still there, less happy to see that it sits abandoned, overgrown with weeds and surrounded by a chain link fence.

The Hingston mansion on Sherbrooke Street was sold shortly after Lady

Hingston died and became a boarding house for university students until it was demolished in 1974 to make way for a luxury hotel, today the Omni.

The headquarters of the Montreal City & District Saving Bank where Hingston had an office is still stands but the building has been renovated into the elegant XIX Siècle boutique hotel. The bank itself was sold in 1987 and continues today as the Laurentian Bank of Canada.

Medicine has made great strides in the past century, But Sir William would still be able to make his way through the Hôtel-Dieu hospital on Pine Avenue and feel at home there. He was, for his time, a first-rate doctor and the city will forever be in his debt for the fight he waged against smallpox. A man of deep faith, he was widely respected as an innovative surgeon who by the sheer force of his personality took on the opponents of vaccination and helped reduce the severe mortality rate.

When Hingston left office in 1877, the *Canada Lancet* remarked that as mayor he would compare favourably to anyone "who may have preceded or who may after follow ... in so far as education, gentlemanly manner, dignity of bearing, social standing, honesty of purpose and thorough business habits."

That bold assessment has proven prescient. Hingston's name remains consistently high on any list of the city's best chief magistrates, up there with the likes of Honoré Beaugrand, the journalist and man of letters who distinguished himself during the 1885 smallpox epidemic, Camillien Houde, the colourful and compassionate mayor who guided Montreal through The Depression or Jean Drapeau, who presided over both a Worlds Fair and the Olympics. Hingston would recognize the controversies at city hall in this century as many of the same ones he was engaged in as mayor. He moved effortlessly but not always comfortably in the French-Catholic and English Protestant milieu as few can, but over time each side assumed he belonged to the other, and he slipped through the cracks of history. But he touched the lives of his sons, and proved to be a good mentor.

He was an autocrat, a man of conviction, and a politician who embraced qualities of moral and pragmatic leadership. He helped shaped medical history and because he did, we today, remain in his debt.

Hingston Gathering, Donald and Lillian Hingston's 40th Wedding Anniversary 1948: BACK: Harry S. Dolan MD, Robert P. Vaughan, Kenneth Purtill, Elizabeth (Betty) Hingston Daly, George A. Daly, Bea MacDougall Ewan, Rev. William H. Hingston SJ, Berthe Larocque Hingston (widow of Basil Hingston), Cynthia Hingston Vaughan, Donald Gray-Donald, Harold W. Hingston. CENTRE: Donald Alexander Hingston, Lillian Peterson Hingston. SEATED FRONT: Aileen Hingston Purtill, Andrea Hingston Dolan, Katherine Hingston Gallery, Osla Hingston Gray-Donald.

Aknowledgements

Few projects have been as challenging or as satisfying as working on this book. It could not have been written without the enthusiastic support of Brian O'Neill Gallery, the exuberant keeper of the Hingston family flame who commissioned the work, and provided encouragment every step of the way. To his credit, he never once interfered with the content or attempted to direct the manuscript. For that alone, I am doubly grateful. The book and whatever errors are in it, are mine and mine alone. Not one word of it would have been written had an old broadcasting colleague, CJAD's Derek Lind, not suggested that I might be up to the task. Much of the primary resource material was assembled by Frank Fontaine who several years ago wrote the script for an as yet unproduced television series on the subject, which he generously shared. I am also indebted to William Hingston who embarked with me on the genealogical scavenger hunt, followed the manuscript through various stages and was there for both the difficult and fun times to offer the supportive prodding and provocative analysis only a friend could provide. Because of him it is a better book than it might have been. I am indebted to Graeme Decarie for enlightening me on the War of 1812 and for his introduction to this book.

The biggest frustration was in knowing that Sir William, Aileen and Donald Hingston each kept personal diaries but an exhaustive search failed to find them. One keeps hoping they might eventually turn up and provide material for a revised edition.

The largest collection of catalogued Hingston material is at the Concordia University Archives in Montreal, but various Hingston descendants scattered throughout the country each have pertinent papers of their own. I am grateful to his great-grandchildren, William (Bill) Hingston III and Geraldine Kingston Purtill Wallace in Ottawa, Judy Hingston Dingle and Harriet Hingston Stairs in Toronto and Evelyn Hingston in Montreal and Lillian Gallery Porter in Ottawa, whose collections of family memorabilia were invaluable in solving certain pieces of the puzzle. Other key documents, photographs and valuable research material were provided by Brian

O'Neill Gallery, Andrea Hingston Dolan McNally, and the late Edgar Andrew Collard. Jean-Marc Laporte, at the Canadian Institute of Jesuit Studies, Liliane Reid Lafleur and the Canadian War Museum, Elizabeth Gibson at the McGill University Library, Gordon Burr at the McGill University Archives, Nancy Marrelli and Vincent Ouellette, Caroline Sigouin and Nathalie Hodgson at the Concordia University Archives, Lucie Pelletier, Archives Ville de Montréal, *Gazette* colleague Frank Mackey, who happily was living with me in the 19th century doing research on his own book, Jennifer Keelan in Toronto, Pamela Miller and the staff of The Osler Library of Medical History, Cornelia Hingston Molson, Janet Macklem, Lucinda Boyd, Bruce Bolton at the Stewart Museum, Robert Stewart, Sunhee Ro, United Church of Canada Archives, Victoria Dickenson at the McCord Museum, Nicole Bussières, archivist with the Religieuses Hospitalières de Saint-Joseph, Mary McGovern, at St. Patrick's Basilica, Anna M. Grant at the Archives and special collections at Bishop's University, University of Edinburgh Archives, Michael Dawe at the Red Deer (Alta) District Archives and Adam Taves at the Pratt Library of Victoria University and Michele Courtemanche of the Canadian Museum of Civilization.

Eber Rice of Ottawa and Caroline Simmonds of Philadelphia also helped shape the text.

I am especially grateful to Michael Ballantyne, for an outstanding job of editing. Publisher Michael Price and his son, David, have been souls of patience and understanding. Graphic artist and page layout coordinator Ted Sancton personifies grace under pressure. I am also obliged to *Gazette* colleague Susan Ferguson for the elegant design of the dustjacket. I am also obliged to the former *Gazette* publisher Larry Smith and former editor-in-chief Peter Stockland, for their support and especially to my immediate supervisor at the paper, former city editor George Kalogerakis, who permitted me to work around his schedule giving me the time to complete the manuscript on time.

The Gazette's overworked and often under-appreciated librarians, Michael Porritt, Pat Duggan, and Elizabeth Ferguson have again demonstrated their weight in gold. Robert Ramsay helped solve some of the systems problems I encountered along the way.

I also have to thank Stéphane-Lajoie Plante who made the daily grind of writing a lot more fun.

Alan Hustak
A.M.D.G.

BIBLIOGRAPHY

BECOMING A PHYSICIAN, MEDICAL EDUCATION IN BRITAIN, FRANCE, GERMANY AND THE UNITED STATES, Thomas Neville Bonner, Oxford University Press, 1995.

BIBLIOGRAPHIE CANADIENNE, edited by Philéas Gagnon, 1895

BISHOP'S MEDICAL COLLEGE, by E. H. Bensley, M.D.

CANADA, ARDUOUS DESTINY, 1874-1896, P.B. Waite, McClelland and Stewart, 1971, ISBN 0-7710-8800-0

CYCLOPEDIA OF REPRESENTATIVE CANADIANS: CHIEFLY MEN OF THE TIME, Rose Publishing Company, Toronto, 1888.

DÉCISION SUR LA QUESTION ENTRE L'UNIVERSITÉ LAVAL ET LA SUCCURSALE ET L'ÉCOLE DE MÉDICINE DE MONTRÉAL, Aug 23, 1884.

DES ÎLES DU SAINT-LAURENT, Lorraine Guay, Septentrion, 2003

DOCTOR IN CANADA, THE WHEREABOUTS AND THE LAWS WHICH GOVERN THEM, Robert Wynyard Powell, Gazette printing company, 1890.

HISTORY OF THE COUNTY OF HUNTINGDON AND OF THE SEIGNIORIES OF CHATEAUGUAY & BEAUHARNOIS FROM THEIR FIRST SETTLEMENT TO THE YEAR 1838, by Robert Sellar, first published in 1888. Chateauguay Valley Historical Society.

FUTURE OF HISTORIC COUNTRY HOME THREATENED, Mayfair, Dec. 1950

HINCHINBROOKE – MONTREAL, SIR WILLIAM HALES HINGSTON, by J. Y. Touchette, Chateauguay Valley Historical Society Annual, 1995.

MEDICAL EVIDENCE IN THE WELLINGTON STREET MURDER CASE, Hingston, William H. Feb 1, 1860, from the original publication held by the Bibliothèque National du Québec. ISBN 0665446977. #44697 microfiche, Humanities & Social Sciences.

L'HOTEL DIEU DE MONTRÉAL, 1642-1973, Robert Lahaise, Les Cahiers du Québec, Hurtubise, 1973,

LES MÉMOIRS DU SÉNATEUR RAOUL DANDURAND, 1861-1942 Laval University Press, 1967.

THE MEDICAL INSTITUTIONS OF BERLIN, Hingston, William H.Art XVI, September, 1853, Hannah Microfiche of Canadian Medical Journals, Osler Library, 144/2

THE MEDICAL INSTITUTIONS OF PARIS, Hingston, William H.

HISTORY OF THE MONTREAL GENERAL HOSPITAL, H. E. MacDermot.

HISTORY OF THE FORMATION OF THE MEDICAL FACULTY UNIVERSITY OF BISHOP'S COLLEGE IN MONTREAL, by Francis Wayland Campbell. J.H. Osgood, 1900.

THE BISHOP'S MEDICAL FACULTY MONTREAL, 1871-1905, by Elizabeth Hearn Milner, René Prince Imprimeur, Inc. 1985.

MINUTE BOOK OF THE MEDICAL FACULTY OF McGILL COLLEGE, 1842-1852 McGill University Archives.

McGILL MEDICINE, THE FIRST HALF CENTURY, 1829-1885, by Joseph Hanaway and Richard Cruess, McGill Queen's University Press, 1996.

MEDICAL EDUCATION IN THE UNITED STATES AND CANADA, A REPORT TO THE CARNEGIE FOUNDATION, BULLETIN 4, 1910, by Abraham Flexner.

L'UNION MÉDICALE DU CANADA, by D. Mignault, 1926.

THE MORGANS OF MONTREAL, by David Morgan, Privately printed, ISBN 0-9696676-0-4.

MÉMOIRE SOUMIS AUX EMINENTISSIMES SEIGNEURS CARDINAUX DE LA SACRÉE CONGRÉGA-TION DE LA PROPAGANDE, TOUCHANT LES DIFFICULTÉS ENTRE L'UNIVERSITÉ LAVAL DE

QUÉBEC ET L'ÉCOLE DE MÉDICINE ET DE CHIRURGIE DE MONTRÉAL: 1880, Ths. E. d'Odet d'Orsonnens, McGill Rare Books division folio LE3 L32 077.

REMEMBRANCE OF GRANDEUR, THE ANGLO-PROTESTANT ELITE OF MONTREAL, by Margaret W. Westly, Éditions Libre Expression, 1990, ISBN 2-89111-439-6

PERSONNEL OF THE SENATE AND HOUSE OF COMMONS, EIGHTH PARLIAMENT OF CANADA, John Lovell and Son, Montreal, 1898

PUBLIC HEALTH IN MONTREAL, 1870-1930, MEDICINE IN CANADIAN SOCIETY, edited by S.E.D. Shortt. McGill Queen's University Press, 1981

REPORTS OF THE MEDICAL OFFICER OF HEALTH, CITY OF MONTREAL, FOR THE YEARS ENDING 1875, 1876, 1885. Archives Municipales. V.001.4

RAPPORT DE L'OFFICIER DE SANTÉ, 1875-1885, by A.B. Laroque, Louis Perrault & Cie.

ROUGES, REBELS AND GENIUSES, THE STORY OF CANADIAN MEDICINE, Donald Jack, Doubleday, 1981

PLAGUE, A STORY OF SMALLPOX IN MONTREAL, by Michael Bliss, HarperCollins, 1991 ISBN 0-00-215693-8.

SAINT MARY'S HOSPITAL by J.J. Dinan, Optimum Publishing, 1987.

TYPES OF CANADIAN WOMEN AND OF WOMEN WHO ARE OR HAVE BEEN CONNECTED WITH CANADA, Edited by Henry James Morgan, William Briggs 1903.

UNE VISITE À L'HÔTEL-DIEU, 1887, Léon Ledieu.

WILLIAM HALES HINGSTON, M.D., (1829-1907) by Rev. William H. Hingston, S.J. Privately published.

WILLIAM OSLER, A LIFE IN MEDICINE, by Michael Bliss, University of Toronto Press, 1999, ISBN 0-8020-4349-6.

INDEX

Aberdeen, 29, 185
Abord-à-Plouffe, 83
Academic Hall, 189
Acton, William, 126
Adventures of Huckleberry Finn, 145
Agnostics, 45
Alcohol, 143
Alexandra Hotel, 198
Alexandria, 82, 183
Allan Steamship Liner, 173, 196
American Civil War, 66-68, 151
American Consul-General, 135
American interference, 63
American Journal of Insanity, 49
American Medical Association, 132
American Revolution, 31
Amherst, 105
Amiens, 208
Amputation, 142
Anarchy, 35, 103
Anderson, John, 63
Anesthesia, 33, 44
Anglican, 29, 32, 36, 63, 74, 152, 204
Anglo-Irish, 23
Anglo-Saxons, 35, 127
Anima, 126
Ankylosis, 45
Annexation, 29, 36
Annual Saint-Jean-Baptiste Parade, 89
Anthropology, 143
Anti-Catholic sentiment, 41
Anti-Catholic, 41
Anti-vaccinateur, 156
Anti-vaccination, 118
Anti-vaccinationist, 151
Antibiotics, 21
Antigonish, 216
Antiquarian, 172
Antiseptic, 15, 117, 125, 132
Antoine Ward, 83-84, 115
Apostoli, Georges, 162
Apothecary, 31, 46
Appendectomies, 15, 125
Appendicitis, 183
Archbishop Paul Bruchési, 185, 202, 204, 206, 216

Archbishop Elzéar Taschereau, 112, 132, 139
Archbishop John Lynch, 99
Architect of French Catholic nationalism, 31
Arizona, 221
Army Hospitals, 51
Arnhem Oosterbeek War Cemetery, 218
Arnhem, 218
Arteries, 177
Association of English-speaking doctors, 57
Astronomy, 30
Asylums, 49, 65
Athanase-David Pavilion, 178
Atheists, 45
Athelstan, 27
Athens of the North, 42
Atlantic crossing, 69
Atoms, 126
Atwater Avenue, 105
Augustin Grisolle's *Pratique de Pathologie Interne*, 66
Aylwin, Thomas Cushing, 56
B.C. fir, 213
Bacteria, 83
Bacteriology, 69
Baker, Hariette, 197
Ball, 110, 131, 136, 185, 194
Balmoral Street, 205
Baltimore, 15, 184
Bank of Commerce, 109
Bank of Montreal, 221
Bank of Spain, 185
Bankruptcy, 212
Banque Jacques-Cartier, 85
Barbados, 81
Barbeau, Henri-Jacques, 130, 194
Baron Lister of Lyme Regis, 184
Baron Longueuil, 74
Baron Shaughnessy, 189, 215
Baroness Stanislas d'Halewyn, 206
Barry, James, 51-52
Batoche, 152
Battalion Canadian Expeditionary Force, 208
Battle of Amiens, 208
Battle of Chippewa, 25
Battle of the Boyne, 109, 114

Battle of Ypres, 17, 207
Bavaria, 76
Bay, The, 165
Beaudry, Jean-Louis, 85-86, 120, 134-135, 205
Beaugrand, Honoré, 222
Beauharnois Regiment, 27
Beauharnois, 27
Beaujon, 49
Beaver Hall Hill, 36, 104, 142
Bel-Air Jockey, 166
Belleville, 176
Bennington, Elizabeth, 201
Berlin, 44-45, 218
Bermuda, 204
Bernard, Aldis, 84, 86, 114
Bernard, Edmond, 104
Bertram, Alexander, 92
Best, Geoffrey, 23
Bethanian Hospital, 44
Betrothal, 28
Bibakiba, 101
Bibliographie Canadienne, 145
Billiards, 215
Birmingham, 15, 75
Birth of Irish nationalist Daniel O'Connell, 90
Bishop Bourget's body, 152
Bishop Bourget's declarations, 97
Bishop Bourget's humiliation, 91
Bishop Bourget's intention, 77
Bishop Édouard-Charles Fabre, 128, 139, 141, 161
Bishop Ignace Bourget, 30, 51, 58, 73, 152
Bishop of Montreal, 30, 85, 93, 103, 112, 114
Bishop's fledgling medical school, 75
Bishop's medical school, 75
Bishop's medical students, 75, 164
Bishop's University reunion banquet, 157
Bishop's University, 74-75, 128, 157, 164
Black Rock, 25
Blackwood, Frederick Temple, 81
Blaserie, Jean-Baptiste Duratteau de la, 29

Bliss, Michael, 155
Bloodletting, 33
Boa-constrictor, 143
Board of Health, 89, 103, 117, 120, 151, 154, 157
Board of Sewage Commissioners, 121
Board of Trade, 84
Board of Trustees, 75
Body of Joseph Guibord, 73, 92
Boer War, 190
Bon Dieu, 182
Bond, William Bennett, 63
Bonneau, Justine 129
Bonsecours Market, 87, 90, 104, 111
Bonsecours Street, 36
Borden, Frederick, 196
Boston, 45, 50, 105
Boulton, Charles Arkel, 183
Bourget's bravado, 134
Bourget's judgment, 73
Bourget's mouthpiece, 134
Bourget's Papal Zouaves, 85
Bourget's prestige, 134
Bourget's ultramontanism, 152
Bourget, Ignace, 30, 51, 58, 73, 152
Bout de l'Isle, 57
Bowell, Mackenzie, 176, 178-179, 181
Boxing, 205
Boyhood, 58
Boyne, 109, 114
Brahma, 45
Brahma, Herman, 45
Branches, 29, 174, 220
Braun, Antoine-Nicolas, 77
Brazil's unassuming emperor, 113
Breast star of a Knight Commander, 196
Brewer, 130
Breweries, 48
Brigantines, 23
Brims, Daniel, 50
Britain's Vaccination Act, 117
Britain, 34, 43, 48-49, 51, 117, 144, 196
British Ambassador, 131
British army, 218
British Association, 15, 109, 143, 173, 184
British colonies, 51
British Empire, 45, 104
British Guiana, 81
British Medical Association, 15, 173, 184
British Medical Journal, 174
British North America, 22, 24-25, 33, 35, 109, 176

British Parliament, 88
Brosseau, Alfred-Toussaint, 128, 134
Brown, Fayette, 206-207
Brown, Henriette, 102
Brown, Leighton, 206
Bruchési, 185, 202, 204, 206, 216
Brunelle, Joseph-Antoine Stanislas, 76, 125, 194
Brunet, Joseph, 87
Burial of Monsieur Guibord, 103
Burke's Landed Gentry, 23
Burlington, 83
By-election, 178-179, 181
Cadavers, 33
Caesarean, 43, 55
Calgary Herald, The, 109
California, 114
Callaghan, Luke, 216
Cambridgeshire, 24
Campbell, Thomas Edmond, 75
Campion College, 217
Canada Lancet, 133, 136, 222
Canada Medical Record, 164-165, 175-178
Canada's climate, 145
Canada's conscription laws, 212
Canada's first foray, 189
Canada's foremost graphic artist, 202
Canada's governor-general, 81
Canadian Cardinal, 161
Canadian Centre, 215
Canadian Club, 201
Canadian Confederation, 180
Canadian economy, 183
Canadian Eucharistic Congress, 205
Canadian Foundation, 221
Canadian Handicrafts Guild, 214
Canadian Illustrated News, 48, 58, 110, 118
Canadian Knight, 16
Canadian Medical Association, 15, 69, 125, 130, 132, 143, 175, 183
Canadian Medical Journal, 48, 68, 76
Canadian Messenger, The, 216
Canadian National Railways, 221
Canadian Pacific Railway, 84, 145, 189, 204, 206
Canadian Parliament, 59, 201
Canadian Patriotes, 29
Canadian Patriotic Fund, 214
Canadian securities, 84

Canadian Senate, 37
Cancer, 59, 76
Canon Callaghan, 216
Canterbury, 205
Cap Saint-Michel, 74
Capital of the United Canadas, 34
Capitalists, 154
Carbolic, 66, 117, 125, 127, 132, 184
Cardinal Gaetano Bisleti, 216
Cardinal Giovanni Siméoni, 140, 161
Cardinal Lodovicio Jacobini, 161
Cardinal Newman, 131
Carey, Margaret, 25
Carey, Patrick, 59
Caribbean, 32
Carlin, Patrick, 127
Casgrain, Charles Eusèbe, 37
Cassidy, Francis, 84
Catholic cemetery, 73, 92-93, 102
Catholic community newspaper, 217
Catholic doctrinal purity, 125
Catholic Literature League, 205
Catholic Quebec, 128, 152, 162, 178-179
Catholic schools, 178
Catholic Social Service Guild, 216
Catholic Theatre Guild, 205
Catholic universities, 78, 162
Catholic University of America, 216
Catholic Women's League, 212
Cavendish, Winifred, 24
Caxton Street, 190
Cecilian Society, 189
Cemetery Street, 87
Central Board of Health, 154
Chambre de Commerce, 84
Champs de Mars, 25, 35, 51, 101, 150, 155
Chapleau, Joseph-Adolphe, 134, 177
Charlevoix, 202
Château Ramezay, 132, 185
Chateauguay, 27
Chemistry, 33, 42, 44, 117
Chief medical officer of the Grand Trunk Railway, 149
Chief of the College, 41
Children of France, 144
Childs, George, 87
Chippewa, 25
Chirurgie de Montréal, 58-59, 75, 112

Chloroform, 43-44, 50, 76, 127, 142, 177, 190

Chomedey de Maisonneuve, 46, 172

Christmas Story, A, 195

Church of England, 152

Church of Rome, 33

Church of the Ascension, 220

Church of the Immaculate Conception, 205

Cigarette, 195

Cigars, 143, 215

Cistercian monk, 141

Citizens Ball, 131

Citizens' Taxpayers Association, 115

City & District Savings Bank, 17, 101, 130, 179, 185, 194, 201, 205, 218, 220

City of Montreal, 17, 22, 81, 84, 101, 105, 130, 179, 194, 222

City Passenger Railway, 142

City's Exhibition Grounds, 154

City's greatest promoter of Roman Catholicism, 152

City's Irish businessmen, 50

City's Public Health Officer, 150

Civil Code, 50

Civil War, 23, 64, 66-68, 151

Clendenning, William, 87

Climate of Canada, 143-145

Clinical Professor of Surgery, 117, 136, 184

CMA, 69, 130

Cobourg, 68-69, 133

Collège de Montréal, 23, 29, 163

Collège Henri IV, 59

College Medical Students Dinner, 164

College of Christ, 217

College of Medical Doctors of Quebec, 85

College of Physicians, 41, 47, 57, 154

Collège St, 190, 213, 216

Collège St. Marie, 77, 128, 190

Columbus, 163, 211, 214

Command of Phineas Riall, 25

Commander of Boulton's Scouts, 183

Commemorative memorial medals, 202

Commendations, 111

Commissioner's Square, 23

Commonwealth War Dead Cemetery, 218

Con, George, 127

Concordia University, 17

Condora, 150

Confederacy, 67

Confederate, 151

Conference of Women, 212

Congregation of Seminaries, 216

Connell, James, 55, 75

Conscription, 212

Consecration of the city's first Roman Catholic Cathedral, 99

Conservative candidate, 178

Conservative government, 131

Conservative Member of Parliament, 15

Conservatives, 84, 134

Consolidated Bank, 130

Constantinople, 131

Construction of the Canadian Pacific Railway, 145

Construction of the Victoria Bridge, 64

Consul-general, 135

Consumption, 151

Contagious, 88, 99, 116, 134, 150, 164

Convention of the American Medical Association, 132

Convocation, 37

Corn Exchange, 84

Corn Laws, 34

Cornwall, 82, 193

Coroner, 136

Côte-des-Neiges, 97

Council of the Victorian Order, 214

Countess of Minto, 194

County Cork, 24-25

County of Dublin Regiment, 25

Coursol, Charles, 83-84, 100

Court of Common Pleas, 64

Courtney, William, 35

Cowpox, 88

Craik, Robert, 16, 56, 117

Crawford, James, 33, 41

Creation of a Small Pox hospital, 91

Crévier, Joseph, 87

Cricket, 84

Crimson Chamber, 201

Cromwell, 23, 175

Cross pro Ecclesia et Pontifice, 174

Cruess, Richard, 68

Cunard steamships, 195

Curran, John Joseph, 179

Custer, General George Armstrong, 114

Cystoscope, 125

Dagenais, Adolphe, 87

Daily Witness, 90, 102

Dandurand, Raoul, 101

Darwin, 132

David, Aaron Hart, 46, 65, 74

David, Ferdinand, 87

David, Laurent-Olivier, 84

Davidson's funeral, 204

Davidson, John, 50

Davidson, Sarah, 65

Davidson, Shirley, 203-204

Davis, Jefferson, 67

Dawson, Michael P., 216

de Lamellae, Jobber, 49

de Maisonneuve, Paul de Chomedey, 46

de Maricourt, Paul Le Moyne, 185

de Martigny, Sieur, 74

Dean of Bishop's, 75

Dean of Edinburgh's medical faculty, 42

Dean of the Medical Faculty, 16

Dean of Victoria College, 141

Dean of Victoria University, 165

Debt of Montreal, 115

Decorative Art, 129

Defender of French-Canadian culture, 152

Depression, 27, 34, 84-85, 103, 115, 126, 216, 222

Description of First Nations' peoples, 143

Desjardins, Alphonse, 179

Desjardins, Louis-Édouard, 140, 142

Deslauriers Island, 203

Diagnosis of Doctor Rodger, 158

Diarrhea, 46-47

Dickens, Charles, 43

Diocese of Montreal, 85, 114, 128, 134

Diphtheria, 21, 89

Director of the CMA's education committee, 130

Director of the Export Development Corporation, 221

Diseases of Women, 43

Disfigurement, 118

Disinfectants, 69, 117

Disorders, 64, 175

Divorce, 197

d'Odet d'Orsonnens, Edmond, 59, 133, 141

Doctor Aaron Hart David, 46, 74

Doctor Alphonse-Barnabé Larocque, 90

Doctor Archibald Hall, 56

Doctor Armand Larocque, 117

Doctor Charles Smallwood, 75

Doctor Coderre, 59, 90, 134, 151
Doctor Craik, 16, 56, 75
Doctor d'Odet d'Orsonnens, 133, 141
Doctor David, 46, 74-75
Doctor Duncan C. MacCallum, 41
Doctor Edward Trenholme, 75
Doctor Émery-Coderre, 73, 89, 151, 156, 165
Doctor Emmanuel-Persillier Lachapelle, 16
Doctor Eugène-Hercule Trudel, 129, 141
Doctor Francis Wayland Campbell, 68
Doctor George Campbell, 33, 142
Doctor George Fenwick Campbell, 142
Doctor Hector Peltier, 56, 59
Doctor Henry Howard, 47, 152
Doctor James Barry, 52
Doctor James Crawford, 33
Doctor James Grant, 15
Doctor James Guérin, 16, 154
Doctor James Simpson, 43
Doctor James Walsh, 217
Doctor Jean-Philippe Trefflé-Rottot, 16, 165
Doctor Joseph Émery-Coderre, 59, 73, 89, 151, 165
Doctor Joseph-Antoine Stanislas Brunelle, 194
Doctor Juenken, 44
Doctor Lawson Tait, 15
Doctor Louis-Edouard Desjardins, 140
Doctor Munro, 60, 78, 128
Doctor Patrick Sheridan, 16
Doctor Robert Craik, 16, 56
Doctor Rodger, 149, 157-158
Doctor Simpson, 43, 45
Doctor Thomas George Roddick, 15
Doctor Thomas Rodger, 157
Doctor William Elijah Bessey, 150
Doctor William Fuller, 100
Doctor William Henry Drummond, 16
Doctor William Osler, 15
Dom Joseph-Gauthier-Henri Smeulders, 141
Dom Pedro II, 113
Dom Smeulders, 141
Domaine du Cap Saint-Michel, 74

Dominion Medical Association, 135
Dominion Medical Convention, 90
Dominion Square, 84
Donald, Day, 196
Donegani Hotel, 36, 134
Dorchester Boulevard, 34, 215
Dorchester Street, 176
Doré, Jean, 86
Dorion, Antoine-Aimé, 63
Dowd, Patrick, 140, 163
Downing Street, 104
Dr. Campbell, 37
Dr. James Grant, 117
Drapeau, Jean, 222
Drowned, 203-204, 221
Drummond, George, 44, 63, 166
Duchess of Cornwall, 193
Duck Lake, 152
Dufferin, Harriot, 81, 111, 131
Duhamel, Joseph, 87, 89-90
Duplessis, Maurice, 218
Dupuis, Isaac, 155-156
Earl of Dufferin, 81
Eastern Townships, 74, 89
Easton, 32
Eccentricities, 173
Ecchymosis, 55
Ecole de Médecine et de Chirurgie de Montréal, 58-59, 75, 112
Écoles Ménagères, 214
Eczematous, 76
Edema, 44
Edmond, Marcel, 104
Einnan's Cathedral, 183
Eleanor, Katherine, 136
Elected president of Montreal's MedicoChirurgical Society, 132
Elected president of the Canadian Medical Association, 125
Elected president of the Montreal Parks, 198
Elizabeth of Hungary, 82
Embryology, 212
Émery-Coderre, Joseph, 73, 89, 128, 151, 165
End, Mile, 101
Endsleigh Palace Hospital, 208
Enemas, 31
English Protestants, 22-23
English-speaking Catholic population, 211
English-speaking Catholic university, 216
English-speaking Catholics of Montreal, 211

English-speaking community, 22, 36, 103, 142, 189, 193
English-speaking physicians, 15, 46
English-speaking Protestant community, 22, 103
English-speaking Roman Catholic doctor, 17
English-speaking Roman Catholic university, 216
English-speaking Tories, 34
Epilepsy, 56, 183
Ermins Hotel, 190
Erysipelas, 150-151
Excommunication, 31, 140
Execution of Louis Riel, 155
Executive of the Red Cross, 214
Executor, 211
Existence of God, 45
Export Development Corporation, 221
Fabre, Édouard-Charles, 112, 114, 128, 139
Faculty of Medicine, 33, 133, 165, 167
"Faithful Watchdog", 87
Family's coat of arms, 23
Famine, 23, 32
Father Dawson, 216
Father Dowd, 163
Father Marcel Toupin, 163
Faubourg Saint-Honoré, 49
Fenster, Julie, 69
Fetish, 151
First Baroness of Longueuil, 185
First Canadian separatist, 152
First Earl of Dufferin, 81
First Franco-Ontarian, 37
First head of the General Hospital, 41
First International Eucharistic Congress, 205
First Mass, 167, 205
First Nations, 143
First premier of Ontario, 82
First president of the Canadian Foundation, 221
First president of the Montreal's Parks, 214
First Quebec doctor, 140
First successful kidney operation, 70
First World War, 17
Fitzpatrick, Charles, 212
Flagellation, 56
Fleming, Sandford, 35
Fletcher, John, 100
Forbes, J. Colin, 193
Ford's Theatre, 85

Forerunner of the National Capital Commission, 194

Former prime minister of the United Canadas, 81

Former residence of Canada's third prime minister, 189

Fort Erie, 25

Fort Munroe, 67

Foster, Thomas, 87

Founders of the City & District Savings Bank, 205

Fourth Battalion of the Beauharnois Regiment, 27

Fourth Conservative prime minister, 178

Franchère, Joseph-Charles, 197

Francis Xavier University, 216

Fraser, Catherine, 82

Fredericton, 109

French Canada's patron saint, 89

Friends of Catholic higher education, 178

Frog Lake, 152

Frostbite, 46

Fundamentalists, 43

Gabriel Street Presbyterian Church, 25

Gaetz, Leonard, 109, 114

Gagnon, Philéas, 145

Gallery, Brian O'Neill, 221

Galt, 145

Galt, Alexander Tilloch, 145

Gazette, The, 27, 32, 34-36, 47, 55, 64, 77, 87, 90-91, 104, 139, 146, 152, 155, 178, 204, 220

General Hospital, 23, 34, 41, 56, 75, 88, 117, 125, 142, 149, 157

Gentlemen of St. Sulpice, 106

George Square, 42

Germany, 45, 49, 125, 218

Glackemeyer, Charles, 104-105

Glasgow Royal Infirmary, 66

Glengarry County, 82

Globe, The, 99, 181

Goderich Signal, The, 204

Golden Jubilee, 163

Gomorra, 45

Goulet, Napoléon, 155

Government House, 99

Governor of Nouvelle-France, 175

Governor-General Aberdeen, 185

Governor-General of Barbados, 81

Governor-General's Ball, 136

Governors of the Quebec College, 154

Governors-General, 15

Graduates, Loyola, 214

Grand Master of British North America, 176

Grand Master of Upper Canada, 176

Grand Rapids, 151

Grand Seminary, 127

Grand Trunk Railway, 64, 67, 130, 149

Grant, James, 15, 81, 117

Gray-Donald, Katherine, 221

Great Britain, 49, 144, 196

Great Lakes Dredging Company, 212

Great St. James Methodist Church, 109

Greenway, Thomas, 182

Grenier, Jacques, 87, 120

Grey Nuns, 23, 134, 140, 215-216

Griffintown, 23, 48, 88, 99, 102, 105, 179

Grisolle, Augustin, 66

Grosse-Isle, 32

Guelph, 212, 217

Guérin, James, 16, 154

Guibord, 73, 84, 91-93, 97, 100-105, 109, 141

Guibord, Joseph, 73, 92

Guiteau, Charles, 135

Gustav Simon of Heidelberg, 70

Guy Street, 46

Guy, Louis, 28

Guy, Marie-Amélie, 28

Gynecologist, 75, 162, 172

Gynecology, 16

H Battery of the Fourth Battalion, 51

Haemorrhaging, 172

Hague, 85

Hall House hospital, 113

Hall Institute, 63

Halton County, 150

Hamel, Abbé Thomas Etienne, 132

Hamilton, Harriot Rowan, 81

Harper's Weekly, 156

Hébert, Louis Philippe, 172

Hébert, Philippe, 172, 202

Heidelberg, 45, 70

Herald, The, 86, 97, 109, 116-118, 153, 155, 185, 196, 202

Heyfelder, Johann Ferdinand, 49

Hinchinbrooke, 27

Hincks, Francis, 81, 85, 101, 110, 115, 145, 153

Hingston Avenue, 65, 184, 205

Hingston family tree, 24

Hingston Hall, 142, 220

Hingston's faith, 152

Hingston's fortunes, 44

Hingston's knowledge of German, 67

Hingston's life-long conviction, 202

Hingston's medical office, 23

Hingston's mother, 50, 65, 69, 206

Hingston's motion, 198

Hingston's pamphlet, 154, 156

Hingston's regiment, 25

Hingston, Aileen, birth of, 139, death of 203

Hingston, Aileen (Basil's daughter) 208

Hingston, Andrea Aileen, 204

Hingston, Basil Reginald, birth of, 152, marriage, death, 208

Hingston, Basil, Jr. 208

Hingston, Cynthia Ann, 204

Hingston, Donald Alexander, Dr. birth of 129, marriage of 204, founder of St. Mary's Hospital, 215, death of 220

Hingston, Eleanor, (McGrath) 25, 69

Hingston, Eleanor, 27

Hingston, Fayette Williams Brown George (Billy) 207

Hingston, Harold Ramsay, birth of, 164, WWI 207, death of, 221

Hingston, Katherine Isabel, 204

Hingston Margaret

Hingston, Mary Ann 27

Hingston Mary Elizabeth, 204

Hingston, Osla, 204

HIngston, Samuel Col. 24, 25, 27

HIngston, Samuel James, 28, 44, 130

Hingston, Thomas, 27

Hingston, William Hales Peter, birth of 27, education, 33, burning of parliament, 35, graduation, 36, in Edinburgh, 42, election as mayor, 86, marriage, 99, in byelection, 178, appointed to Senate, 181, 50th anniversary as a doctor, 193, death of 202.

Hingston, William, Rev. S.J. birth of 120, ordination of, 205, WWI, 212, Rector of Loyola College, 212 death of 220

Hingston, Winnifred, (Cavendish) 24

Hingston-Smith, Edward, 117

Historical Fancy Dress Ball, 185
Holland, Richard, 87
Holmes, Andrew Fernando, 33
Homeopathy, 33
Homosexual, 132
Honey, John, 65
Hôpital Beaujon, 49
Hôpital Général de Montréal, 23
Hôpital Général, 23
Hôpital Notre-Dame, 16, 134
Hôtel-Dieu Hospital museum, 197
Hôtel-Dieu Hospital, 15, 17, 46, 56, 58, 128, 132, 134, 149, 197, 215, 222
Hôtel-Dieu's medical school, 75, 133
Hôtel-Dieu, 15, 17, 46, 48, 56, 58-59, 64, 68-70, 75, 78, 88, 111, 125, 127-129, 132-136, 139, 142, 149-150, 152, 154, 157, 163, 167, 183, 193, 197, 201, 211, 215, 220, 222
Houde, Camillien, 222
House of Assembly, 35, 50
House of Commons, 36, 132, 152
House, Benjamin Hall, 99
Howard, Henry, 47, 65, 152
Howard, Robert Palmer, 55
Howell, Margaret, 67
Humphrey, Robert, 221
Hungary, 82
Huntingdon, 28-29, 37
Hyde Park Corner, 198
Hydrotherapist, 151
Hysteria, 154
Ice, 87, 150
Ile Ronde, 113
Imperial Leopold Academy, 45, 50
Imperial Order of the Daughters, 190, 212
Inaugurated Université Laval's, 177
India, 131
Indian Terrority, 114
Influence of the Climate, 143
Influenza, 190, 213
Influx of Irish immigrants, 84
Infringement of Hygienic law, 49
Inheritance, 57
Insanity, 49
International Medical Conference, 117
International Surgical Congress, 198
Invasion of Normandy, 218
Invasion of Quebec, 32

IODE, 190
Irish Canadian Rangers, 207
Irish Catholic, 41, 105
Irish Roman Catholics, 22
Iroquois, 185
Jamaica, 50
Jamdudum, 164
James II, 109
Jefferson Jr. Margaret Howell, 67
Jehovah's Witnesses, 218
Jesuit College, 77, 201, 217
Jesuit School, 77, 216-217
Jesuit seminary, 217
Jobin, Gérard, 211
Jodoin, Amable, 87
Johns Hopkins University, 15, 184
Joliette, 59
Jubilee celebrations, 184
Jubilee Mass, 77
Judah, Henry Hague, 85
Judicial Committee of the Privy Council, 73
Julien, Henri, 202
Kansas City, 50
Killarney Irish, 15
Kinder Hospital, 44
King Edward VII, 57
King's College, 29
Kingston, 47, 143, 150, 164, 175, 197, 216
Knight Bachelor of the Realm, 176
Knight Commander of St. Gregory, 196
Knights of Columbus, 163, 211, 214
L'Aile de la Providence, 48
L'Annuaire de l'Institut Canadien, 73
L'École de médecine et de chirurgie de Montréal, 58-59, 112
L'Hospice de la Maternité, 48
La Presse, 202
Laberge, Louis, 151
Lachine Canal, 104
Lacolle, 76
Ladies Auxiliary, 214-215
Ladies of the Hôtel-Dieu, 139
Lady Dufferin, 81, 111
Lafontaine, Louis-Hippolyte, 34, 81, 101
Larocque, Berthe, 205
Larocque, François-Antoine Chartier, 205
Latent French-Canadian nationalist, 189
Laurentian Bank of Canada, 17, 222
Laurier, Wilfrid, 73, 182, 184

Laval episode, 161
Laval University, 134, 136
Le Monde, 134
Leacock, Stephen, 17
Leeches, 31
Legislative Assembly, 32, 34
Legislative Council of Lower Canada, 28
Legislative Council, 28, 36
Leipzig, 218
Lennoxville, 74-75
Les Hospitalières de Saint-Joseph, 46
Liberal children of Protestantism, 73
Liberia, 64
Lincoln, Abraham, 85
Lister's antiseptic carbolic spray, 125
Lister's carbolic spray, 125, 132, 184
Lister, Joseph, 15, 66, 117, 184
Listerism, 132
Listerites, 125
Lithotomies, 51
Little Big Horn, 114
Longley, George, 149
Longue Pointe Asylum, 152
Longueuil, 74, 185
Loranger, Alderman Louis Onésime, 87, 90, 115
Lord Dufferin, 110, 194
Lord Elgin, 34
Lord Shand of Edinburgh, 43
Lord Thomas Shaughnessy, 189, 206, 213-214
Louisiana Purchase Exposition, 196
Lovell, Robert, 65, 67
Loyal Orange Association of British North America, 109
Loyalist, 59
Loyola College, 17, 206, 211-213, 220
Loyola of Montreal, 189, 212
Lynch, Catherine, 59
Lynch, John Joseph, 93
Macdonald, Donald Alexander, 81, 136, 183
Macdonald, John A., 17, 51, 81, 84, 131, 163, 175
Macdonald, John Sandfield, 17, 82
Macdonald, Margaret, 17, 81-82, 93, 136
Mackay Street, 176
MacKenzie, Alexander, 85, 98, 101
Madison, James, 24
Magog, 31
Major Melchior Alphonse de Salaberry, 28

Mance, Jeanne, 46
Manifesto, 36
Manitoba School Question, 178, 182
Manning, Henry Edward, Cardinal, 152
Marot, Clement, 197
Marquis of Lorne, 132
Martin, Abraham, 205
Mary Queen of the World, 201
Masonic Hall, 114
Massachusetts, 70
Massacre of General George Armstrong Custer, 114
Masturbation, 49
Mayor Beaudry, 85, 134-135, 205
Mayor Charles Coursol, 83-84
Mayor Street, 150
Mayor William Workman, 85-86
McCambridge, Alexander, 87
McCord Museum, 57
McCord, David Ross, 87
McGee, Arcy, 50
McGill Street, 21, 23, 31, 46, 48, 50
McGill University Alumni Society, 57
McGill University's Medical school, 68
McGill University, 16, 32-33, 57, 68, 117, 135, 143, 163, 178, 217, 221
McGrath, Eleanor, 25
McGrath, Owen, 25
McLaren, John, 87
McNally, Andrea Dolan, 221
McNally, Margaret, 214
McShane, Alderman, 105
Mechanics' Hall Institute, 63, 115
Medical Department of Victoria University, 136
Medical Health Office, 155
Medical School, 42, 68, 74-75, 133, 136, 139, 141, 165
Medicare, 142
Medico-Chirurgical Society, 57, 150, 177
Melancholy, 59
Member of Parliament, 15, 152, 181
Member of the L'Institut des Écoles Ménagères, 214
Member of the Legislative Council, 28
Member of the Medico-Chirurgical Society, 57
Member of the Privy Council, 176

Member of the Quebec legislature, 84
Member of the Royal College, 195
Members of the Antiquarian, 172
Members of the Sulpician fraternity, 22
Mendelssohn's Wedding March, 99
Mental Hygiene Committee, 214
Mercier, Honoré, 167
Meunier, Pierre, 171
Michigan, 151
Microbiology, 66
Microscope, 132
Microscopy, 125
Middelboro, 70
Midwife, 43, 46
Midwifery, 33, 43, 56
Mignault, Louis D., 17
Migneault, L. G., 142
Military Cemetery of Villers-Bretonneux, 208
Mills, John Easton, 32
Minister of Public Works, 51, 180
Molson, John Jr., 130
Monarchists, 30
Moncton Transcript, 179
Monsieur Guibord, 103
Mont Sainte-Marie, 65
Montreal Amateur Athletic Association, 203, 205
Montreal Athletic Social Club, 57
Montreal Bar, 201
Montreal campus of Université de Laval, 162
Montreal City & District Savings Bank, 17, 101, 130, 179, 185, 194, 218
Montreal City Hall, 202
Montreal Evening Star, The, 114
Montreal Field Battery, 112
Montreal Field Rifles, 46
Montreal General Hospital, 34, 41, 56, 75, 117, 125, 142, 149
Montreal Hunt Club, 57
Montreal Maternity Hospital, 194
Montreal Medical Journal, 184-185
Montreal Orangemen, 110
Montreal Parks, 198, 214
Montreal School of Medicine, 139
Montreal Snowshoe Club, 110
Montreal Standard, The 202
Montreal Star, 114, 202

Montreal Street Railway, 121, 173
Montreal West, 51
Montreal Witness, 87
Montreal's first Orange parade, 114
Montreal's formidable resident anti-vaccinationist, 151
Montreal's Irish Catholics, 22
Montreal's Jesuit school, 77
Montreal's Square Mile, 165
Morgan, Colin, 165
Morrissey, Helen, 211
Mother Justine Bonneau, 129
Mount Royal Boulevard, 154
Mount Royal Cemetery, 73, 91-92, 101, 153
Mount Royal Club, 189, 193, 201, 215, 220
Mount Royal Park, 84, 88, 112, 154
Mount, John William, 37
Mountain View, 194
Moyne, Charles Le, 185
Moyne, Jacques Le, 74
Mucoperiosteal, 45
Mullally, Emmett, 196
Mullarky, Michael Cromwell, 175
Mulligan Guards, 101
Mulroney, Brian, 221
Municipal Board of Health, 103, 117
Munro, Pierre Antoine Confrey, 58-59, 136
Murray, Margaret Folson, 189
Nasopharyngeal, 76
National Capital Commission, 194
Natural History Society, 47, 143
Nebraska, 135
Needlework Guild of Canada, 214
Nephrectomy, 70
New France, 185
New Jersey, 24
New York Herald, 97
New York State Women's Hospital, 176
New York, 51, 59, 97, 99, 105, 132, 151, 156, 176, 194, 201
Newman, John Henry, Cardinal, 152
Nicotine, 143
Nolan, Sarah, 55-56
Nordheimer's Hall, 114, 154
Normandy, 218
Notre Dame Church, 152
Notre Dame Street, 134, 155

Notre-Dame-des-Neiges
    Cemetery, 69, 73, 91, 100,
    102, 136, 173, 202
Nottingham, 173
Numismatic Society, 172
Obituaries, 115
Obituary, 27
Obstetrical, 50
Obstetrician, 66, 75
Obstetrics, 16, 59
Ogilvie, Ian, 221
Ohio, 135
Olmstead, 113
Olmsted, 104, 112-113
Olmsted, Frederick Law, 104,
    112
Ontario Street, 155-156
Oosterbeek, 218
Operating-room, 69
Operations, 33, 66, 69, 77,
    125, 127, 172, 174, 220
Ophthalmology, 140
Opium, 31, 55-56
Orange Day, 114
Orange Lodge, 114
Orange Ontario, 179
Orange Parade, 109-110, 114
Orangemen, 109-110, 175-6
Oregon, 217
Orphan, 163, 212
Orphanage, 163
Osler, William, 15, 117, 125,
    184
Ottawa Improvement
    Commission, 194
Ottawa Journal, 189
Ouimet, Joseph-Aldéric, 180
Outbreak of an Asiatic cholera,
    47
Outbreak of the Great War,
    211
Outhouses, 117
Outremont, 97
Ovariectomy, 70
Ovaries, 177
Ovariotomies, 51
Ovariotomy, 135
Pagé, Marie, 58, 75, 78, 129
Palace of Electricity, 196
Pallbearer, 194
Palliative, 23
Pamphlet, 154, 156, 218
Pandemic, 118
Papal Bull, 112
Papineau, Louis-Joseph, 34,
    101
Paradis, Hercule, 155
Paralysis, 183
Parks Committee, 113
Parliament Hill, 202
Parliament House, 35, 51
Passchendaele, 208

Pasteur, Louis, 66, 184
Pathology of the Eye, 47
Pathology, 33, 47, 57
Patriote, 30, 41, 112
Peacock Alley, 15
Peltier, Hector, 56, 59, 69, 75,
    129
Pennsylvania, 117
Penton, Fred, 104
People's Jimmy, 87, 179
Père Jean, 58, 195
Peritoneum, 172
Perry, Alfred, 35, 115
Peterson, Lillian, 204
Petit Séminaire, 29, 31
Petit-Côte-de-la-Visitation, 83
Pharmacology, 32-33
Pharmacopeia, 31
Pharmacy, 33
Pharynx, 171
Philadelphia, 117
Phillips Square, 65, 86, 130,
    165, 211
Physiology, 45, 47
Pierce-Smith, Richard, 50
Pine Avenue, 65, 222
Place d'Armes, 30, 83, 99, 114,
    150, 172
Place Jacques Cartier, 117, 155
Place Victoria, 83
Plains of Abraham, 22, 205
Plattsburgh, 25, 36
Playgrounds Association, 198,
    214
Point St. Charles, 32, 100, 105,
    149
Pointe-au-Pic, 202
Poison, 47
Pope Gregory XVI, 196
Pope Leo XIII, 161
Pope Pius IX, 112
Port Arthur, 217
Portuguese Embassy, 218
Post-graduate, 42
Post-operative, 76
Postmortem, 55
Postpartum, 64
Premier Honoré Mercier, 167
Premier Oliver Mowat, 98
President Lincoln, 151
President of the Canadian
    Medical Association, 15, 125
President of the Canadian
    Pacific Railway, 206
President of the Grand Trunk
    Railway, 67
President of the Great Lakes
    Dredging Company, 212
President of the Montreal City
    & District Savings Bank, 17,
    179, 220

President of the Protestant
    Society, 151
President of Université Laval,
    16
Prime Minister Bowell, 178,
    181
Prime Minister John A.
    Macdonald, 163
Prime Minister Lafontaine, 36
Prime Minister MacKenzie
    Bowell, 178
Prime Minister Thompson,
    175
Prime Minister Wilfrid
    Laurier, 73, 184
Prince Edward Island, 196
Prince Leopold, 43
Prince of Wales Rifles, 68, 110
Prince of Wales Terrace, 165
Prince of Wales, 57, 68, 110,
    165
Prince Regent, 25
Princess Louise, 132
Princess of Wales, 43-44
Principles of modern surgery,
    48
Privy Council, 64, 73, 91, 100,
    176, 178
Progressive Conservative, 221
Protection of Orthodox
    Christians, 48
Protection of Women, 151
Protestant Sisters of Charity,
    44
Provincial Health Department,
    156
Public Health Journal, 102
Quarantine, 32, 88, 99, 157,
    207
Quebec City, 22, 24, 32, 68,
    77, 103, 118, 133, 162, 165,
    205
Quebec College of Physicians,
    154
Quebec Legislature, 16, 84,
    103
Queen Victoria, 15-16, 32, 35,
    43, 99, 103, 132, 176, 184,
    193
Queen's Hall, 136, 145
Queen's University, 15
Queenstown, 42
Quinine, 31
Quinn, Michael Joseph
    Francis, 181
Rector of Cobh, 24
Rector of Loyola College, 212
Rector of Queenstown, 42
Rector of Youghal, 24
Rectum, 172, 177
Red & White Revue, 217
Red Cross, 214

Redpath, Helen, 63
Redpath, John, 44, 63
Redpath, Peter, 85
Regiopolis College, 216
Regis College, 217
René Lévesque Boulevard, 46
Requiem Mass, 202, 220
Reverend David Shaw Ramsay, 164
Reverend George Cotter Hingston, 42
Revolutionary War, 24, 59
Rexford, Rice W., 31
Rheumatism, 46
Riall, Phineas, 25
Richelieu River, 67
Rideau Hall, 110
Riel Rebellion, 151-152
Riel, Louis, 151, 155
Rimouski, 128
Riot Act, 104
Robichaud, Pélagie, 150
Roddick, Thomas George, 15, 184
Roddick, Thomas, 15, 117, 125, 184
Rodger, Tom, 149
Rodier, Charles Séraphin, 63, 85
Roosevelt, Franklin Delano, 221
Root, Elihu, 201
Rose Room Banquet Hall, 15
Rose, John, 29, 31, 36, 51
Ross, Alexander Milton, 151
Rottot, Jean-Philippe, 128
Rousselot, Benjamin Victor, 92
Rousselot, Victor, 92, 100
Rowat, Donald, 163
Roy Thomson Hall, 99
Roy, Alfred Jr., 87
Royal Canadian Academy, 205
Royal Canadian Air Force, 217
Royal Canadian Infantry Corps, 218
Royal College of Surgeons, 195
Royal Commission of Inquiry, 212
Royal Infirmary, 33, 66
Royal Irish Artillery, 24
Royal North West Mounted Police, 152
Royal Trust Company, 218
Royal Victoria Hospital, 15, 113, 178
Rumilly, Robert, 17, 175
Russell, Charles T., 218
Sackett's Harbour, 25, 36
Sacred Heart, 216
Saint-Jean-Baptiste Parade, 89
Saint-Pierre, Henri, 90

Samaritan Hospital, 176
Saskatchewan, 217
Sault-au-Récollet, 189
Schizophrenic, 133
Schoenlein, Johann Lukas, 44
Scotland, 83, 143
Scott, Adam Sherriff, 28
Scott, General Winfield, 25
Scott, Richard, 110
Scottish Catholics, 82
Semmelweis, Ignac, 66
Senator Edward Murphy, 179
Senator George Brown, 99
Senator Lieut.-Colonel Charles Arkel Boulton, 183
Senator Louis Forget, 189
Senator Michael Sullivan, 15, 197
Senator Thomas Ryan, 85
Sepsis, 66
Shand, Alexander Burns, 43
Shaw, Francis, 197
Sherbrooke Gazette, 91
Sherbrooke Street, 29, 105, 127, 136, 165, 204, 211, 221
Simeoni, Giovanni Cardinal, 140, 161
Simpson, James, 43-45, 66, 69, 190
Sir Alan McNab, 36
Sir Charles Tupper, 180-181
Sir Farrer Herschell, 133
Sir Francis Hincks, 81, 85, 110, 115, 145, 153
Sir George Étienne Cartier, 51
Sir James Simpson, 69
Sir John A. Macdonald, 51, 81, 131, 175
Sir John Abbott, 175, 189
Sir Peers Davidson, 203
Sir Wilfrid Laurier, 182
Sir William Hales Hingston, 15, 221
Sir William Hingston Memorial Hospital, 211
Sir William Hingston, 15-17, 176, 183, 185, 211, 215, 221
Sisters of Charity, 44, 134
Slopes of Mount Royal, 22, 83
Small Pox, 91, 116, 118, 154, 157-158
Smallpox, 21, 85, 87-89, 91, 99-100, 103, 105, 111, 113, 116-118, 120-121, 125, 149-158, 164, 184, 222
Smallwood, Charles, 75, 143
Smeulders solution, 142
Smith, Edward Hingston, 135
Smith, Francis, 214
Smith, John Quincy, 135
Smith, Lapthorn, 142
Smith, Richard H. W., 65

Snowshoe, 110, 150
Society of Decorative Art, 129
Society of Jesus, 189
South Africa, 189-190
South Shields, 164
South Staffordshire Airborne Battallion, 218
Sparrow, John, 174
St-Hyacinthe, 128
St. Ann, 83
St. Anne, 23, 35, 99
St. Antoine Street, 47
St. Antoine Ward, 83-84, 115
St. Antoine, 47, 83-84, 97, 115
St. Augustine, 32
St. Catherine Street, 90
St. Denis Street, 114, 177
St. Einnan, 183
St. Elizabeth of Hungary, 82
St. Ermins Hotel, 190
St. Famille, 34, 65
St. Francis Xavier University, 216
St. Gabriel Street Presbyterian Church, 25
St. George, 118, 204
St. Helen, 104
St. Hilaire, 67
St. Ignatius, 216
St. James Cathedral, 98-99
St. James Street, 109, 114, 130
St. Jean Baptiste Society, 37
St. Jean Baptiste, 83, 97
St. Jean-Baptiste Village, 102
St. Joachim, 70
St. Lawrence Boulevard, 101
St. Lawrence Hall Hotel, 81, 164
St. Lawrence River, 23, 74, 113
St. Lawrence School of Medicine, 47
St. Louis, 97, 189, 196
St. Marie, 83
St. Martin Creek, 47, 88
St. Patrick's Church (Basilica), 23, 36, 69, 99, 129, 140, 163, 167, 179, 193, 202, 204-206, 208, 211, 215, 221
St. Patrick's Day (Parade), 109, 111, 213
St. Patrick's Hospital, 46-48, 58, 65
St. Patrick's Orphanage Asylum, 163
St. Patrick's Society, 84
St. Paul, 29, 90, 216
St. Peter, 27, 63, 83, 204
St. Petersburg, 131
St. Philippe, 58, 129
St. Roch Street, 221
Staffordshire, 218
Stairs, Harriet Hingston, 221

Star, The, 86, 88, 93, 99, 105, 110, 114, 127, 130, 141, 153, 161, 193, 202, 206
Steamship, 173
Stephens, George Washington, 87, 93
Stephens, Washington, 87, 93
Stroud, Alderman William Dicker, 151
Suicide, 89, 136, 204
Sulpician, 22, 29-30
Superior of Les Hospitalières, 58
Superior of the Sulpicians, 162
Surgical gloves, 197
Switzerland, 198, 206
Sylvan, Rich, 113
Syme, James, 42
Syphilis, 46, 89, 151
Taschereau, Alexandre Elzéar, 77, 161
Taschereau, Elzéar Alexandre, 77, 161
Taschereau, Elzéar, 77, 112, 132, 139, 161
Taxpayers Association, 115
Telegram, 75, 140, 181
Telephone, 117
Theatre Royal, 110
Thoroughbreds, 166
Three Rivers, 118
Tobogganing, 150
Torching of Parliament, 36
Toronto School of Medicine, 136
Toronto University, 136
Tower of London, 190
Township of Hinchinbrooke, 27
Trefflé-Rottot, Jean-Philippe, 16, 69
Tremblay, Patrice, 155
Tribalism of the French Canadians, 36
Trinity Anglican Church, 36
Trois-Rivières, 128
Trudel, François-Xavier, 134
Tuberculosis, 46
Turkey, 48
Turney, Rebecca, 50
Twain, Mark, 145
Typewriting, 117
Typhoid, 89
Typhus, 21-22, 32, 46
U.S. Centennial Exhibition, 117
U.S. President James A. Garfield, 135
U.S. President Theodore Roosevelt, 201
U.S. Seventh Cavalry, 114
U.S. War Department, 75

Ulcer, 76
Ultramontane, 31
Ultramontanism, 110, 152
Umbria, 195
Uncle Willie, 120
Undy Academy Grammar School, 29
Unitarian, 101
United Empire Loyalist, 59
United Kingdom, 180, 184
United Province of Canada, 17, 82
Université de Laval, 162
Université de Montréal, 17, 162, 167, 205, 216
Université du Québec à Montréal, 178
Université Laval à Montréal, 165, 212, 216
University of Edinburgh, 33, 46
University of Ottawa, 189
University of Pennsylvania, 117
University of Victoria, 129, 136, 139, 142, 151, 165
Unsanitary, 47
Upper Lachine Road, 113
Urethra, 177
Urologist, 70
Usefulness of the Upper House, 183
Uterus, 175
Vaccination Act, 88, 117
Vaccination, 88-91, 111, 116-118, 120-121, 150-151, 154-156, 222
Vagina, 172, 177
Valedictory, 37, 163
Van Horne, William, 145
Vancouver, 216-217
Vanier, Georges Philias, 189
Varias Sollicitudines, 112, 128
Varicella, 157
Varioloid, 149, 157
Varennes, 74, 135, 152, 167, 173, 185, 193, 198, 203, 211, 221
Vatican, 77, 112, 135, 140, 161
Vaughan, Cornelia Hingston Molson, 221
Vein, 145
Venereal, 46
Viaticum, 46
Vice-chairman of Canadian National Railways, 221
Vice-president of the City Passenger Railway, 142
Vice-president of the Montreal Street Railway, 120, 173
Vice-president of the Needlework Guild, 214

Vice-rector of Université Laval, 162
Victims of the French Revolution, 30
Victoria Bridge, 57, 64
Victoria College, 136, 141
Victoria Rifles, 208
Victoria Rink, 57, 82, 110
Victoria Square, 23, 114, 155
Victoria Universty, 128
Victorian Order of Nurses, 190, 214
Vienna, 45, 84
Ville Marie Bank, 130
Virginia, 67
Von Esenbeck, Christian Gottfried Daniel Knees, 50
Von Langenbeck, Bernard Rudolf Konrad, 44
Waite, Peter B., 16
War, Crimean, 50
Wayland, Francis, 68, 74-75
Wellington Street, 55
Wesleyan Methodists, 68
Westminister Cathedral, 205
WHH, 149
White House, 135, 151
White Revue, 217
Whitechurch, 24
William Hingston High School, 221
Wilson, Thomas, 87
Windsor Hotel, 15, 131, 150, 157, 178, 185, 190, 201
Women's Historical Society, 129
Workman, William, 85-86, 101
X-rays, 196
Ziegle Strasse, 44

AGMV Marquis

MEMBER OF SCABRINI MEDIA

Quebec, Canada
2004